T4-AHE-283

TRADERS AND MERCHANTS

Panorama of International Commodity Trading

Revised and Updated
Second Edition

PHILIPPE CHALMIN

Research Centre on World Commodity Markets
Conservatoire National des Arts et Métiers, Paris

Translated from the French by
Erica E. Long-Michalke

harwood academic publishers

chur · london · paris · new york · melbourne

HF
1051
.C42B

1987

333.7
C43t2

© 1987 by Harwood Academic Publishers GmbH Poststrasse 22, 7000 Chur, Switzerland. All rights reserved.

Harwood Academic Publishers

Post Office Box 197
London WC2E 9PX
England

58, rue Lhomond
75005 Paris
France

Post Office Box 786
Cooper Station
New York, New York 10276
United States of America

Private Bag 8
Camberwell, Victoria 3124
Australia

Originally published in French as *Négociants et chargeurs: La saga du négoce international des matières premières* by Editions Economica, Paris, 1985, © 1985 Editions Economica.

Library of Congress Cataloging-in-Publication Data

Chalmin, Philippe, 1951–
   Traders and Merchants.

   Translation of: Négociants et chargeurs.
   Bibliography: p.
   Includes index.
   1. Raw Materials. 2. Commerce. 3. Trading companies. I. Title.
   HF15051.C4213   1987   333.7   87-26074
   ISBN 3-7186-0435-3

ISBN 3-7186-0435-3 No part of this book may be reproduced or utilized in any form or by any means, electronic or mechanical, including photocopying and recording, or by any information storage or retrieval system, without permission in writing from publisher. Printed in Great Britain by Bell and Bain Ltd., Glasgow.

CONTENTS

University Libraries
Carnegie Mellon University
Pittsburgh, Pennsylvania 15213

FOREWORD TO THE ENGLISH EDITION

This book was first published in French in 1983, and the second edition (1985) was updated for the English translation in September 1986. The general climate of international commodity markets has not changed much since then: prices are depressed, in some cases at their lowest levels since the thirties. In this context, traders have experienced hard times, and some companies, hitherto untouched, have suffered. This text does not take into account what happened in 1987 (Jacobs-Suchard's participation in Ed. and F. Man, for example), as its main interest for the reader is a description of the unchanging characteristics of international commodity trading in a changing world.

Philippe CHALMIN
September 1987

INTRODUCTION

The role of international trading companies in the evolution of trade since 1945 and the specific case of commodities

An unprecedented expansion and development has taken place in international trade since 1945. The expansion was due, in the initial stages, to the disappearance of the colonial empires, and their currency and financial areas as well as to the collapse of the Bretton Woods system at the beginning of the Seventies. The development resulted from the redistribution of industrial activity on a worldwide scale (which some prefer to call the new international division of labour) and the quest for new sources of agricultural and mineral raw materials[1].

The system of commerce inherited from the Thirties was, however, ill-adapted to managing and serving these new forms of trade. The still extremely atomized and dispersed trade mechanism of the times — result of a gradual evolution since the end of the 18th century — was split-up among vertically integrated industrial and commercial firms, merchant companies, the more or less direct descendants of the old chartered companies, import or export traders and merchants, often based in the ports themselves, and finally brokers and other middlemen working on commission. The laying of submarine cables at the end of the 19th century had somewhat reduced the distances between producer and consumer markets, and a certain number of futures markets had been established in the old commodity exchanges. But in the aftermath of the 1929 slump, as the tides of liberalism receded, public structures began to exert their influence on the very functioning of international trade.

Admittedly, most attempts at reaching international agreements or setting-up producer cartels were — and still are — of no avail. But regardless of the dominant ideology of the regime in question, government has come to show an increasing tendency to take the place of private initiative in the import and export trade, both directly and indirectly by means of producer cooperatives which it controls.

This movement, begun in the Thirties, was almost institutionalized during the Second World War: among the Allies, the United States organized production and trade on a worldwide level. After the war, some nations maintained and even strengthened the existing structures, while a large number of others found themselves under Communist control.

The dominant characteristic of world trade after 1945 has therefore been this increased presence of parastatal organizations, both in import and export, especially for commodities. This development could only exacerbate the general inflexibility already evident in the very functioning of international trade.

Whereas a smoothly functioning chain of middlemen, most often with a rather small financial base[2], had been in a position to meet the needs of trade rather effectively before the war, the emergence of a monopolistic state structure at one point in the chain after 1945 threw the existing balance out of kilter. As a result the old structures rapidly proved to be ineffective.

In fact, what was increasingly needed was a participant capable of providing a permanent link between the structures of supply and demand, for shipments of ever increasing size (due no doubt to bureaucracy but also to the increase in the size of transport units).

This participant, who began to appear at the end of the Forties but whose real development goes back to the splitting-up of the colonial empires, (with the attendant nationalizations and socializations) and the disappearance of traditional merchants, is *the international trader*.

The international trader is the vital link ensuring the physical exchange of goods between an importer and a final exporter who are separated both by time and by distance and who most often do not share the same nationality.

The functions assumed by the international trader have also evolved with time: what were originally logistic functions in the days when a product needed only to be transported, have become increasingly financial. The trader assumes, as it were, the risks of price and currency fluctuations in the later stages of the operations and guarantees their successful outcome.

Clearly, we have come a long way from the import or export merchants of old who were attached to a market-place or port. For the sake of efficiency, today's international trader has to span the world with a tight network of agents, warehouses, informants, in short, of 'contacts'.

Aided by the increasing instability of world markets, huge multi-national firms soon began to emerge. Although very little is known about them by the public at large and even by specialists, owing to the secrecy with which they carry out their activities, these firms constitute at present one of the most dynamic poles of international capitalism. In effect, most of them have reinvested the profits derived from trade in related upstream and downstream activities and have gradually built themselves up into industrial empires.

Trading companies, necessary vectors of international trade, especially that of commodities, have now attained such a level of development that they in no way resemble the anecdotal description which one normally attaches to this type of firm. Paradoxically, traders have now taken the place in trade once occupied by the great merchant families of the 15th century (the Fuggers of Augsburg for example), a place which in the following centuries had been gradually obscured by their production activities. It is therefore important first of all to place the trading firms in their historical context by tracing their evolution back to the 11th century with the aid of the numerous studies recently made on the subject. It will also be useful to put them in their commercial context by trying to define, as clearly as possible, the different types of functions which they exercise and their evolution. It will then become clear that the international trading firms deal mainly in commodities — which in value terms amount to half of all international trade — and it is precisely along these lines that we shall develop our study after having put the major trends of the international commodity trade in context. This will be the First Part of the book.

Part Two will take a look at how a trading firm works. Using practical examples, we shall try to show the different aspects — financial, logistic, commercial or legal — of the daily running of such firms and shall discuss the problems of risk-taking and of the extremely ambivalent relationship between the trader and the speculator.

Essentially descriptive in nature, Part Three will present the major trading firms in their product-environment, from grains to oil, before trying to classify them according to the types of transaction they handle and their geographical or historical origin.

The foregoing may help us to find an answer to the question which remains at the core of these discussions: what is the real influence of these firms on international trade, in particular that of commodities, and can some form of control not be exercised over their activities? This was the very problem faced in the 15th century by a certain number of monarchs of Christendom confronted with the power of early merchant capitalism. . .

PART ONE

GENESIS AND DEFINITION

Chapter 1

EVOLUTION OF PRACTICES, METHODS AND STRUCTURES OF INTERNATIONAL TRADE SINCE THE ELEVENTH CENTURY

The fall of the Roman Empire and the concomitant decline of the Western economy radically changed the routes taken by international trade. New middlemen, the Arabs, appeared on the route to the Orient, Byzantium gained importance at the expense of Rome, and previously great urban (hence trading) centres disappeared. This decline was less significant in Italy where, beginning in the 7th and 8th centuries, a few small ports became the keystones of East–West trade: Amalfi and Pisa until the end of the 8th century, Venice and Genoa in particular, and Bari at least until the Norman conquest.

The merchant or tradesman was at that time essentially a navigator, or at least a ship-owner, whose role was to ensure the transport, barter or resale of raw materials or manufactures. The same could be said about the first *societa maris* found from the 11th century onwards in Italian ports. This was a two-handed partnership between a *socius stans* who remained on the spot, and a *socius tractator* who traveled in person on the ship[1]. The notion of the merchant going on an 'adventure' (the merchant adventurer) was gradually replaced at the end of the 8th century by sedentary trade and the setting-up of trading-posts networks.

Trade inside Europe was essentially based on direct contacts: it was the Golden Age of fairs and notably of the famous fairs of Champagne which provided the link between Italy and the Low Countries. The importance of these fairs diminished in the 13th century, when the circumnavigation of Spain became possible, and new fairs then developed in Antwerp and most notably in Geneva and later in Lyons. Other important routes were the Low Countries–England link and the Baltic–Low Countries–England connection.

Most often the merchants and tradesmen dealing with foreign markets grouped themselves according to nationality to the point of creating separate legal entities whose members were in a way partners. Based on this model were the famous 'regulated companies' of Britain to which all British merchants of a sector had to belong. The best known of these were the Merchant Adventurers, cloth wholesalers, and the Merchants of the Staple, wool exporters[2]. Although they were not merchant associations but merchant towns, we could also mention the members of the Hanseatic league which covered the North of Germany and the Baltic and had its main trading posts in Novgorod, Bergen, London and Bruges. These cannot however be rightly termed international trading firms. They were at most importer and exporter associations.

Totally different in nature were, however, the often family-founded trading companies which, in the 12th century, began to spread their networks all over Europe.

The first international trading firms: 12th–17th century

As early as the 12th century a certain number of groupings, most often based on family units, had begun to weave a web of contacts, trading posts and even banks both in Europe and abroad. Conditions were, at that time, relatively favourable: state structures were weak and susceptible to the influence of foreign groups (although they had the power to tax these should the need arise). Moreover, in spite of the fact that mercantilist ideology had already begun to emerge in the economic thinking of the 15th century, it was not until the end of the 16th century that it was really applied. Finally, so high were the risks involved in international trade that only a few large multinational concerns could enter into partnership with governments always on the lookout for new sources of capital (see below).

It was therefore, in a way, the 'Golden Age' of 'stateless' merchants and bankers. The first were the Italians especially the Lombards[3] followed by the Florentines. 'Companies' such as those belonging to the Bardis or the Peruzzis and later the Medicis literally dominated economic and financial Europe until the bankruptcies of the middle of the 14th century (as a result of rash loans made to the English Crown). These merchants were replaced by the Venetians and the Genovese, the Catalans and the Majorcans as well as by the Provençals, dominated in the 15th century by the figure of Jacques Coeur who organized trade with the East. On the European continent the only companies comparable to the Italian ones — and which were to eclipse them by the middle of the 15th century — were the large concerns of Southern Germany such as the Fuggers of Augsburg (1450–1620), the *Ravensburger Gesellschaft* (1380–1530) and the Welsers of Augsburg.

The Fugger fortune was, in all probability, the one which left the most significant mark on its era, especially during the first half of the 16th century. The family stemmed from one Hans Fugger, a weaver, who settled in Augsburg in 1367 and became a wool and clothing merchant. The international expansion of the company, however, was the achievement of his descendant Jacob Fugger, the Rich, (1459–1525) who set up the first trading post in Venice in 1478. At the same time the Fuggers became interested in metals produced in Tyrol (and began to lend money to the Habsburgs) and later in Hungarian metals especially copper). At the beginning of the 16th century, the Fuggers dominated the European metal trade, were in control of production since many governments were indebted to them[4], had agencies all over Europe and had already secured a foothold in the Spanish and Portuguese empires. In 1499 the Fuggers had a virtual monopoly of the copper trade in Europe. At the death of Jacob in 1525, the Fugger 'concern' was worth some 1,500,000 gold florins and constituted the largest fortune in all of Christendom. The family's prosperity reached its zenith in 1546 after which the company's fortunes, like those of Spain and the Empire with which the Fuggers had probably been too closely associated, began to decline.

The *Ravensburger Gesellschaft* (also known as the *Magna Societas*) was an older company but its inability to adapt to the new trends in trade caused by the great discoveries brought about its relatively early disappearance. It was a grouping of associates dominated by three families (from Ravensburg, Constance and Buchorn). It specialized in the wholesale trade and owned a network of trading posts covering the whole of Europe from Barcelona and Saragossa to Bruges and Cologne. Also worthy of mention are the Tripps, Dutch merchants who later rose to pre-eminence in the iron, arms, and copper trade (they virtually controlled the Swedish economy) from Holland to the Middle East, Scandinavia and Russia[5].

Among the other trading companies whose names have been transmitted to us we should not forget the Ruiz family of Medina del Campo in Spain, the delle Failles of Antwerp, the Welsers and the Pallers of Augsburg and of course, that remarkable figure, the frenchman Jacques Coeur.

A graphic example of the range of their activities is the case of the Portuguese pepper trade at the end of the 16th century. At that time, Portugal had a quasi-monopoly in supplying Europe with pepper (the main spice then required for the preservation of food) after having supplanted Venice at the beginning of the century. Since 1506 the monarchs, first of Portugal and later of Spain, had retained a monopoly in this trade, which they in turn leased to local capitalists and especially to foreigners: Italians or Germans. The 'farming out' took the form of two contracts: the Asian contract which included the buying of the pepper in the Indies and reselling it to the Crown warehouses in Lisbon, and the European contract concerning the resale of this pepper to the North via the trading posts of Antwerp and Bruges. In 1585, the Asian contract was awarded to a group of capitalists, among them the Fuggers and the Welsers. In 1591 the European contract was awarded to an international consortium including the Fuggers who received seven out of thirty-two shares, the Welsers (6), the Italians Rovalesca (4), the Spaniard Pedro Malvenda (4), and the Portuguese Ximenes (11)[sic]. The organizer of the entire transaction was Matthaus Welser[6].

But the lifetime of these great trader–bankers was also to see the appearance of a new type of trade with the setting up of the first joint stock companies (often controlled by the great families we have just mentioned: the Tripps and the Dutch East India Company for example). It would be safe to assume that the notion of owning 'shares' in ships or in mining undertakings was, at that time, already a familiar one. Shortly afterward a few banking institutions had developed along this model (the *Casa de San Gorgio* of Genoa, for example) but, from the historical point of view, it would seem that the first joint stock company ever formed was the Muscovy Company, founded in London in 1553 to trade with Russia and which disappeared around 1620. The Levant Company founded in the middle of the 16th century to trade with the Mediterranean followed the same model.

But the appearance of these enterprises already signalled the advent of a new era, one in which public initiative would replace and manage private initiative, in which trade would become the tool of policy. The Levant Company was already receiving assistance from the British Crown (as had the Merchant Adventurers since 1564 when they were granted the monopoly of the textile trade with the Low Countries and Hamburg). The great companies which were to develop in the 17th and 18th centuries would owe their prosperity to the trade monopolies granted to them by their states of origin. This was the beginning of the era of the East India Companies.

The great merchant companies of the 17th and 18th centuries

'The great merchant companies were born of trade monopolies', writes F. Braudel[7]. They were therefore the result of the ties existing between capital and government. A government would grant a trade monopoly in a specific zone discovered or yet to be discovered to a group of capitalists (bankers, merchants). In point of fact, these companies often (but not always) relied heavily upon the existing or about–to–be–established colonial empires of states practising non-interventionist economic policies: the most famous companies were therefore those of British and Dutch origin whereas there were to be none of Spanish or Portuguese origin and the vague desires of the French never took concrete form.

It would be tedious to enumerate all the companies created since the beginning of the 17th century. These joint stock companies, as they were called, were the driving force behind the first stock exchanges. They were the privileged recipients of royal charters granting them a trade monopoly for a specific region at the expense of the already existing circuits as well as of the rest of the trading community. The most famous of these was the British East India Company (founded in

1599 and having obtained its monopoly in 1600), the Dutch *Oost Indische Compagnie* founded in 1602 and finally the French *Compagnie des Indes Orientales* founded in 1664. But there were also Danish, Italian and German East India Companies. . . These undertakings were managed like private firms and it is a fact that they were run for a long period by the same few families. In their respective monopoly areas, however, they were to become a sort of public institution: until 1864 British India was governed by the East India Company, in a perfect marriage of political and commercial interests.

To refer to an example already mentioned, the pepper market was marked from 1620 onwards by the struggles between the British and the Dutch. From 1640 Amsterdam was the undisputed capital of the pepper distribution trade in Europe.

But as one often has occasion to note, a monopoly's management is rarely dynamic in nature since, rather than seeking to expand, it is apt to try and conserve the income which is ensured by its very position on the market. The founders' heirs often did not inherit the former's taste for risk and adventure and the monopoly generally became an obstacle to freedom of trade.

From the end of the 17th century, depending on the prevailing policies, these monopolies were called into question: the monopoly of the East India Company was suspended during the 1688 Revolution and was only restored ten years later. In 1673 trade between Great Britain and Scandinavia was liberalized and at the end of the century it was the turn of Africa, Russia and Newfoundland. In France the monopoly of the *Compagnie des Indes* was withdrawn in 1682, later re-established, then definitively revoked in 1769. In fact the life-span of a monopoly did not only depend on government policy but also on the economic zone in which it exercised its prerogatives: whilst Asia and Africa were the two main regions of operation of this type of firm, it enjoyed little success in Central America and in the West Indies.

In general the companies practised a barter and exchange economy: they either bought through the channel of local merchants (hence the merchant dynasties installed in most of the Indian ports) or they resorted to more or less forced labour on plantations (spices in Indonesia). Futhermore it was not long before they graduated to a form of territorial imperialism: from 1619 onwards the Dutch strengthened their position in Batavia and their example was followed, in 1680, by the British in India[8].

The India chartered companies possessed import monopolies for the home market: the East India Company's monopoly of tea imports from China (the only tea available to Europeans at the time) lasted until 1834. As a rule, their goods were sold by auction (in Amsterdam and London). In London, sales took place on a quarterly basis: tea sales for example were held in March, June, September and December and in the 17th century they were still done 'by the candle'.

The 18th century therefore marked both the zenith and the beginning of the decline of the chartered companies: in a number of countries they lost a great deal of their commercial credibility on becoming an integral part of royal policies: as can be seen from the use made in France of the *Compagnie d'Occident* within Law's system[9]. Although trade had been liberalized almost everywhere in Europe, new forms of protectionism were on the rise (the British Navigation Acts, Colbertism. . .) even as certain colonial empires were opening up: 1713 saw the founding of the *Compania de Asiento* (later the South Sea Company) which was granted the privilege of supplying Spanish America with black slaves.

But the companies were hard pressed to ride out revolutionary upheavals. Only the British maintained the formula and made it one of the pillars of their colonization system. Although the privilege — and therefore the control of India — enjoyed by the East India Company was abolished as late as 1864, new companies were created in the 1880's for Africa and Asia: the British North Borneo Company in 1881, the Royal Niger Company in 1886 and especially the British South Africa Company, the famous 'Chartered' of Cecil Rhodes[10]. Although by the beginning of the 20th century practically all the chartered companies had disappeared, a few companies had managed to survive the revocation of their charters, among them, the Hudson Bay Company. This firm, founded in 1670, was relieved of its privilege in 1857 but remains active in Canada today, especially in the fur trade and in distribution.

Although this system had lasted for three centuries and had been, at the very beginning, responsible for the rapid commercial penetration of Western imperialism, it subsequently became a factor of rigidity and even of retrogression. Consequently, it comes as no surprise that, from the end of the 17th century, other commercial circuits developed either alongside them, in competition with them, in 'free' regions or in the wholesale trade using the very same method of company auctions.

Table 1.1 Some major chartered companies

Country	Date founded	Name	Date of disappearance or withdrawal of privilege
Denmark	1732	Danish Asiatic Company	
France	1664	Compagnie des Indes Occidentales	1674
	1664	Compagnie des Indes Orientales	1682 (final disappearance 1790)
	1670	Compagnie du Levant	1672
	1669	Compagnie du Nord	
Germany		Deutsche Ostafrika Gesellschaft	
Great Britain	1553	Merchant Adventurers	1689
	1581	Muscovy Company	1620
	1599	Levant Company	1825
		East India Company	1834 (end of privilege)
			1864 (end of privilege in India)
	1670	Hudson's Bay Company	1857 (end of privilege)
	1713	South Seas Company	1720
	1553-1660	African Company (became Royal Africa Company)	1752
	1555	Russia Company	end 18th c.
	1881	British North Borneo Company	1946
	1886	Royal Niger Company	1899 (end of monopoly)
	1888	Imperial British East Africa Company	1894
	1889	Chartered British South Africa Company	1923 (end of administrative tasks in Rhodesia)
Netherlands	1602	Oost Indische Compagnie	1798
		West Indies Company	

Before touching on this aspect it should be pointed out that the chartered companies, along the lines of the East India Company, were the forerunners of the great trading posts companies which were to flourish in the colonial empires of the 19th and 20th centuries. But there was little to distinguish one from the other. The monopolies, of course, disappeared, but within the empires no competition from non-nationals was allowed. Only certain zones were the object of fierce competition among companies of different nationalities. The most graphic example of the times is provided by China: the British firms in Hong Kong and Shanghai (Jardine and Matheson, Butterfield and Swire) came up against competition from French (the *Compagnie Olivier*) or German firms[11]. But within the different empires a few firms were in complete control: the *Compagnie Française de l'Afrique de l'Ouest* (founded in 1834 in Marseilles) and the SCOA (*Société Commerciale de l'Ouest Africain*) for France, and the United Africa Company, the East Africa Trading Company, John Holt and Co. for British Africa[12], *Internatio* (founded in 1863) for Dutch Indonesia. The situation was the same in the settlement colonies: founded in 1842 in Melbourne, Dalgety delivered supplies to farmers and bought up the wool they produced. Such firms collected the local produce (coffee and cocoa in Africa) with the aid of their networks of trading posts and thus appeared on the international markets as important exporters of tropical products, the transport of which they often ensured all the way to the home market.

In 1929 the United Africa Company, which resulted from the merger of the Niger Company and the African and Eastern Trading Company, accounted for 60% of the palm-oil, 45% of the palm cabbage, 60% of the ground-nuts and 50% of the cocoa exports of the British West African colonies (Nigeria, Ghana, Sierra Leone) and the Ivory Coast[13].

As we can see, the old system of two-way trading economy survived well beyond the 19th century and, if it ever did disappear, then it was not before 1960 or thereabouts.

The development of international trade: 18th and 19th centuries

It might be deemed audacious to speak of the development of international trade. It is rather a question of the development of trade mechanisms and the delineation of functions which were to survive without major changes until the 1950's.

The influence of the chartered companies in this evolution is less important than it might appear. What we feel was fundamental to this development was the formation of trade circuits in physical or other markets and the establishment of a chain of intermediaries whose size, relative to one another, was limited by the very splintering of these markets.

The development of the major companies was accompanied first of all by the growth of wholesale trade: it was then that the first harbour entrepots appeared, created by the first commodity exchanges. It should not be forgotten that the importance of the early commodity exchanges depended on the size of the stocks they were able to hold since these dictated the volume not only of the import trade but especially of the re-export trade. Antwerp was therefore destined to become the centre of gravity of the sugar world from 1550 to 1585, followed, after the seizure of Antwerp by Farnese, by Amsterdam until 1650 at least. The markets subsequently scattered to the French ports and those of London, Hamburg, and to those ports of Prussia, Poland, Russia, and Austria which had been granted import monopolies.

It was, moreover, at Antwerp that relatively sophisticated forward dealings took place for the first time (on cargoes 'due to arrive'[14]. This type of transaction was used subsequently in Amsterdam for herrings, cereals, spices, whale oil, salt and, in the 18th century, for cocoa, coffee, and saltpetre[15]. The first real futures markets appeared only at the end of the 19th century in Chicago.

A complex wholesale trade network was thus taking shape at one end of the chain: merchant dynasties, whose function was to manage and redirect imports (and to do so already on a European level) were appearing in all the major ports. Given the weakness of the banking system, the main problem was to manage to round off operations by dealing in merchandise for the homeward leg of the journey; (it was this need to round off operations which gave rise to the famous triangular trade). Moreover the irregularity with which supplies became available resulted in severe market instability which encouraged speculation, at least in times of war. Under the *Directoire* the Parisian trading and banking circles earned most of their profits through speculation in commodities, notably in cotton, indigo and

Spanish wools[16]. Similarly, according to F. Braudel, an essential feature of the 18th century as a whole was the struggle between merchants and the financial community to set up monopolies at both ends of the chain. In the words of Braudel: 'the VOC [the Dutch East India Company] was a machine which stopped where the profits of trade monopolies began'[17]. Since the Dutch merchants were past masters in that art, Amsterdam, with its huge warehouses, was destined to become the leading entrepot of Europe where a merchant would stock in slump times to re-sell when the market was buoyant.

But before long, by the beginning of the 18th century in fact, international trade was to undergo a number of changes. As trade became increasingly direct, the influence of the chartered companies diminished and, in many areas, even disappeared.

From that point on, international trade began to take on an appearance which could be termed 'modern'. Let us take a look at how the chain leading from producer to consumer was henceforth formed.

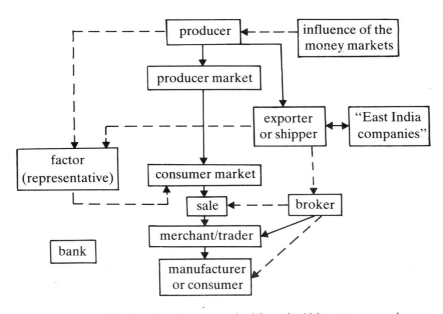

Figure 1.1 International trade as it was organized from the 18th century onwards.

At the very top we have the producer who can take one of two forms: he could be a large-scale planter with enough capital to do his own marketing (the case of most plantation or mining economies) or he could be a small producer selling his produce at the door of his farm to a merchant or to a marketing syndicate (the case of the barter economies but also, paradoxically, that of the grain producers).

Few producers' markets existed in the 18th century owing to a lack of the necessary banking and commercial facilities. There was therefore no producers' market for West Indian cane sugar in the 18th century: as a rule planters sold directly to ship-captains (who were about to make the third leg of their triangular trade) or, if they were sufficiently large, directly on the home market through correspondents or 'factors'[18].

The first facility set up in the production centres was a collection network: there were a number of export merchants who, with their network of correspondents and warehouses, reproduced the above-mentioned model of the merchant companies and the India chartered companies. It was, moreover, usually the general merchants who carried out a form of barter trade. At the beginning of the 19th century

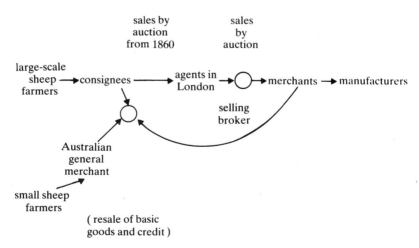

Figure 1.2 The wool circuit (Australia–England) around 1850–1900. (From REES (G.L.), *Britain's Commodity Markets*, London, 1974, pp. 322 *sq.*).

the Australian wool trade which functioned along those lines, was, consequently, in the hands of a number of wholesale merchants (Dalgety, Elder Smith and Co.). After 1850, these merchants were increasingly called upon to play the role of consignment agents, also in charge of the transport of merchandise. From 1860 they also organized auctions in Australia itself, thus creating a producers' market which would continue to grow. In spite of this development, their position (especially Dalgety's) was later to be strengthened by the extension of their links with the great colonial banks (Union Bank of Australia, Bank of New Zealand) which were, in the Nineteen Thirties, the main importers on the British market.

This pattern was duplicated in the cotton trade in Egypt and in the United States (figures 1.3 and 1.4), in the cocoa trade on the African coast, the tea trade in China and later in the Indies, and the silk trade in Sicily which had been monopolised in the 17th century by the Genoese. Cotton trade out of the United States was dominated during the first third of the 19th century by a few Anglo-American firms such as Alexander Brown and Sons, or Baring Brothers, who acted as exporters, shippers and bankers[19].

In the British West Indies, a number of firms bought sugar, rum, cocoa and spices on the estates, sorted them into lots and shipped them off to England. Firms like Booker Bros, McConnel, Frame and Co., and D.Q. Henriques gradually succeeded in dominating these islands' economy and came to acquire their own estates. As a result, Booker and McConnel, in time, came to own most of the sugar plantations in British Guyana. In the British colonies in Asia, with McLaine Watson, Rogers and Co., and Guthrie, the situation was the same. Whether

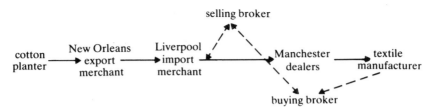

Figure 1.3 The Cotton circuit United States–England around 1850. (G.L. REES, *Britain's Commodity Markets*, pp. 322 sq.)

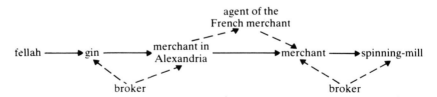

Figure 1.4 The cotton circuit Egypt–France around 1900. (F. MAURETTE, *Les Grands marchés de matières premières,* Paris, 1940, p. 94.)

owner of the goods or merely the consignee thereof, the merchant shipper had correspondents or branches on the consumer markets (in general those of his home country) which continued to have the upper hand until 1880.

The introduction of submarine cables in 1880 was to bring about profound changes in this state of affairs in facilitating the development of producers' markets which were now only a matter of hours away from the consumer markets.

As sales could now be carried out directly, the consignment system gradually disappeared and the Sydney and Adelaide auctions for wool, the New Orleans market for cotton and finally the grains exchange in Chicago managed to assert themselves. Of significance for sugar were the markets of Magdeburg and, in particular, of Hamburg which was, at the time, the leading world market-place.

In the Dutch Indies, 'freed' from the monopoly of the VOC (*Vereenigde Oost-Indische Compagnie*) at the end of the 19th century, producer markets for spices, copra, manioc, and later on for rubber and sugar, were organized at a very early stage (around 1850). The chambers of commerce of Surabaya, of Semarang and especially of Batavia drew up standard forms of contract which speculating European, Arab or Chinese merchants exchanged with one another. These markets reached their zenith in the Nineteen Thirties when it was not unusual for the chain of a single contract to contain some twenty operators[20].

The Chinese silk trade of the 19th century was controlled by Chinese traders (the *hongs*) and Chinese brokers who sold to the great foreign

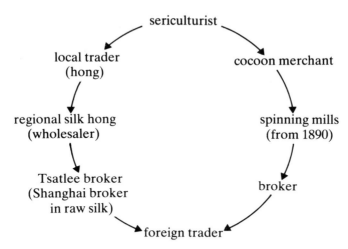

Figure 1.5 The silk export trade in China in the 19th century. (From LI (Lilian M.), *China's Silk Trade: Traditional Industry in the Modern World 1842–1937,* Harvard, 1981).

firms established in Shanghai (and which, like Jardine and Matheson, sometimes had their own spinning-mills). Until 1868 almost all Chinese silk passed through London. It was around that time that the end-users — the French first of all — began to buy directly.

Unlike their Japanese counterparts from 1890 onwards, the most important Chinese firms in Shanghai (there were about ten of them), merely acted as brokers (*compradores*) for foreign firms and strove to maintain a very speculative climate on the market. For example, in 1882 the *comprador* Hu Kuang Yun attempted to corner the market by buying up and hoarding 15,000 bales of raw silk only to have his manoeuvre frustrated by a bumper Italian harvest.

The case of grains merits special treatment. In the 19th century, the two great export centres were North America and, even more so, Russia (Argentina and Australia came to the fore only around 1920). Until 1913 it was Russian wheat which filled the breadbaskets of Europe. From the 18th century, the Russian wheat trade was control-led by Greek merchants who dispatched shipments from the port of

Odessa: around 1850 the Baltic Exchange of London, then the nerve centre of the grain trade in Europe, counted some 300 Greek members out of a total of 400[21].

It was in 1818 that John and Eustratio Ralli set up in London and began to deal in silk and grains. The Rallis were a family of five brothers: John and Eustratio in London, Auguste in Marseilles, Thomas in Constantinople, Pandia in London at first and later in Odessa. In 1850 they opened branches in Calcutta and then in Bombay[22].

From 1870 Anglo-Greek firms began to encounter serious competition from European firms. Léopold Louis Dreyfus, originally from Alsace, had started out in 1850 as a grain merchant in Basel. From 1860 he dealt with the countries along the Danube. In 1872 he settled in Marseilles and began to take an interest in Russian wheat, setting up an agency in Odessa. In 1902 he had his first ship built and around the same time opened a banking department[23].

The British were no less active: the firm Ross T. Smith and Co. of Liverpool, had branches in Trieste, New York, Odessa, Rostoff, Karachi and Buenos Aires. Of equal importance were firms such as William Rathbone and Co., or Balfour Williamson, of Liverpool. In 1877 the *Crédit Lyonnais,* which had just set up operations in Russia, even envisaged extending its activities to wheat by shipping Ukrainian wheats through the Baltic ports. The project never materialized[24]. The main problem at the Russian end of the chain was the lack of an effective collection and storage system: in 1913 the Russian Agricultural Bank decided to finance the construction of 83 elevators (13 of which were constructed by July 1914[25]).

Early North American grain trade was dominated by the great cotton shippers, such as Alexander Brown and Sons or Baring Brothers. By 1850, most of those firms shifted from trading to either shipping or banking activities. Baring Brothers remained active in the grain trade till around 1880, before concentrating on banking, for which they are known today. The general shift away from being general merchants profited more specialized traders like those who dominated the Californian wheat trade (one George W. Menear was known as the 'Wheat King' of the West Coast throughout the 1880's[26]). The main effect, however, was due to the appearance of indigenous traders who built an elaborate grain collection system connecting local silos to terminals on all the major routes. The American merchants: Rosenbaum who dominated the Chicago market, P.N. Gray associated from 1920 with Bunge, Cargill in the Great Plains, were, nevertheless, by no means active in international trade before 1935.

Argentinian grain exports were dominated by foreign firms: in 1910, three firms accounted for 80% of exports: Bunge and Born, founded in 1884 in Buenos Aires and associated with Bunge SA of Antwerp (founded in Amsterdam in 1818), *Louis Dreyfus et Cie.,* and Weil Brothers[27]. At the end of the Nineteen Twenties, Bunge and Born accounted for one-third of all Argentinian grain exports.

All the same, the grain trade offered the only examples, before 1939, of multinational undertakings, as most of the 'merchant princes' of the ealry 19th century had vanished in banking, shipping, etc.: some firms were in fact present both on the producer markets and on certain consumer markets. We have already cited Ross T. Smith and Ralli Brothers, but it would not do to overlook Louis Dreyfus, present in the Balkans and in Argentina, Bunge and Born, based in Antwerp, in Buenos Aires and subsequently in Australia, Canada and the USA, and Continental, founded later by the Fribourgs and based primarily in New York. But these were small firms and outside Argentina their influence was negligible. As was the case for other products, their activities were enhanced by the fact that they operated under conditions of great instability: wars, crises, revolutions. The Fribourgs got their start during the Spanish civil war when Continental was called upon to provide supplies for the Republicans.

Of much greater importance were those manufacturing firms which had integrated production: the first to follow this idea through to its logical conclusion was the British soap-maker William Lever who bought plantations in the Solomon Islands in 1905 (copra), and in the Belgian Congo in 1901 (palm oil), before expanding to barter trading. A comparable example is that of the tyre manufacturers (Firestone in Liberia, Dunlop in Malaysia, Michelin in Indochina. . .), the sugar refiners (Tate and Lyle in the West Indies from 1937), the banana companies (United Fruit, Standard Brands, and Del Monte which took over the Central American market at the beginning of the 20th century) and finally the major mining firms which have integrated processing operations in the developed countries. If the internal transfer prices are artificial, these operations along vertical lines virtually by-pass the channels of international trade.

In addition to this, producer groupings in the form of trusts or cartels

had already succeeded in organizing a number of national and international markets at a fairly early stage. The early groupings which gave
rise to the major oil and iron and steel companies (and which are
involved in a number of other sectors such as sugar refining in the USA
with Amstar) will not be discussed here. In the realm of international
trade, copper provides an instructive example of how a cartel operates:
in 1887 the world price of copper was so low that the majority of
producers were selling below production costs; after a number of
fruitless attempts to reach an agreement, the main European processor, the French *Société Industrielle et Commerciale des Métaux*, run
by one Hyacinthe Secrétan and supported by loan capital from banks
(the *Comptoir d'Escompte*, the Rothschilds, the Barings, the *Crédit
Lyonnais*. . .), attempted to purchase all the marketable copper
available, not only in Europe, but in the rest of the world. In exchange,
producers undertook to limit production. This copper syndicate was
unable to hold its ground, however, and collapsed in 1889 bringing
down with it the *Comptoir d'Escompte*. Until 1914, the efforts made by
the international financial community (especially the Rothschilds) to
come to some sort of agreement failed to modify the general trend.
After the war, renewed attempts to form an international cartel led, in
1926, to the signing of an agreement regrouping 32 producers
essentially around Anaconda (Rockfeller group), Kennecott, Phelps
Dodge, the *Union Minière du Haut Katanga*, and the Rio Tinto
Company. Officially, the main aim of the cartel was to 'stabilize' prices
and to eliminate speculation and middlemen. But before long
(according to Keynes' opinion in 1929), they were essentially carrying
out 'monopolistic' manoeuvres. The price of 18 cents per pound fixed
by the cartel was almost double the official production price. At the
end of 1932 the cartel was unable to maintain its position and collapsed
with the world price at 4 to 5 cents per pound![28].
    The trade in a number of other metals followed the same course:
zinc (controlled by a syndicate with headquarters at Vieille Montagne
in Belgium from 1885 to 1894, and later by the zinc cartel from 1928 to
1932), aluminium (1926), potash, natural and chemical nitrates, mercury (1928–1932) and sulphur. Around the same period (end of the
19th century) the first shipping conferences, which were no less than
cartels of shipping companies on a given route, began to emerge.
    At this stage the product under consideration has moved from the
producer's warehouse to the hold of a ship which is transporting it to a
consumer market. At this point in time, it is either still the property of

the producer or that of a merchant–exporter or a merchant company. The reader will recall that the consumer markets had been organised far earlier than the producer markets. From the 16th century onward Antwerp had been the primary market of the North of Europe and already boasted of a commodity exchange. Although the first Royal Exchange was built in London as early as 1571, for a long time transactions continued to be carried out in the coffee houses of the City before the markets specific to each commodity were built. Until 1900 or thereabouts, consumer markets, with the exception of London (England pursued a resolute free-trade policy), were strictly national. The French, German and Dutch markets had little impact outside their national borders and the American markets only began to take on an international dimension in 1920.

These were markets for 'actuals' and sales by auction were still frequently held. The forward and later futures markets (with produce clearing houses) were still restricted to the largest market centres, although there was no longer a market-place monopoly (as in eighteenth-century Amsterdam). Most often, exporters and importers traded directly with one another so that there was no international trade in the strict sense of the term.

At the centre of all trading activity was the broker. Before 1945, he was the international middleman *par excellence*, who received a commission for transactions which he carried out on behalf of another. Business would be conducted either on behalf of the buyer (the buying broker) or that of the seller (the selling broker). Very often it was he who organized the auctions (still along the model of those of the East India Company). The London Commercial Sale Rooms at Mincing Lane in London opened their doors in 1811 and continued to function until 1920; today, however, eight brokerage firms are responsible for the tea auctions which are held in London. Goods imported within the framework of the East India Companies' monopolies were generally sold by auction on the company premises.

The broker circulated information, organized auctions or, quite to the contrary, represented industrialists in the conduct of business with importers. But the role of the broker can only be fully understood through a closer study of some of these operations.

• James Man, born in 1754 started out as a cooper[29]. In 1792 he joined up with another cooper, William Humphrey, and became a broker. And so it was that on the 26th of March 1795 they were selling 'by the candle' at Garraway's coffee house in London, the following merchandise:

     50 hogsheads of refined sugar for export
   250 hogsheads of refined sugar for export
   100 bags of black and white ginger
    20 'goads' of Barbados aloes
 1200 skins from the West Indies
    50 bags of cocoa.

On the 11th of February 1796, James Man advertised for sale on his own premises:

    25 hogsheads of sugar
  205 casks and 60 bags of Jamaican coffee
  237 bags of black ginger
   84 bags of white ginger
   36 bags of cotton
   30 tonnes of bark
   30 'goads' of Barbados aloes
    1 cask of tortoise shell
    8 casks of indigo
   50 barrels of Carolina rice.

The merchandise for sale was generally recorded in a catalogue which the broker prepared and distributed on the eve of the sales.

The broker therefore acted either on behalf of the producer or the merchant-exporter with whose assistance he established a catalogue and estimated the value of the lots. The broker's commission, payable by the seller, was generally O.5%.

Under various company names, the Mans continued their brokerage activities throughout the 19th century moving, in 1808, to Mincing Lane which was at the time — and has remained to a great extent — the centre of the London commodities trade. Man remained first and foremost a colonial broker specializing gradually in sugar, rum (in 1870 the company became a broker for the Admiralty procuring the rum distributed daily to the sailors), cocoa, coffee and spices. Twice monthly Man published a circular containing information on the market. Gradually the auctions were abandoned and the company became a middleman operating on order both in actuals and in futures.

• Mark Woodhouse started out as a sugar broker around 1767. Before long he became a factor for a number of Jamaican planters the sale of whose sugar he ensured. There is a record of a sale 'by the candle' of pepper, ginger, coffee and cocoa, which he organized on the 7th of August 1816. The Woodhouse firm continued to grow, specializing in the Nineteen Twenties in the sale of coffee from Central America. In 1926 it merged with Carey and Browne (James Carey had been a coffee broker since 1825). In 1899 Carey and Browne had organized the largest auction of coffee in human memory: 13,121 bags were sold in three days. In the Nineteen Thirties, Woodhouse Carey and Browne became involved in trade, notably in sugar. But this brings us to the dawn of a new period[30].

• It was in 1775 that Robert Lewis began to organize auctions of colonial produce. His son Arthur pursued these activities, holding sales at the famous Garraway coffee house. Renamed Lewis and Peat in 1846, the firm continued to expand, opening an office in Singapore in 1919. In the Nineteen Twenties it was the largest produce broker in the City.

• London's foremost sugar broker around 1880 was C. Czarnikow and Co. founded in 1861 by a German emigrant, Cesar Czarnikow who started out as a sworn broker. Czarnikow gradually took charge of sales for a number of West Indian producers — and even those of the Colonial Company from 1897 — and before long began to publish a *Weekly Price Current* which was the major source of information on the market. He was the first to introduce beet sugar trading in Great Britain and opened branches in Glasgow (1871), Liverpool (1881), and New York (1891). Following his death in 1909 the firm continued to grow and was, in all likelihood, the world's foremost sugar broker in the Nineteen Thirties[31]. The sugar broker was responsible for bringing the more or less regrouped exporters into contact with one another. Thus Czarnikow was, from 1923, the exclusive agent of Colonial Sugar Refining, the company which accounted for all Australian sugar exports. Brokers also played a fundamental role in the circulation of information. As a rule, each brokerage firm published a weekly bulletin on the markets of the products which it traded: thus for sugar there was Czarnikow in London and Lamborn and Farr in New York.

In the field of sugar and colonial produce there were also a number of particularly outstanding Anglo-Saxon firms:

Table 1.2 Some major Anglo-Saxon brokerage firms.

Original company name	Present name	Founded in	Activity
Allen and Woodhouse	Woodhouse Drake & Carey	1748	colonial
Robert Lewis	Lewis and Peat	1775	general
Humphrey and Man	Ed. and F. Man	1792	colonial
Rucker and Bencraft	(disappeared)	1780	general
Hale and Sons	(disappeared)	1780	general
Paines and Read	(disappeared)	1815	general
James Carey	Woodhouse Drake & Carey	1825	coffee
John Drake	Woodhouse Drake & Carey	1820	colonial
J. Rouse	R.J. Rouse (Mercantile House)	1840	general
Arthur B. Hodge	Ed. and F. Man	1850	sugar
Czarnikow	Czarnikow Ltd.	1861	sugar
Golodetz	Golodetz	1908	sugar
Farr (New York)	(disappeared)	1920	sugar

Prominent among the French firms was *Duclos et Fils*, founded by Maurice Duclos in 1874 with a range of dealing activities extending from non-ferrous metals to colonial foodstuffs through a royal Siamese elephant and a portion of the gold from the roofs of the Kremlin churches sold to the West by the Soviets around 1920[32].

The first French broker to enter the grain trade was J.A. Goldschmidt. Founded in 1866 in Mulhouse by Elie and Aron Goldschmidt, the firm specialized in the brokerage of wheats and flours. Having started on the domestic market, the Goldschmidts expanded to the international market at the end of the century and opened branches in Antwerp (1908), Naples (1919), Marseilles (1920). At that time Goldschmidt represented in France some ten American and (before 1914) Russian export firms selling either directly to millers or to merchant–importers. During a meeting with this writer, Michel Goldschmidt described how a typical transaction was executed in the Nineteen Thirties: at 11 p.m. the Paris office would receive coded cables from Chicago. After they had been decoded offers would be dispatched at midnight to the Mediterranean Basin for reply on the following day at 2 p.m., in time for the opening of the Chicago market at 3.30 p.m. (Paris time). The operations were small ones: very often 1,000 quarters, the equivalent of 217 tonnes. Until about 1930, Australian wheats were transported in 300–500 tonne sail-boats making it possible for the end-users — the millers — to import directly[33]. Transactions were carried out according to the standard forms of contracts established by the GAFTA in London which contained provisions for all possible disputes[34].

As we can see, in view of the quantities dealt in and the general climate of commercial security which prevailed, it was possible to import or export directly, a development which rendered superfluous the services of the international trader. It was the broker who acted as middleman although he never appeared as principal in the transactions, his responsiblility coming to an end as soon as the contract was signed.

In general the broker was also active on the futures market and in France he was known as the *commissionaire*. Most often he also had to guarantee the successful outcome of transactions inasmuch as produce clearing houses were in general not prevalent until much later and using them was not necessarily compulsory. Although the London clearing houses were established as early as the end of the 19th century, that of the Parisian market for example was only created in the Nineteen Twenties. The broker was therefore under the obligation to protect himself by making regular margin calls on his clients. Notwithstnding, this could be a rather risky activity especially when the market was prey to speculation: speculation on the European sugar markets caused many a brokerage firm to go out of business especially in 1905[35].

On the other hand brokers only infrequently doubled as traders. They would, however, do so on occasion, especially when precise regulations called for it, but in general the separation of the professions was rather strict and the brokers — at least those who managed to survive over a long period of time — likewise refrained from speculating for their own accounts. But it is difficult to generalize on this level: Czarnikow, whom we have mentioned above, was not only the worlds's foremost sugar broker, he also possessed a 'produce' department responsible for a number of other products and was, especially in the Nineteen Thirties, the world's foremost pepper merchant, handling almost 55% of world exports[36].

Brokers were, not infrequently, called upon to deal in several products at the same time: a distinction was made in fact between the colonial brokers whose range of activities ran the gamut from sugar to coffee through spices, the grain brokers (who also dealt in certain oilseeds), and the metal brokers. . . Finally, alongside the major international firms, there were numerous national, 'departmental' (in France) and even county-based brokerage firms!

The broker, whose basic capital was the possession of information and the control of the means of communication, reached the height of his development at the end of the 19th century and the beginning of the 20th century. As soon as this capital had lost its strategic value, the broker's function was stripped of its importance. Between the 16th century, the age of the merchant and the 19th century, the age of the broker, there was a transition from goods to 'services', just as in a parallel field there was a transition from goods to banking with the introduction of acceptances and bills of exchange.

As we said before, the importer was often the end-user. This was the case of the mill-owners, the sugar refiners, the texile manufacturers. . . The harbour merchants with their warehousing facilities retained nevertheless a very important position, especially in the Anglo-Saxon countries. The following quotation taken from Thiers and dating from 1851 illustrates this difference of approach if applied to the buying function:

'In England the manufacturer is not allowed to be a merchant. In France the manufacturer from Roubaix or from Lille leaves his workers on the job and comes to Paris; he plays a dual role: he is manufacturer and to a certain extent merchant and there is no middleman separating him from the retailer. . . In Britain, two or three middlemen have taken up position between the large producers and the consumer, and it is they who pocket all the profits'[37].

This should help to explain why cotton shipments would pass through the hands of importers in Liverpool and dealers in Manchester, before reaching the owners of the spinning-mills. All the same, there was a tendency for these channels to simplify even here, especially with the increase in the speed of communications owing to the laying of submarine cables. Thus from 1880 onwards the Manchester merchant began to offer brokerage services to the spinning-mills and in Le Havre where, in the coffee trade, it was normal to distinguish between the *importateurs–arbitragistes* or pure importers and the *importateurs–commissionnaires* or distributors, the two professions gradually merged into one[38].

And here too, it was indisputably brokerage services which tended to replace commercial activities. At the beginning of the 20th century, oilseeds arriving in Marseilles were 'received by importers who delivered to the manufacturer through the agency of the broker'[39].

Nonetheless colonial trade continued to maintain its originality and vitality: in France the firm *Maurice Hecht Frères et Cie* founded in 1847 began to specialize in the rubber trade (from the end of the century) and gradually abandoned its activities in spices, cocoa and ivory. . . In 1914 it changed its name to Alcan et Cie.

In 1826, the German trader Frederic Foerster founded a firm in Le Havre with the purpose of trading in coffee. Renamed *Raoul Duval et Cie* in 1889, the company was to become the main importer in Le Havre in the 20th century, maintaining special contacts with Africa, particularly with the Ivory Coast.

In Great Britain, on the other hand, a number of large wholesale distributors for food products were on the rise. Joseph Travers and Sons, a very old-established company going back at least to the Great Fire of London in 1666, is one of the most interesting examples of such undertakings. In 1779 it was known under the name of Smith, Nash, Kemble and Travers and was located in Cannon Street, 'at the Sugar Loaf'. The main products handled were tea and sugar, later spices and dried fruit. The firm of Travers owned and published the *Produce's Market Review* which was, with the *Public Ledger,* one of the chief organs of the fiercely free-trader British commercial community. In 1899 it opened a branch in Singapore for the purpose of exporting spices and tinned pineapple. Other agencies were subsequently opened in Malaysia, Indonesia and later in Borneo. Thus around 1930, Travers began to develop into a veritable international trader in spices and tropical fruits[40]. Other major firms were James Budgett of London, the Berisfords of Manchester, the Billingtons of Liverpool, the Swiffens of Birmingham. S. and W. Berisford were already one of the largest domestic traders in refined sugar. In Switzerland, the firm founded by Georges André in 1877 was, in 1914, one of the major grain importers in the country.

Such was the state of international commodity trade in 1939. Admittedly, our approach is by no means a rigorous and systematic one. Our aim is merely to help the reader get a feel for the general evolution from the 18th to the 20th century. And in fact there were few changes during that period: an acceleration of the trading process owing to innovations in the field of communications, resulting in a simplification of the systems as well as the transformation of numerous commercial functions into brokerage ones. Moreover, in the same period, markets became formalized and centred around a few major market-places.

But even before 1939 new elements were to appear bringing in their wake marked changes in the practices obtaining in international trade. The most important novelty was indisputably government intervention in the marketing of commodities.

The new conditions prevailing in international commodity trading: 1930–1970.

We have already stressed in the introduction the radical changes which have taken place in international trade in commodities since 1945. We shall not dwell on the physical growth in quantities traded. Two points strike us as being of particular importance: the appearance of government in commodity marketing on the one hand, and on the other, the opening up of the various geo-economic regions of the world to an international market prey to an increasingly chronic instability.

There was of course nothing new about government intervention in the commodity marketing chain. In fact, since the dawn of modern times, government has not only actively encouraged private initiative but, when necessary, supplanted it. We are familiar with the Spanish and Portuguese state monopolies, the *Casa de India* of Lisbon, the *Casa de Contratacion* of Seville and later of Cadiz. Moreover, we know that never has private initiative been so prosperous as when it has been able to lean on the discreetly protective arm of a protectionist government. Furthermore, many a state — often for budget and tax purposes — has doubled as manufacturer or trader in order to take over the management of some particularly interesting monopoly. So it was with certain nations of continental Europe which created sugar monopolies in the 19th century: the first beet sugar refineries — those of Achard in Prussia at the end of the 18th century — were state undertakings. Finally one would have to go back to the more general framework of the 'obligatory membership' guilds which were abolished in France by the French Revolution but survived in Austria-Hungary until 1859.

But the economic theories of the 19th century were not consonant with this function of the state as entrepreneur and trader. It was held that government was at most to serve as a safety net and, in the view of pure liberals, even this function was hardly desirable. Thus, before 1914, the direct intervention of government in a domestic market (outside the traditional monopolies of alcohol, tobacco or matches) was extremely rare. In certain cases it confined itself to strengthening

— at times even taking over from — the trusts and cartels formed by private industry. By means of the *Norminovka,* as that system was called, the Russian state was able to achieve just that in the sugar trade from 1895 onwards: the state granted each factory a quota on the local market and one on the export market. In certain sectors, especially in mining, we find governments operating as producers: the Spanish mercury mines for example. But although this case is a relatively exceptional one, government has never hindered and has even encouraged the formation of national or even international trusts and cartels.

The First World War provided many governments with the opportunity to take a closer interest in the management of markets. This, and the return to normalcy which followed, coupled with the Great Crash of 1929 and the surplus-induced depression of agricultural prices whose origins went as far back as 1924, all conspired to radically change this conception of the role of the state. Faced with the bankruptcy of the market economy and of private initiative, the state was obliged to expand its role, reassure producers by providing them with its guarantee and slash what at the time were considered to be the excessively large profits generated by trade. On the international level the Thirties were characterized by a number of abortive attempts to stabilize the markets[41]. On the national level the Soviet example, implemented from 1917, took on a new significance in 1928, and although the Western countries were by no means about to follow the same path, they had nevertheless, as early as the Twenties, begun to address themselves to solving their agricultural problems. One of the first solutions advanced was the establishment, with a certain amount of state encouragement, of producer cooperatives which would bypass the first stages of the trading process. Thus in June 1929 the Agricultural Marketing Act of the very liberal President Hoover provided for the creation of a $500 million fund to finance the setting up of cooperative storage bodies. Note that this came after President Coolidge had vetoed two laws voted by Congress, aimed at endowing the United States with a system comparable to the present EEC Common Agricultural Policy (purchase at a guaranteed price, export monopoly. . .). Thereafter the Commodity Credit Corporation, created by the Agricultural Adjustment Act of Roosevelt in 1933 and strengthened in 1938, developed a lending scheme which made it possible for farmers to stock their produce while awaiting a rise in prices. Government involvement was more discreet in Canada where the coopera-

tives also carried more weight: in the inter-war period, five-sevenths of
Canadian wheat exports were handled by the Canadian Cooperative
Wheat Producers[42]. A first Farm Board had existed during the war but
had been dissolved in 1920. In 1931, faced with the magnitude of the
crisis, a new Farm Board (as of 1945, the Canadian Wheat Board) was
created as the sole body responsible for regulating the Canadian grain
market. The same process took place in France where the *Front
Populaire* created the *Office National Interprofessionnel du Blé* leading
to the birth of a *de facto* monopoly benefitting the cooperatives.
Similarly in Great Britain the beet industry was practically nationalized and merged into the British Sugar Corporation (1936). As a
major exporter of agricultural produce Brazil was also suffering from
depressed world prices. During the early Thirties the government
therefore decided to create 'institutes' to manage the markets and to
export produce: the *Instituto do Azucar e Alcohol* (1933) and the
Instituto Brazileiro do Cafe. Finally, certain colonial administrators,
concerned about the instability of their revenues, created the first
caisses de stabilisation (in French-speaking Africa)[43] and Marketing
Boards (in English-speaking Africa). The first was the West African
Cocoa control Board created in 1939 in British West Africa.

We can well imagine that the Board met a need, to judge by the
curious poem written in 1944 on the Burma front by a soldier from the
Gold Coast who was familiar with the Twenty-third Psalm[44]:

> The European trader is my shepherd; I am in want.
> He maketh me to live in the cocoa plantations;
> He leadeth me beside the waters of great need;
> He bringeth a revival of my doubts about the good working of the 'pools'.
>
> He leadeth me in the paths of destruction
> For his finances' sake.
> Yea whilst I walk through the valley of starvation I shall fear everything,
> For thou art like me:
> The generating agents and the profiteers
> They frighten me.
>
> Thou preparest a reduction of my salary in the presence of my creditors;
> Thou anointest my income with taxes;
> My expense runneth over my revenue.
>
> Surely unemployment and poverty shall follow me all the days of the 'pools'
>   life:
> and I shall dwell in a rented house forever.

Unfortunately the disappearance of the trading posts did not necessarily improve the fate of the producers. In the same vein, we can refer

to the works of fiction written by the Brazilian Jorge Amado, dealing with the cocoa growers' situation in Bahia during the Nineteen Thirties.

In Great Britain and in the principal dominions (South Africa, Australia, New Zealand. . .) marketing Boards came into existence. These were interprofessional bodies to which the government granted a trading monopoly (and over which it maintained a substantial control). The first ones were created in Australia and New Zealand in the Twenties.

For very different motives, all trade in Germany from 1934 was regulated by distribution boards. But here we are already dealing with a war economy.

As during the First World War, international trade during the Second World War, especially in the case of the Allies, was placed under state control; besides, the men who really made the wheels of trade turn were generally former brokers and traders who doubled as civil servants: the director of the Sugar Division of the British Ministry of Food was none other than William Rook, general manager of Czarnikow. The Combined Food Board created by the United States and the United Kingdom administered the food supplies of the entire allied zone and, from 1944–45 until 1948, of almost the entire world![45].

But while this form of state action on an international level was not here to stay, the situation was not quite the same on the national level. On the one hand the centralized management of the economy attracted new followers: Eastern Europe and China thus disappeared from the trading chessboard. On the other hand, many states organized, if not their domestic trade, at least their foreign trade on models previously tried and proven in the pre-war period (and curiously enough many reforms carried out by dirigiste and corporative governments in the 1930–45 period were maintained by their liberal heirs).

The Anglo-Saxon marketing and produce boards became common practice for agricultural produce. From 1962, the Common Agricultural Policy totally isolated the EEC from the major world markets. In the United States the P.L. 480, voted in 1954, contained provisions for dealing with agricultural surpluses and for channelling food aid to the Third World.

A look at the wheat supply on the world market today will therefore reflect the marked bias towards state control evidenced by the proliferation of government agencies: in Australia, the Australian Wheat

Board; for the European Community, the Brussels Commission; in Canada, the Canadian Wheat Commission; in the United States, the USDA (Ministry of Agriculture) which controls all shipments above 50,000 tonnes. The only exception is Argentina where the *Junta Nacional de Granos* was gradually stripped of its power after the fall of the Peron regime (yet it now appears to regain a certain degree of activity). The situation is more or less identical for coffee and cocoa.

Finally 1947 and subsequent years ushered in a new era of independence for a number of states. This meant not only a transfer of authority and responsibility but also a rather sudden wave of nationalizations of the means of production (plantations and mines) and the creation of marketing boards. This process was slow to evolve between 1945 and 1960, but rapidly gained momentum in the following decade regardless of the political or ideological direction of the regimes in power. Let us take a look at a few examples:

- in 1945 'colonial' sugar production based on sugar cane was almost everywhere controlled by foreign interests: American (in Cuba, in the Dominican Republic, in the Philippines), British (West Indies, Guyana), Australian (Fiji), even South African (Rhodesia), and Dutch interests (Java). But by 1980 this was a thing of the past. From Indonesia (1948) right down to the Dominican Republic (1979) all traces of it were removed, leaving only British Honduras and Mauritius partly as remnants of the colonial era. Everywhere in the world today, almost all of the sugar-cane supply is accounted for by state-controlled or parastatal structures[46];

- even more characteristic than sugar was the trade in copper, which was in the hands of a few international groups (Anaconda, *Union Minière du Haut Katanga,* Rio Tinto Zinc. . .). These groups operated on the basis of an intense vertical integration which meant that they were established in several countries and were in a position to concentrate supply. Here too the winds of nationalization have swept everything away, diluting supply among a multitude of producer nations (Peru, Chile, Zambia, Zaire, founders of the *Consero Internacional de los Paises Exportadores de Cuper* or CIPEC) and leaving very little other than the mines of the Rio Tinto Company in Papua New Guinea and the rather peculiar case of Australia.

The logical upshot of these changes was therefore the adaptation — if not the disappearance — of two-way trading and that of the integrated groups. The export trade survived only — and under a stiff yoke of authorisations and regulations — in the United States and to a lesser extent in Europe[47]. Moreover the situation was practically the same for the import trade since, there too, most of the new states immediately took matters into their own hands. One of the main consequences was a reduced flexibility in international trade since government structures are apt to be much less flexible in their approach to problems than private ones. Another result was a clear increase in the unit tonnages of operations and a more widespread use of f.o.b. sales and c.i.f. purchases.

The second significant change in international trade in commodities after 1945, was the appearance of a true world market. The old empires disappeared taking with them their currency areas and their relative calm. The Japanese empire collapsed in 1945 followed by the Dutch empire and then bit by bit the French and British empires. These were replaced for a time by the dollar empire but one might safely assume that at present — and since 1973 — the latter practically no longer exists.

Great expanses have therefore opened up and thanks to developments in the field of communications (telephone, telex), the unification of the market has been achieved. Formerly, the concept of a world market had been based on a number of different real elements and on a collection of separate markets, being in fact the synthesis of these realities: the 'world price' itself only concerned a small portion of international trade. In 1954, for example, the share of the free market (and hence that to which the 'world price' was applicable) in world sugar exports was only 42.90%. By 1978 this share had risen to 62.74%, an evolution which could be observed for most commodities.

But, and this is of paramount importance, the present world market is unique in that operators the world over have access to the market at any given time. Moreover, it is on the international level that supply meets demand, since, generally speaking, the logistics of transport no longer pose a problem. The preferred meeting places for supply and demand are the major futures markets, which have experienced a spectacular development since 1960: the Chicago Board of Trade, the Chicago Mercantile Exchange, The New York Sugar and Coffee

Table 1.3 Chronological table of Marketing Boards, *Caisses de Stabilisation* and public bodies

Date	Country	Institution	Product handled
1931	Canada	Farm Board	Grains
1936	New Zealand	Marketing Department (replaced in 1947 by the Dairy Products Marketing Commission)	All agricultural products (but especially dairy produce)
1939	Australia	Marketing Board	Wheat
1939-1942	British West Africa	West African Cocoa Control Board	Cocoa
1942-1949	—	West African Produce Control Board	Cocoa, groundnuts, oil-palm
1947	Ghana	Cocoa Marketing Board	Cocoa
	Nigeria	Cocoa Marketing Board	Cocoa
	Burma	National Agricultural Marketing Board	All products (especially rice)
	Australia	Wheat Board	Grain
1949	Ghana	Produce Marketing Board (renamed in 1955 Ghana Agricultural and Fisheries Development Corp.)	All products except cocoa
	Nigeria	4 Marketing Boards (transformed in 1954 into regional boards controlled by an umbrella organization, the Nigeria Produce Marketing Company Ltd)	Groundnuts, oil-palm, cotton, cocoa, sesame, soya
	Sierra-Leone	Sierra Produce Marketing Board	Oil-palm, cocoa, sesame, coppra, groundnuts (since 1961, coffee and ginger)
	Uganda	Lint Marketing Board	Cotton
	Gambia	Gambia Oilseeds M.B.	Palm cabbage, groundnuts
1953	Uganda	Coffee Marketing Board	Coffee
1960	Ghana	Timber Marketing Board	Wood
1962	EEC	Commission of European Communities	Grain, sugar, dairy products…
1963	Argentina	Junta Nacional de Granos	Grain

(This is of course by no means an exhaustive list!)

Exchange, The London Metal Exchange, have become the undisputed centres of international trade in commodities.

The extension of world market frontiers, the concentration of supply and demand in the hands of public structures, with their very understandable lack of flexibility, improved circulation of information and the concomitant improvement in the accuracy of forecasting and anticipation, have combined to increase the market's propensity to fluctuate. In order to protect themselves from these fluctuations, dealers are obliged to almost systematically resort to hedging and therefore to use futures markets. Furthermore, since 1970 and with the 'establishment' of the international monetary disorder, futures have come to be used as financial instruments by banking establishments or institutional investors. Yves Simon[48] has pointed out that the volume of transactions on the major American and British Commodity exchanges has increased since 1968 at a rate of 20% per annum: in the United States from 3.9 million contracts in 1959, to 9.3 million in 1968, 58.5 million in 1978, and to almost 140 million in 1983! The world price is now one which is fixed by speculators (or investors) who arrive at a decision on the basis of their anticipations of possible variations in real supply and demand levels. The decisive factor is to control, but more importantly to understand, the information available.

There are few products whose world price is not fixed on a futures market: products which are not easily fungible such as tea or which have a very limited market such as many non-ferrous metals, and which are still governed by a system of producer prices. But here too an evolution is taking place: for copper, mentioned above, the producer price system which obtained until the beginning of the Seventies has given way to a price fixed on the London Metal Exchange. The same change has already taken place for aluminium and nickel and it is quite likely that in the near future, world oil prices will be fixed on the New York futures exchange.

Finally we should like to point out that all the efforts made, especially by UNCTAD since 1976, to stabilize these markets have been to no avail. In the event, world monetary instability, which began in 1973 and continued with the widespread floating of currencies, has exacerbated the instability prevailing in international trade.

These new conditions obtaining in international trade have, of course, effected marked changes in the various commercial professions. The function of the international broker has lost importance; the import and export traders have joined forces and powerful cooperative associations have appeared in agriculture. Finally, a new middleman has risen from the ashes of brokerage and domestic trade: the international trader.

Before proceeding any further with the discussion of international traders, however, we should like, on the one hand to undertake a precise analysis of the various functions which at present play a role in international trade, and on the other, to clarify our analysis of international trade in commodities.

Chapter 2

THE DIFFERENT FUNCTIONS IN INTERNATIONAL TRADE

Broker, dealer, trader on the one hand, *courtier, négociant, commissionnaire* on the other, so many words which take on very different meanings according to the context. The next logical step after this brief historical overview, would be to define the limits of the different functions which play a role in international trade today.

One essential distinction must be drawn between the middlemen who work on commission or for a fixed consideration and who do not appear as principals in a transaction, and those middlemen who deal or trade on their own account and who at a given time are sole owners of the goods traded.

The problem is that very often these two commercial functions are carried out by one and the same operator who, for example, can be a broker one day and a merchant the next. The difference lies more in the size of the undertaking, the methods employed and the way in which problems are tackled. For our part, we propose to look successively at:

– the brokers, *courtiers* and their variants

– the export houses (*commissionnaires–exportateurs*) and the specialist buyers (*bureaux d'achat*)

– the international trading companies (merchant houses or agencies)

– the traders specializing in two-way trading
– the international traders in commodities and semi-finished goods who are the subject of this study.

The brokers, *courtiers,* and their variants

As we have seen in the preceding chapter, the broker exercises a long-established function in international trade which reached its high-water mark between 1850 and 1950.

The international broker as we have described him has practically become a thing of the past in an era of such effortless communications. On the strictly international level there are nevertheless a number of significant relics:

● on the one hand the brokerage firms continue to monopolize the organization of auctions (tea in London[1], diamonds in the case of the Central Selling Organization[2]) or the management of specific markets (the fixing of gold prices in London);

● on the other hand certain firms continue to handle sales for the major producers on the international market (Czarkinow for the Australian CSR, Ed. and F. Man for South African sugar);

● finally in many sectors the international broker continues to carry out his activities under a serious time constraint, at the mercy of his two telephones.

It is estimated that 5–10% of all grain transactions are handled by a few international brokerage firms. Apart from the French company Montenay, special mention should be made of Pasternak-Baum, originally an American firm. This company, which boasts of a hundred employees betweeen Geneva, New York, Kuala Lumpur, Sao Paolo, and Buenos Aires, possesses its own integrated telecommunications network. Its effectiveness hinges on the rapidity with which it receives information: a broker's offer is rarely firm for more that a quarter of an hour! In the grains sector commisssions are fixed at 10–15 cents per tonne (1–1.5%), 20–25 cents per tonne for soya (beans and cakes) and $1 per tonne for oils (0.25%). Pasternak's office in Geneva alone handles a yearly average of 6 million tonnes of soya, 5 million tonnes of maize, 5 million tonnes of cakes and 500,000 tonnes of soya oil. Since the grain embargo in 1980, the Eastern Bloc countries and especially the USSR, increasingly resort to the services of brokers. But in all these operations the broker merely acts as an interface. He does not make any in-depth analysis. Almost without exception, he has lost practically all of his strategic importance save for certain markets (minor metals in particular) where there is a paucity of information. Very often in fact, the broker is to some extent the official organ of the market, especially when public quotations are not held. This is probably what led the French firm Duclos to gradually specialize in 'minor products' such as glycerine, essential oils, and reptile skins! On the whole one could say that over the past few years brokers have been making a progressive shift towards merchanting. They have gradually tended to take futures positions and later to become traders themselves, a process which has taken place faster in some regions and for some products than for others. In the coffee trade there are still a number of Le Havre brokers (Jacques Louis Delamare for example), agents for Brazilian or Central American shippers. They represent their producers in a non-exclusive manner in dealings with the major French coffee roasters or distributors. On the other hand, coffee from Indonesia is always handled by traders (mainly of British or Dutch nationality). Finally, as a favour to clients, brokers, on occasion, operate as merchants (as the principal) for 'back to back operations'. In the final analysis the broker is first and foremost a go-between who makes it possible for people who do not know each other — and often have no desire to do so — to reach an agreement. His role as a contact is an essential one; the career of Jean-Baptiste Doumeng, who was until his death in 1987 the privileged middleman of the countries of the Eastern Bloc, leaves no doubt as to his importance.

It is clearly difficult to generalize and the possibility remains that the brokerage profession will demonstrate a capacity for survival which is not evident at first glance.

Alongside the international produce broker whose very existence is moot[3], there are sworn brokers (with an official status), exchange brokers and other financial middlemen.

In many countries certain brokers, (whether they hold office or not) are raised to the status of public officers once they have taken the oath and are allowed to organise auctions of both government-owned and impounded goods and to fix prices or quotations. These are the French 'courtiers assermentés'[4]), the British 'sworn brokers' and the Italian *pubblici mediatori*. . .

In maritime affairs, international shipping brokers (in France, Barry Rogliano Salles for example) bring together ship-owners and shippers and negotiate the main elements of the charterparty (not to be confused, however, with the French *courtiers maritimes*, public officers who are based in the ports and have a monopoly there).

The broker is therefore, as a rule, independent (guarantee of a certain neutrality) even in cases where he acts on behalf of a specific buyer or seller. The factor or *commissionnaire*, on the other hand, resembles more a representative.

But before we go any further, the financial aspect of brokerage operations on the futures markets — because of its recent development — deserves our consideration.

The financial middlemen

On the futures markets, transactions are handled through brokers who have a market-place monopoly. These are the French *commissionnaires agréés*, and the Anglo-Saxon brokers.

In the financial world the Anglo-Saxon concept of 'broker' or 'commission house' is an extremely broad one covering activities as dissimilar as those of the stock broker, the *commissionnaire agréé*, (chartered commission agent or factor), the merchant banks. . . The activities on the futures markets are but a small part of a range of services which constitute a sort of financial supermarket. However the development of the futures markets (especially the markets for financial instruments) has revived the interest of these firms in commodities[5]. This renewed interest has been particularly noticeable in the United States with the mushrooming of investment houses and commission houses.

With around 17,000 employees, Merrill Lynch and Co. Inc. is the largest financial services company om Wall Street and in the world. Its revenue in 1985 was over $7 billion with a net profit of $224 million: it is the largestbroker on the American futures markets with an income from these activities of $103 million in 1979. Merrill Lynch and a few other firms of this type constitute in fact one of the only real powers on the commodities futures markets. Owing to the size and the number of portfolios which they administer or in whose management they have a say, the company can have a direct influence on the prices in Chicago or in New York[6]. Until 1981 the chairman was Donald T. Regan who then was in put charge of the Treasury in the Reagan Administration, before becoming the White House's Chief of Staff until February 1987. Among the other major firms which are particularly active in raw materials (and which are responsible in particular for administering commodity funds), there is Bache (bought in 1980 by the Prudential Insurance Company), Goldman Sachs (which, in 1981, paid over $100 million for the trader, Jack Aron, a specialist in coffee, cotton, and precious metals), Salomon Brothers, associated with Phibro one of whose vice-presidents Henry Kaufman ranks among the gurus of Wall Street, Donaldson Lufkin and Jeanrette (they purchased the world's leading coffee trader ACLI, also in 1981, sold their trading division to Cargill in 1984 and were themselves bought November 1984 by the Equitable Life Insurance Company).But for the last few years, the 'commission house' most active on commodity futures markets (and probably the world's biggest in that field) has been Refco, which in 1984 fully bought Conti Commodities.

Table 2.1 The ten principal financial houses on Wall Street (in $million)

		Capital	
		1980	1979
1	Merrill Lynch	1,065.00	784.20
2	Shearson Loeb Rhodes	469.80	246.3
	(bought in 1981 by American Express)		
3	EF Hutton Group	448.00	238.00
4	Salomon Brothers	330.70	228.70
	(bought in 1981 by Philip Brothers)		
5	Paine Webber	243.00	236.00
6	Bache Halsey Stuart Shields	233.80	162.50
	(bought in 1980 by Prudential Ins.)		
7	Goldman Sachs	219.00	181.00
	(purchased J. Aron in 1981)		
8	Dean Witter Reynolds	216.30	193.70
9	Stephens	167.30	145.10
10	First Boston Group	153.20	127.20

Source: *Institutional Investor.*
(This classification changes somewhat when seen in terms of issue management: in 1983, in $ billion subscribed: Salomon Brothers (15), Merrill Lynch Capital Markets (11), Goldman Sachs (11), First Boston (9.9), Morgan Stanley (8.8), Drexel Burnham Lambert (7.6), Lehman Bros. Kuhn Loeb (5.9), Kidder Peabody (3.4). . . In June 1984, American Express which had already bought Shearson in 1981, took over Lehman Bros Kuhn Loeb).

Among the British firms worthy of mention, note the spectacular rise of the Mercantile House group which bought a subsidiary in Chicago in 1980 (Woodstock Commodities) and one in London in 1981 (R.J. Rouse). Note also the take-over of Wallace Brother Commodities, since 1972 part of the Brooke Bond Group, by Johnson Mathey Bankers before the near collapse of the latter in 1984 and its rescue by the Bank of England.

For most commodity trading firms, however, the development of brokerage activities in futures was not only dictated by their own needs but also by those of an external clientele: e.g. Conti Commodity Services created by the Continental Grain Company (United States). In this direction Philip Brothers has probably gone the furthest in buying out the Wall Street broker Salomon Brothers in 1981. We shall pursue this point at a later stage, but it would seem that we are about to witness the advent of a new category of transnational financial middlemen present on the traditional financial markets and on the major commodity markets, both as brokers and traders[7].

In any event, the power of the 'commission houses' on the futures markets has been on the increase over the past few years. Abnormal market behaviour due to the concentration of speculators around a few commodity funds has been a source of concern to the American farming community in recent years. According to *Business Week* (12th March 1984): 'A firm like Merryl Lynch, by selling a new commodity fund, can modify price trends more fundamentally than can the arrival of a fleet of tankers'.

The export commission houses and the specialist buyers

This type of operator, not very often found in commodity trading, acts on behalf of the buyer, who is generally foreign, in dealings with manufacturers. He may take the form of:

– a wholesaler dealing on world scale (but then in his own name),
– a large retail business with branches abroad which have to be supplied (but here too the purchase is firm),
– the integrated agency of a retail chain or of a trading posts company,
– the representative of a foreign buyer in a given country (usually his own).

The most famous example of the last mentioned is the British Crown Agents, a financial group responsible in the past for all purchases made by the various colonial administrations and which has retained a large clientele in the countries of the Commonwealth[8]. In the French context, there are the export commission houses (selling or buying), and in Germany, the *Export Vertreter* (who represent German manufacturers in dealings with trading firms). Sometimes the representative guarantees the fulfillment of the buyer's undertakings to the manufacturer, in which role he is known as a confirming house in Britain, or a *commissionnaire ducroire* in France. These are, moreover, principally financial bodies which also act as forwarding agents when the need arises. It remains to be pointed out that — in connection with engineering contracts — engineering consultant firms often take the place of the specialist buyers for overseas clients[9].

But the most outstanding feature of numerous international trading companies is that they perform the dual function of agencies and of specialist buyers.

International trading companies

The first international trading companies on a global level were in fact the great East India companies of the 16th and the 18th centuries. They were succeeded — as we have seen — by the mercantile houses and later by the merchant firms. The latter underwent profound changes from 1950 during the decolonization process and, while some of them managed to adapt, others fell by the wayside.

At present the share of international trade (all goods taken together) controlled by the international trading companies varies considerably by country: almost 80% of Japan's foreign trade but only 10% of that of the United States's, for example.

International trading companies are multi-faceted. In days gone by, the colonial type of company was a specialist in barter trade: it purchased local raw materials, produce and handicraft through its trading posts and shipped them to the home country while exporting back to the trading posts, the manufactured goods which it purchased on the home market. The opposite model was at the origin of the Japanese firms: they were created at the beginning of the Meiji era to check the growth of foreign companies and started off by managing

Japan's imports of raw cotton before taking charge of its exports. There is an import–export character to the Japanese firms which is much less apparent in the old colonial companies.

Let us take a look at how an international trading company functions from a given country: in general it has a system of agencies and subsidiary companies all over the world or at least in a given geographical zone. These agencies either distribute directly (supermarket chains for example), prospect potential markets or carry out manufacturing or other activities on the spot. They receive supplies through the parent company or through its subsidiaries on the production sites. The last mentioned serve to a certain extent as specialist buyers. Such companies are often the exclusive representatives for a specific brand on a given market (SCOA or Optorg for the French car maker Peugeot in Sub-Saharan Africa for example), but the subsidiaries also export local produce either to the firm's home country or to an international merchant, although most of the international trading companies also trade rather extensively in commodities themselves. This general description has so far served our purposes, but a better understanding of these trends requires a country-by-country analysis at this stage.

● **Japan**: to give honour where honour is due, we shall begin with Japan whose general traders, the *sogo shosa*, are by far the largest on the international scene. Most of them were founded in the years which immediately followed the opening up of the country to the outside world (the Meiji era, 1868 onward). At that time, Japan's foreign trade was entirely controlled by foreign firms and the Government encouraged the local capitalists and industrialists to set up trading companies. The latter underwent a spectacular development especially from 1890 when they began to import cotton. As a rule such firms relied on the large, more or less feudal, industrial groups, the *zaibatzu*. In 1874 the *shosa* accounted for 1% of Japan's foreign trade, but by 1918, this figure had risen to 80%. In 1946 Mitsui and Mitsubishi, the two largest *zaibatzu*, which at that time literally dominated Japan's foreign and domestic trade, were dissolved as were, in July 1947, some of the mercantile companies belonging to these two groups.

This provided the opportunity needed by a number of other companies such as C. Itoh or Marubeni, which, as of 1950, were able to develop international trading activities. Mitsubishi and Mitsui were able to resume their activities in 1954 and 1959 respectively.

At present there are almost 6,000 trading companies in Japan but 9 of them — those presently called the *sogo shosa* — account on their own for 50% of Japan's foreign trade, with a combined turnover equivalent to 22% of the country's GNP in 1980. Of these 9 companies the two largest, Mitsui and Mitsubishi, had turnovers of over $70 billion in 1980-81.

A look at Tables 2.2 and 2.3 will reveal the main characteristics of these groups:

– their dealings are not limited to the domestic market although they do in fact dominate Japanese domestic trade which accounts for 40% of their activities. Their domestic activities provide them with a powerful commercial base which is cemented by their ties with Japanese industrial and financial structures: in the absence of a formal reconstitution the *zaibatzu* have retained informal links with each other (for example the Monday conference of all the Mitsui company directors). Moreover, a very complex system of crossed financial connections allows them to maintain very close links with the major Japanese banks[10] which lend them their support (the *sogo shosa* are rather 'loose' structures with a proportion of net worth to working capital of two to four percents!).

– They control a substantial share of Japan's foreign trade and have a quasi-monopoly of a certain number of commodities such as coal, iron, oil, cotton, timber, pulp, grain[11]. They have not hesitated to participate in mining joint ventures in Australia (coal, iron, bauxite, aluminium), in the Philippines (copper and nickel), in the United States (copper. . .), in Brasil (iron), or in agro-industrial or forestry projects[12]. In 1980, they accounted for 52% of Japan's imports and 48% of its total exports.

– We shall not deal, at this point, with the problem of exports but we should underscore the large number of activities which the *sogo shosa* carry out on an 'offshore' basis, that is, in third countries. This is particularly the case for commodities such as grain where the Japanese firms are often in the leading position in international trade. Marubeni carried out 70% of its grain transactions in third countries, trading 4 million tonnes of wheat, 4 million tonnes of other grains, 2.3 million tonnes of soya beans and 70,000 tonnes of palm-oil in 1980. In the trade sector the Japanese firms make good use of their privileged access to Asian markets and in particular to the Chinese market. Moreover,

Table 2.2 The nine Japanese *sogo shosa*

Company	Founding date	1983 turnover in $ billion	Net profit in $ million	Number of foreign offices	Number of subsidiary companies	Group	Number of employees
Mitsubishi Corp.	1870-1954	63.6	77.2	148		Mitsubishi	17,000
Mitsui and Co. Ltd	1876-1959	59.7	44	130		Mitsui	13,000
C. Itoh and co. Ltd	1858-1949	52.9	13		406	DKB	10,200
Marubeni Corp.	1858-1949-77	49	1.5	154	212+162	Fuyo	9,000
Sumitumo Corp.	1919	48.1	72.8	120		Sumitumo	7,500
Nissho Iwai Corp.	1928-62-68	33.9	33.7	166		Sanwa	8,000
Toyo Menka Corp.	1920	16.6	8.1	106		Tokai	3,800
Kanematsu Gosho Ltd	1889	14.7	4.2	100		DKB	3,400
Nichimen Co. Ltd	1892	13.8	5.9			Sanwa	3,500

Source : Annual reports of the firms under consideration for the year ending 31.3.1983. For the year ending 31.3.1984, Mitsubishi was about to publish net profits of $107 million.

Table 2.3 The distribution of turnover among the main *sogo shosa* (in %)

COMPANY	domestic trade	import	export	off shore	oil products	chemicals	ferrous metals	non-ferrous metals	machinery and construction	agricultural produce	general	textiles
Mitsubishi Corp.	40.7	31.7	17	10.6	26.1	8.6	17.9	7.6	16.9	14.1	5.8	3.2
Mitsui and Co. Ltd	39	22	18	21	15	12	18	9	15	19	8	4
C. Itoh and co. Ltd	44.2	21.7	19.9	14.2	30.2		10.3		21.9	12.3	6	13.3
Marubeni Corp.	37.5	19.1	25.7	17.7	25.1		22.7		23.7	14.2	7.4	8.9
Sumitomo Corp.					19		33.2		25.5	9	10.7	3.6
Nissho Iwai Corp.	40.3	28.2	17.8	13.7	27.4		33.6		17.1	8.1	8.1	5.7
Toyo Menka Corp.	41.2	23.6	22.6	12.6	22.7		13		20.2	16.8	4.8	16.5
Nichimen Co. Ltd	31.9	22.3	27.3	18.5	28.2				25.5	16.9	6.7	12.2

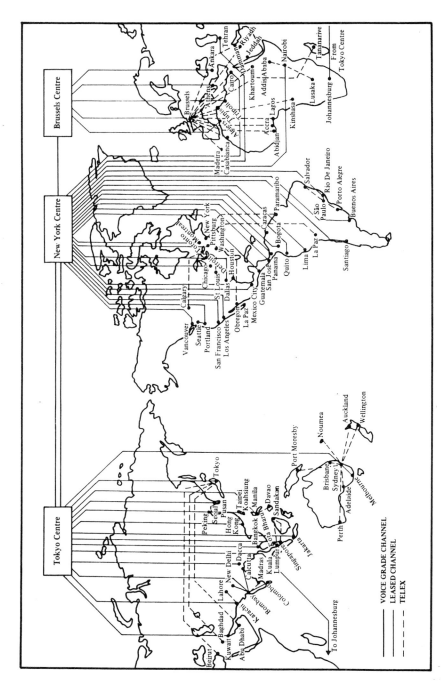

Figure 2.1 The Marubeni communications network.

Marubeni exports coffee from Brazil, C. Itoh is the world's foremost trader in palm oil (from Malaysia) and Toyo Menka is very active in cotton. Finally, most of these firms are present on the markets for precious and non-ferrous metals.

– The *shosa* have no strict rules of operation. They can act as principals or work merely on a commission basis. More or less 70% of Mitsubishi's activites are in trading whereas two-thirds of C. Itoh's are in brokerage. As a rule, the subsidiary companies and agencies are almost totally dependent on the headquarters in Tokyo.

– The *shosa* rely not only on a huge network of offices and subsidiary companies in most countries of the world but also on impressive communications systems which most firms would find it exceedingly difficult to match[13]. They are, moreover, supported by the Japanese banking and industrial community and by the famous MITI (Ministry for International Trade and Industry).

At the beginning of the Eighties (particularly in 1983–84) the major *sogo shosa* were confronted with problems arising from the worldwide recession (Osawa went bankrupt in March 1984, Mitsui ran into problems in Iran). Since 1982, most of them have been experiencing dwindling profits.

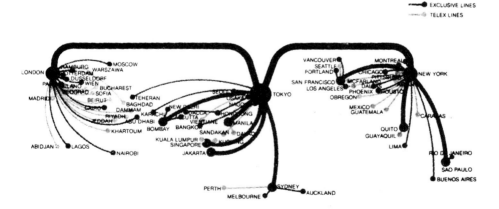

Figure 2.2 The Toyo Menka communications network.

The *sogo shosa* are therefore very peculiar to the Japanese development model. They are, however, perhaps handicapped by the fact that they have remained too Japanese, too 'Nippon-centric', too bilateral. In this sense they have not yet become real multinational enterprises. For many countries they remain, however, an example, a model which it would be very difficult to emulate outside the specific conditions of Japan.

• **Germany**: the tradition of international trading companies of German origin can be traced all the way back to the Hanseatic era. Although the country was not a colonial power, or at least not for long, traders from the North of Germany have been present the world over since the 19th century[14].

At present German international trading companies handle 20–30% of German foreign trade, 50 % in fact, if we only consider long distance trade. Geographically one can distinguish between two groups: the Hanseatics (Hamburg, Bremen, Lübeck), and the subsidiaries of the large groups of the Ruhr coal region, which often have a larger financial base.

There are approximately 4,000 international trading companies in Germany: 3,000 in Hamburg, 600 in Bremen and the rest in the Ruhr. Most of them are small, often still private enterprises. They are active both in export (representing industrial firms as *Export Vertreter*, and in import: they handle 95% of German commodity imports (a figure which includes the specialized traders).

The major companies are those specialized in the products of heavy industry (Stinnes, Klöckner, Thyssen). Worthy of mention among the more classical general traders, are firms such as Breckwoldt, present in some thirty countries (with a 1974 turnover of DM 250 million of which 50% was earned in off-shore operations), SCIPIO (turnover of DM 1 billion) specialized in fresh products, along with a certain number of firms more directly linked to the world of commodities such as Alfred Toppfer (grains) and Tchibo (coffee).

Globally seen, the German traders present the picture of a more dispersed and less conspicuous but very efficient structure. And as we shall see later on, Hamburg is one of the hubs of international trade in commodities.

• **The Netherlands**: With the Netherlands, one enters the realm of those international trading companies with a colonial origin, in this particular case Indonesia and the Dutch West Indies. The first Dutch international trading companies founded around 1850 suffered a fatal blow with the expulsion of the Dutch from Indonesia in 1957. Globally, the sector then turned towards Europe and there are few groups, apart from the three most important firms, which have continued to be active on the world scene.

On the other hand, perhaps due to their relatively small national market, the Dutch international trading companies have found it easier to move into international trade, including commodities. They have been aided in this effort by the position of Rotterdam for oilseeds, and by the presence of industries of first-processing for tropical products.

One of the leading firms is Internatio Muller (with a 1979 turnover of $1.9 billion), the result of the 1970 merger between an old trading firm which dealt with Indonesia (Internatio) and a forwarding agent (Muller). Thirty percent of the firm's turnover comes from international trade (ores, tropical produce, timber, finished goods. . .), 25% from distribution activities in the Netherlands. It has established a network of agencies especially in Australia, South Africa and Hong Kong and is, moreover, probably one of the most active international trading companies dealing in commodities, competing with firms specialized in cocoa (Holco, ceded in 1982 to Ed. and F.Man), in non-ferrous metals (H.P. Thomson), and in rubber (H.A. Astlett). Internatio's turnover in these trades was $750 million in 1979. This firm offers one of the rare examples of a colonial company which has adapted to the new conditions of international commodity trading. Borsumij-Wehry has developed along rather similar lines: the company is the result of a 1961 merger of two merchant houses founded in Indonesia in 1883 and 1867 respectively. Borsumij has reoriented its activities considerably towards Europe but has a substantial turnover from the trade in agricultural produce (coffee, oil, hides) especially from East Africa.

Curacaoshe is, on the other hand, a relatively classical merchant company which has extended its sphere of activites from Curaçao, where it started out, to Central America. Stokvis is most likely the largest firm for technical products in Europe and Hagemeyer, bought over in 1983 by Liem Sioe Liong, the Chinese group from Indonesia, is very active in trade (in January 1986, Sears World Trade, the trading subsidiary of Sears Roebuck, acquired a 20% stake in it).

As we shall see at a later stage, the position enjoyed by the

Netherlands in European commodity trading certainly allows those of its international trading companies which are based there to earn substantial profits simply because of their presence on the market.

- **Great Britain**: this is a country with a glorious past but an increasingly financial and decreasingly commercial present. The international trading companies of British origin have all in all adapted poorly to the decolonized world[15]. Of the 1,300 firms of this type to be found in Great Britain, many operate only as 'confirming houses' or 'factors' (910 in London and 230 in Manchester). The largest and most prestigious of them all is the famous United Africa Company, bought by Unilever in 1929, heir to the chartered companies of West Africa (the Royal Niger Company on the one hand and the African and Eastern Trading Company on the other). The U.A.C. (which controls the *Le Niger Français* company in French-speaking Africa) remains a perfect example of the typical merchant company although it has undertaken a profound redeployment as compared to the colonial era: while it has withdrawn from the traditional form of trading, it now controls new distribution channels (supermarkets. . .) and textile and mechanical industries (in Nigeria, Ghana, the Ivory Coast. . .[16]). The U.A.C. is one of Unilever's major pieces on the international chessboard of commodity trading, especially in the oilseeds sector. The same holds true for John Holt, an African merchant company which became part of the Lonrho group, an originally Rhodesian company whose activities range from hotels, through sugar plantations and newspapers, to postage stamps[17]. Other important British international trading companies are Inchcape[18] and Tozer Kemsley Milbourne. In 1980 Inchcape, which at the outset had directed its energies towards Asia, bought Balfour Williamson, a Liverpool international trading company specialized in trade with Latin America. It continues, however, to focus on the Far East and Souther Asia, where it makes two-thirds of its profits. Tozer Kemsey Millbourne, on the other hand, deals much more with the EEC and Oceania: a sizeable share of its activities are conducted in the international trade in timber and forestry products (Price and Pierce) for which TKM is one of the world's leading traders. Not to be forgotten are also Guiness Peat (whose bad deals caused it to hive off its subsidiary Lewis and Peat, commodities broker), Paterson Zochonis which is present in Nigeria,

Harrison and Crossfield which has recently lost its estates in Malaysia, and James Finlay and its tea estates in India.

But here we have to make a digression to mention those firms of British origin which have focused their attention on a particular region of the Empire: Oceania, Hong Kong, Malaysia. . .

In Australia Dalgety specialized first of all in ensuring supplies for livestock breeders and in marketing their produce (wool, meat). This was the principal activity retained by the firm in Australia and New Zealand as it extended the scope of its activities to industry (purchase of the British flour-milling plant, Spillers, in 1979, aquisition of the agricultural division of Rank Hovis Mac Dougal in Great Britain in 1983), forestry (in Canada) and trading activities (international trade in timber and grains and commodities brokerage with its London subsidiary Goldschmidt and Charteris). Most recently, Dalgety bought the cocoa trader Gill and Duffus.

The position of the Hong Kong-based firms is a rather special one. British in origin and still, for the great part, joint-stock companies, they have dominated China's trade since the withdrawal of the East India Company. They withdrew from Canton and Shanghai to Hong Kong in 1949 and have since then redeployed, dominating the economy of the colony and spreading over the whole of South-East Asia. Known as the *hongs*, they pursue a mixture of industrial and commercial activities while providing services (airlines for example). Acquiring control of these firms is currently at the core of particularly fierce struggles between traditional British capital and the Chinese financial community. The oldest and largest of them, Jardine Matheson, was founded in Canton in 1832 by two Scotsmen. Taking advantage of the abolition of the East India Company's monopoly in 1834, it became the first private trader to ship tea to London and subsequently opened branches in Hong Kong (1841), in Shanghai (1848) and Yokohama (1859). The firm, which had opened the first steam boat line on the Pearl River, continued to pursue its activities in China until 1949. In 1954 Jardine Matheson expanded to South-East Asia, and in 1963 to Australia. The company diversified into real estate (take-over of Hong Kong Land in 1981), insurance brokerage (11th largest agency in the world), sugar production (Theo. H. Davies in Hawaii and in the Philippines). Apart from sugar production and timber, its efforts to expand in the commodities sector have hardly been crowned with success.

In 1983 the Keswick family, descendants of the founders, and who still own 9% of Jardine Matheson's capital, recovered control of the firm, Simon Keswick becoming the *taipan* (chief executive officer). In March 1984, while China and Great Britain were negotiating Hong Kong's status after 1997, Keswick caused a sensation by announcing that Jardine Matheson's registered office was being transferred to Bermuda.

The other *hongs* are Hutchinson Whampoa (controlled since 1978 by local Chinese capital), Swire Pacific, owner of Cathay Pacific Airlines and of the Taikoo sugar refinery in Hongkong[19], and Weelock Marden which carries out particularly extensive activities in the shipping sector.

In Malaysia Sime Darby can no longer be considered a real international trading company. The company (the largest in the country) recently transferred its registered office from London to Kuala Lumpur and has focused its attention on agriculture (oil palm and rubber estates) and on industry (farming equipment in particular). Sime Darby has had little success in commodity trading, especially in oilseeds (it bought the London brokerage firm Faure Fairclough in 1973). Note, moreover, that Malaysia has recently sought to create export companies along the Japanese model (Nastra set up in December 1981, and Matra in January, 1982).

• **Other countries**: first among the other countries with large international trading companies is Denmark, whose leading firm is the East Asiatic Company. Created in March 1897 out of Anderson and Co. which had been founded in Siam in 1884[20], the East Asiatic Company was very active in Asia and was, at the turn of the century, one of the promoters of Chinese soya exports. It subsequently acquired plantations in Malaysia (1905) then in Burma and in Thailand extending the scope of its influence to Oceania and to North America. Today the East Asiatic Company is present, through its 160 subsidiaries, in 40 countries, in shippping and in international trade (rubber, timber, oilseeds. . .). It is one of the world's largest shippers of timber and does more business with China than any other Western country[21].

Among the firms of Swiss origin, Lacoray has also a big presence in the Far East. American trading companies are fairly recent and only got real impetus with the 1982 Trading Act. The most important are General Electric Trading, Sears World Trade, Bank America World Trade. . .

Table 2.4 Some figures on a few international trading companies

(Of course these figures are not comparable with each other and should be seen merely as an indication of size).

Company	Fiscal year ending on the	Turnover $billion	Net Profit ($million)	Employees (thousands)
Mitsubishi	31.03.83	63.60	77.20	17,000
Mitsui	do.	59.70	44.00	13,000
C. Itoh	do.	52.90	13.00	10,200
Marubeni	do.	49.00	1.50	9,000
Sumitumo	do.	48.10	72.80	7,500
Nissho Iwai	do.	33.90	33.70	8,000
Toyo Menka	do.	16.60	8.10	3,800
Kanematsu	do.	7.00	4.20	3,400
Nichimen	do.	13.80	5.90	3,500
Internatio Muller	31.12.79	1.90	3.20	15,800
Borsumij Wehry	do.	0.55	9.30	2,944
United Africa Co.	do.	£0.90	£50.00	—
Inchcape	31.12.83	£1.77	£15.40	—
Tozer Kemsley Milb.	do.	£0.67	£6.50	—
Dalgety	30.06.83	£2.90	£55.00	28,600
Jardine Matheson	31.12.83	1.45	19.00	37,000
Sime Darby	30.06.83	0.93	30.00	50,000
East Asiatic Comp.	31.12.82	3.00	(34.00)	—
Daewoo	31.12.80	1.42†	—	‡
Samsung	31.12.79	1.20†	—	‡
Kukie Corp.	31.12.81	1.00†	—	‡
Hyosung Corp.	31.12.80	0.76†	—	‡
Interbras	31.12.82	2.66	—	—
SCOA	30.09.83	—	(56.00)	13,300
CFAO	31.12.79	FF6.5	142.00	23,315
Optorg	31.12.82	FF2.3	(3.30)	4,712

† figure only for export turnover
‡ total number for the whole sector: 70,000

Not unlike Malaysia, a number of other Third World countries (South Korea, Taiwan, Brazil. . .) have also sought to endow themselves with stuctures more or less similar to the Japanese model. In 1975 the South Korean government set up General Trading Companies to promote Korean expansion abroad. The ten firms of this type which have been established to date are, in general, connected to the most important Korean groups: Daewoo, Samsung, each of which account for 8% of Korean exports, Kukie, Hyosung. . .

In Brazil, Interbras, subsidiary company of the state-owned petroleum group Petrobras, accounts for 8% of all Brazilian exports.

The company, founded in 1976, owed its initial success to the Brazilian soya boom but has since diversified, first to other agricultural produce, followed by manufactured goods and iron and steel products. Interbras rose, not long ago, to the status of a full-fledged trader and its London office is now a member of the major London futures markets. Clearly recourse to international trading companies (at least for export purposes) is becoming increasingly widespread[22], with the exception, however, of France.

● **France**: the French situation is rather similar to that of the British. Most of the trading companies have a predominantly colonial background and in fact are focused on Africa or to some extent on the Far East.

For the majority of these firms, many of which originated in the business communities of the French ports (Marseilles, Bordeaux), the focal point of their activities continues to be distribution in Africa, although they have extended their involvment to a number of countries including some Middle Eastern countries and Brazil and have also invested in France.

The largest firm of this type is SCOA (*Société Commerciale de l'Ouest Africain*), 60% of whose turnover comes from Africa, 25% from Europe and 15% from the rest of the world (it is represented in the Far East by the *Compagnie Olivier* acquired in 1975 and in Australasia by the Sulivan group acquired in 1977). SCOA is involved to a minor extent in the foodstuff trade, in particular that of fresh produce. CFAO (*Compagnie Fançaise pour l'Afrique de l'Ouest*), an important trader in skins and hides, is about the same size as SCOA and carries out 60% and 40% of its activities in Africa and in France respectively. Other firms of this nature include *Optorg*[23] and *Denis Frères*.

As is clearly evidenced by the foregoing, the situation varies considerably from one country to another. In an attempt to classify the various firms, one could draw a distinction between the colonials (such as UAC and SCOA. . .), the major general merchants (*Sogo shosa, hongs*, Sime Darby. . .), and the export merchants (German, Dutch to a limited extent, Brazilian. . .).

A phenomenon which has become widespread, and which is paradoxical in an era when communications are becoming increasingly effortless, is the tendency of the international trading companies to continue to play a role in international trade while focusing their activities increasingly on the national level.

In commodities, (with the exception of the Japanese firms which first penetrated the market in 1970), the international trading companies have practically abandoned their trading role. On the other hand, counter-trading, one of the international trading companies' oldest activities, has had a new lease of life with the growth of trade with the Eastern Bloc countries.

The counter-trading houses

The problem of counter-trading — or barter — occurs when the buyer lacks sufficient amounts of a convertible currency to pay for his purchase. He may — and has an increasing tendency to — propose that the seller accept national products in lieu of some of the currency payable: the outcome will depend on the balance of power between buyer and seller, but very often the seller is forced to accept the buyer's terms, however humiliating they may be, in order to secure access to the market.

Such practices are becoming increasingly common even outside the Eastern Bloc and a number of companies have been created to manage the trade in the often difficult-to-market products resulting from the counter-trading process. They tend to be either the subsidiaries of large industrial firms, or specialized companies which began to emerge from 1960 especially in Germany and Austria: firms from Vienna such as *Allgemeine Warentreuhandel*, Winter and Co., from Germany (*Bankhaus* of Hamburg), from Switzerland (the international grain trader André), and from Great Britain (the trading firm Golodetz. . .). The most well-known example in France is *Interagra*, the firm founded and privately owned by the late J.-B. Doumeng (nicknamed the 'Red Millionaire', he was member of the French C.P. until his death), which trades powdered milk for Russian tractors. . .

Counter-trading has continued to grow phenomenally since the end of the 1970's: in 1984, the US National Foreign Trade Council estimated that if in 1979, 27 countries in the world practised some form or other of counter-trading, by 1984, the number had risen to 88. Most banks, trading firms, and large industrial firms now have their own counter-trading subsidiaries: Renault (whose problems with its coffee operations in Colombia reached the public's attention in the beginning of 1984), the French *Groupe Suez* (associated within *Greficomex* with the Lissauer group). . .

Counter-trading operations grew extraordinarily in the early 1980s because of the international financial crisis and the OPEC-related problems. But the trend seems to have reversed since 1985 (Voest Alpine Intertrading, subsidiary of the Austrian state-owned steel and engineering group, Voest Alpine, made heavy losses on oil trading and its business was nearly taken over in January 1986 by *Metallgesellschaft* (West Germany) and Louis Dreyfus (France), which had already formed a counter-trading joint venture.

In spite of this, counter-trading can still be seen as the only solution for cash-starved countries. Early in 1986, Pakistan agreed to a $400 million counter-trade contract with four partners, whose names are quite evocative: two commodity traders (*Sucre et Denrées* and *Metall-gesellschaft-Dreyfus*), one *sogo shosa* (Mitsubishi), and one commission house (Prudential Bache).

Yet the most spectacular growth experienced by trading firms has, without a doubt, taken place in the field of commodity trading, especially during the Seventies.

Chapter 3

AN APPROACH TO WORLD COMMODITY MARKETS

The foregoing chapters have described the outstanding features of commodity markets today: the influence of government structures both on imports and on exports, and the extension of the sphere of activity covered by a world market managed as often as not from a futures market. It is nevertheless essential to specify again the position of the international market within the framework of a product's itinerary as it passes from the first stage (and even before) — production, to the final stage — consumption. In short, we shall attempt to situate the market within a certain product's complex, or 'chain'[1], the chain that goes from producer to consumer.

For this notion of 'product complex', or 'chain' we propose the following definition[2]:

A chain or complex represents the whole group of economic agents (processors or otherwise), and of administrative and political agents who are directly or indirectly involved in a product's progress from the initial stage — production (and production supplies) — to the final stage — consumption (or at least the stage which results in the loss of the product's identity). The term also encompasses all the interactions which take place among a number of agents who together form a system.

A complex could very well be analysed on a purely national level in which case the international market would be merely residual. Yet however residual this international market might be, its reactions are

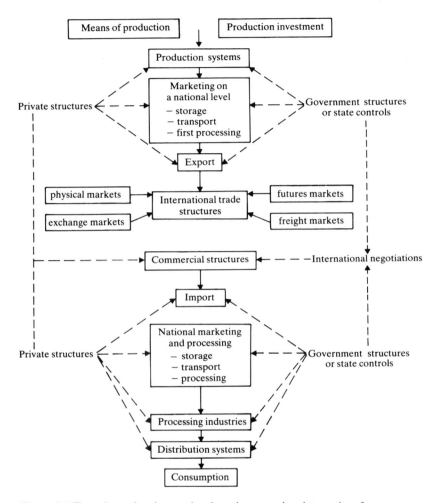

Figure 3.1 Flow-chart of an international product complex, integrating, for one given product, two national chains

dictated by what happens in a number of national complexes. Figure 3.1 gives an example of an international complex, namely, the operators dealing with a product which has been traded on the world market. The international market appears as the outcome of the different national policies and reveals the contrasts existing between the policies of private structures and government entities.

Let us take a short look at the different stages which together make up international trade in commodities, by following a typical chain[3].

Production, production systems and factors of production

Raw materials can be produced by:
  - a single individual (the farmer in Western Europe or in the US),
  - a capitalist-type firm (mines or plantations),
  - the public sector (possibly through producer cooperatives).

We should like to point out here the growing importance of the role of government as a producer both in the socialist and in the recently independent developing countries (see Chapter 1). However, we shall return later to the real significance of this characteristic especially as far as the means of production are concerned.

Without dwelling excessively on this point, we must point out that commodities are nowadays less and less 'primary' and increasingly 'secondary' products, in other words, that an increasing number of external elements enter the production process. Commodity production is becoming more and more a processing activity:

  - in agriculture, the processing of inputs such as seeds, fertilizers, plant care products, agricultural equipment, engineering. . .
  - in mining, the processing of such inputs as engineering, energy, labour.

Although the socialist states have gradually managed to gain control of their production systems, they are far from being in a position to exercise control over the factors of production which are most often in the hands of multinational oligopolies. These firms are all the more powerful since they are in possession not of a good but of a technique, a know-how.

Very often the first stage of processing must take place on the site of production (it is also often integrated into the production complex itself). This may be the case with: beet or cane into sugar, cocoa pods into cocoa beans, ores into more or less finished metals.

A distinction must be made between:

– processing which has to be effected on the site of production (sugar, coffee, cocoa) but which might go no further than simple packaging,

– processing which can be effected either locally (on the site of production) or on the site of consumption.

In fact more and more products are being processed on the spot, at least in the developing countries. This could be complicated by the need for other inputs to produce a 'finished' commodity (for example electricity for the production of alumina and aluminium).

In fact it is the type of product concerned and the customs prevailing on the market which determine how far the first stage of processing goes and where it takes place: on the site of production, the site of consumption or even in a place where energy, manpower and capital can be brought together. This processing can be done by:

– national firms (farming cooperatives. . .),
– state-owned firms,
– transnational firms.

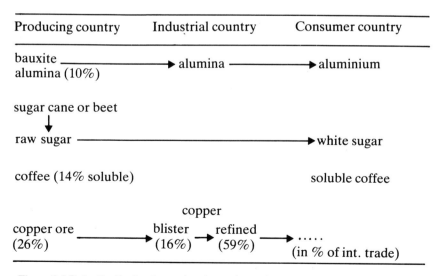

Figure 3.2 Role distribution in products' transformation chains

The share of transnational firms in processing — especially *vis-àvis* industrial commodities — has diminished considerably as compared with twenty years ago.

Supply on the international market

The proportion of production exported varies considerably from product to product. Once more a distinction must be drawn between:

– those products traded essentially on an international level (75–100%):
– coffee, cocoa, tropical fruits, etc. . .
– certain metals (chrome, vanadium, cobalt, nickel, tin. . .),
– those products the major part of which (40–75%) is traded internationally:
– most metals (aluminium, copper, lead, zinc. . .),
– natural rubber, wool, jute, tea. . .
– those products of which a considerable proportion (20–40%) is traded internationally:
– sugar (25%), cotton (27%), iron ore, oilseeds. . .
– finally those products where the percentage traded internationally is limited (0–20%):
– rice (4%), grains (10–15%), beef (6%), etc. . .

Supply on the international market can be analysed on the geopolitical level or on the level of the respective roles played by government structures and national or multinational firms.

It is extremely important to know *how great a role government plays in relation to that of the firm* and whether supply is controlled by the government or by the firm which, more often than not, has subsidiaries all over the globe:

● In agricultural produce state control of exports is more or less widespread and is often exercised through stabilization funds or clearing houses. Freedom of export for sugar producers, for example, exists only in certain Central American or Latin American countries (Argentina). One ought to be able to list the numerous types of relationships which could exist in certain countries between a firm and government. It would seem, nevertheless, that the desire to control resources is virtually unanimous.

Table 3.1 Distribution of supply per commodity

	Developing countries' share when accounting for over 10% of world exports (in % of world exports)	Number of countries concerned	Total share of developing countries (in % of world exports in 1981)	Share (in % of world exports) and name of the main developing country exporter	Producer associations existing in 1984
Bauxite	61.5	3	71	24.8 (Guinea)	IBA
Cocoa	71.5	4	99.9	23.3 (Ghana)	Cocoa Producers Alliance
Coconut Oil	71	1	98.8	71 (Philippines)	Asian & Pacific Coconut Community
Coffee	32.5	2	96.3	17.1 (Brazil)	Bogota Group
Copper	31.1	2	65.1	19.3 (Chile)	CIPEC (Paris)
Copra	54.9	1	99.9	54.9 (Philippines)	
Cotton	—	—	44.7	(Pakistan)	Izmir Group
Fishmeal	33.4	2	45	21.2 (Peru)	
Groundnut oil	63.8	3	76.7	29.4 (Senegal)	African Groundnut Council
Iron	19	1	42.2	19 (Brazil)	APEF (Geneva)
Jute	81.1	2	89.5	69.3 (Bangladesh)	
Linseed oil	62	1	66.1	62.0 (Argentina)	
Manganese	32.5	2	42.9	21.6 (Gabon)	
Palm oil	75.6	2	97.2	59.8 (Malaysia)	
Phosphates	34.4	1	62.3	34.4 (Morocco)	
Rubber	88	3	97.9	51.4 (Malaysia)	Association of Natural Rubber Producing Countries
Sisal	80.3	3	98	42.4 (Brazil)	
Sugar (with the exception of Cuba)	—	—	36.3	(Brazil)	GEPLACEA
Tea	48.7	2	78	27.7 (India)	International Tea Promotion Association
Tin	78.8	4	91	36.4 (Malaysia)	Association of Tin Producing Countries

(World Bank averages, 1977-79, unless otherwise stated).

• It would be more difficult to make such an analysis for ores and metals because of the different processing stages which a metal has to go through and the technological advantage which the major firms possess. Although private companies deal little in products which require only simple technology (such as copper or tin), they continue to play a more fundamental role in:

- aluminium (five firms control 80% of supply),
- nickel,
- platinum,
- diamonds,
- a certain number of minor metals (molybdenum. . .).

On the *geopolitical level* the problem arises of a possible cartelization of the market. In our opinion the cartelization of the market requires the following elements:

- a product which cannot be substituted in the medium term and without which the economies of the consumer countries are unable to function,
- a product which is easily stocked,
- a small number of exporting countries which do not depend excessively on the product for their export earnings and which have cultural, racial and ideological ties with each other.

These were the conditions obtaining on the oil market in 1973 (they no longer do). Let us take a brief look at some of these conditions from the supply side.

Although the developing countries produce a smaller share of primary commodities than the developed countries, the same does not hold true for exports; under these circumstances the relative importance of any particular group varies according to the products in which it deals and when it deals in them; products may fall into one of several categories:

- commodities produced almost solely (75–100%) by the developing countries countries:
    - coffee, cocoa, bauxite, tea, rubber, tin, tropical fruits, jute, phosphates. A surprisingly short list.
- products where there is a balance between the percentages produced by the developing countries, the developed countries and the

socialist bloc (25–75% coming from the developing countries):
- copper, iron, manganese, tungsten, sugar, cotton, tobacco,
- and finally those products of which the developing countries produce only a small quantity:
- grains, wool, lead and zinc, meat and dairy products. . .

The countries of the socialist bloc are rarely involved in international trade except for chrome (22.7%), raw phosphates and potassium (35%), sugar with Cuba and more marginally for sunflower oil. The policies they choose to espouse are also very important in the markets for platinum and precious metals.

Whether a product can be stocked or not depends of course not only on its physical characteristics but also on the storage capacity available in the country it (and the financial means of the producers). The less voluminous the product, the better the possibilities of stocking it. The developing countries often suffer from an acute lack of such storage facilities.

Table 3.2 Some commodities' shares in various countries exports revenue.

Product		Share of total export earnings, in %		
Bauxite	Guinea	63.80		
Cocoa	Ghana	68.70	Ivory Coast	23.80
	Equatorial Guinea	39.90	Togo	23.90
Coffee	Burundi	88.80	Costa Rica	37.10
	Uganda	92.60	Salvador	63.30
	Rwanda	78.30	Ethiopia	72.00
	Colombia	63.10	Guatemala	42.50
Copper	Zambia	88.90	Peru	20.90
	Zaire	44.00	Namibia	71.80
	Chile	50.10		
Cotton	Egypt	22.40	Chad	78.10
	Yemen Arab	41.40	Sudan	51.10
	Republic		Mali	43.50
Iron	Mauritania	81.60	Liberia	57.00
Phosphates	Nauru	98.00	Morocco	33.90
	Togo	43.50		

Source: World Bank, 1981 for the period 1977–1979.

But whether a country can afford to stock or not is also determined by its degree of dependence on the proportion of total export earnings brought in by a single product. Here the figures speak for themselves, although the foregoing table does not take into consideration those countries which are dependent on two or three primary commodities for their export earnings. Finally, we must be aware of the fact that supply is often inelastic because of the length of time it takes to open a mine or to begin to exploit a plantation (a cocoa tree takes five years to begin to bear). It is not rare for 10 years to elapse betweeen the decision to invest and the coming on stream of a plant.

Having seen the main components of the supply of commodities on the international market, we shall now move on to the elements which dictate demand.

Consumption and demand structures

Demand is of course conditioned by consumption, the latter being always determined in the final analysis by the habits of the average earthly dweller. But between the commodity and the end-consumer there is a host of middlemen and processors whose number varies considerably from product to product:

– a few in the case of common foodstuffs (grains, sugar, tropical products) which only require storage and packaging),
– many in the case of metals which often call for extremely complex circuits.

But beyond this aspect, the use to which the product is put and the notion of strategic commodities also come into play. A strategic commodity is, in our eyes, one which is essential to human life or at least to certain aspects thereof (including wars). Seen in this light, grains, non-ferrous metals may be considered strategic. The notion of strategy changes with time (coal and iron were the strategic elements of the industrial revolution in the 19th century) and in some cases is determined by where one is (oil cakes are strategic products for cattle raising in Western Europe).

The main factors which might affect demand are:

– the existence of a monopsony or oligopsony,
– the possiblilty of finding substitutes,
– the possibility of using other commodities.

There is practically no monopsony or oligopsony on the international market. Sometimes an operator's demand can influence a market's performance (with its metal 'stockpiles' the General Services Administration of the United States is in a position to do this).

On the other hand the possibility of using other commodities or substitutes considerably conditions demand. Let us assume that there is in general a ceiling price for each commodity above which it becomes more attractive to use a substitute. In the case of metals the following could be assumed:

Table 3.3 Metals and their substitutes.

Metal	Substitutes
Steel	Aluminium, wood, copper, plastics, titanium, glass, zinc.
Aluminium	Steel, wood, copper, magnesium, plastics, paper, lead, titanium, glass, zinc.
Chrome	Cobalt, nickel, magnesium, tungsten.
Cobalt	Chrome, nickel, molybdenum, vanadium (irreplaceable in permanent magnets).
Copper	Steel, aluminium, plastics, lead.
Tin	Steel, aluminium, plastics, lead, glass (almost irreplaceable for soldering purposes).
Platinum group metals	(almost irreplaceable)
Lead	Aluminium, coppper, tin, plastics.
Titanium	Steel, aluminium, zinc (pigments).
Tungsten	Steel, aluminium, plastics, titanium (pigments).
Zinc	Tantalum, cobalt, nickel, molybdenum, titanium, plastics.

Source: M. OSTERIETH, X. DECLEVE, 'Les marchés des produits de base' in *Etudes et Expansion*, 277, July/September 1978.

For plant products the possibilities of substitution are smaller (we could speak of weak substitutes):

Table 3.4 Agricultural commodities and their substitutes

Sugar	Isoglucose (generally corn, wheat or potato starch based), glucose syrup, lactose.
Grain for animal consumption	Manioc.
Coffee	Chicory.
Wool, cotton, jute, sisal	Synthetic fibres.
Natural rubber	'buna' or synthetic rubber.

Other product families are more or less interchangeable, such as seed oils and protein cakes.

Demand is of course also conditioned by the storage capacities of the user industries (or even by consumer hoarding as a result of the economic situation, as was the case worldwide with sugar in 1974). Consumers might refuse to pay an excessively high price for a product (1974: fall in the consumption of sugar in the United States, where consumption was large all the same — 45kg per head per year). Another factor is the research capacity which the user industries can devote to finding new uses for certain products (alcohol as a source of energy in Brazil since 1977, sugar chemistry in Great Britain).

The very structure of demand is determined either by capitalist firms or by state-controlled agencies or firms. Governments in fact leave the private firms less and less leeway in the choice of their supplies (especially in the case of grains and metals), or at least direct their activities (such is the case of the United States and France (*Groupe d'Importation et de Répartition des Métaux* or GIRM. . .).

For their part the socialist states play a central role in the structure of demand. Since they do not follow the logic of the capitalist system and having no public opinion to satisfy, they can cause serious fluctuations in demand.

The international market

We take this to mean the theoretical moment in the life of a product, when supply meets demand. But before coming to the notion of the 'world market' itself, we have to indicate which products tend to by-pass international trade:

– those products which circulate within the integrated economic zones. The commodities traded within the framework of the EEC or the Comecon, or imported by the EEC within the framework of the Lomé Convention (notably under the Sugar Protocol) by-pass the international market,

– products circulating within vertically concentrated groups which transfer profits internally also escape the logic of the market. Such cases are, we believe, less prevalent today. The old theory of vertical integration seems to be losing ground, the sugar refiners (for example Tate and Lyle) no longer own plantations, and there is a steady

decrease in the number of mines owned by iron and steel manufacturers. Integration remains prevalent, however, in certain metal
industries and in rubber (Firestone in Liberia).

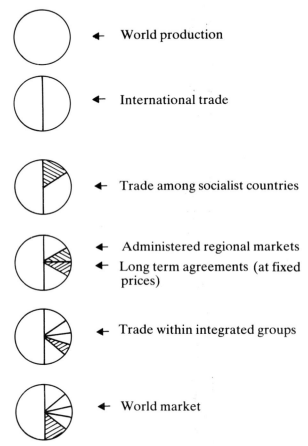

Figure 3.3 From world production to the world market.
Source: Aimé TEYSSIER D'ORFEUIL, 'Pénuries sur les marchés mondiaux des
produits de base', *Tiers Monde*, April–June 1976, p. 379.
Bilateral government-to-government agreements, which come quite close to counter-
trade or barter, should also be included. 50% of all rice traded is exported under
bilateral agreements, 10% as shipments under preferential terms.

– finally long-term delivery agreements between two countries over a period of several years (e.g. the agreeements between Japan and Australia for sugar and certain ores) reduce even more the quantities traded on the market. We are left with a world market which is residual not only in terms of production but also in relation to the quantities exported as can be seen in the diagram devised by Aimé Teyssier d'Orfeuil.

In our characterization of the world market for primary commodities we shall discuss:

– the mechanisms for placing a product on the market,
– the relationship between supply and demand,
– price fluctuations.

● **The mechanisms for placing a product on the market** are numerous. We shall sketchily make a distinction between products with efficient futures markets and those without.

A. A first class of commodities have markets which are governed by a futures market which acts as a yardstick. There are products governed by:

– a single futures market (or at least one which is preponderant): copper, zinc, lead, tin, silver metal (London Metal Exchange in London), maize (Chicago), wheat (Chicago), wool (Sydney), platinum (New York). . .
– a few futures markets carrying out parallel functions: coffee, cocoa, (London, New York), sugar (London, New York, Paris).

Generally speaking, these futures markets ceased to be markets for actuals a long time ago: a mere 1% of transactions (or less) result in delivery on the Chicago Board of trade, 10–15% (at most) on the London Metal Exchange.

Therefore there exist, alongside the futures markets, markets for actuals which are physically located to various degrees:

– production sites: Penang for tin
– importation sites: Rotterdam for oilseeds
– consumption sites: Dundee for jute, Liverpool for cotton, Bradford for wool in the case of the UK; these markets are gradually becoming a thing of the past.

The 'basis', or 'premium' (i.e. the difference between the price on the futures market and the price on the market for actuals) also varies condiderably and, as we shall see in the example given in Chapter 4, the basis is also traded on the market like any other commodity.

Moreover, the futures markets are of paramount importance as they determine the prices of many foodstuffs which are linked to a quoted commodity. The soya quotations in Chicago therefore determine the price of all types of oilseeds.

B. Products having no predominant futures markets. Depending on the balance of power between the operators on these markets the latter fall into the following categories:

– producer markets,
– consumer markets,
– arbitrage markets,
– competitive markets,
– markets by private agreement.

1. *Producer markets*:

One or several producers controlling all or part of exports dominate the market and manage to impose their price. Cases of this type are relatively frequent in the market for mining products. The perfect monopoly is a rather rare occurrence, the closest to it being the diamond trade: the Central Selling Organization (CSO), controlled by the South African firm De Beers, (Anglo-American Corporation) has indeed a virtual monopoly of world raw diamonds sales. But in fact, this monopoly only exists because certain producers — notably the USSR — tolerate it. Moreover it still leaves a certain amount of room for parallel markets in Amsterdam, Tel Aviv or Delhi (though it is true that these deal in partially-cut stones).

Much more often, supply is concentrated in the hands of two or three operators, one of them — a firm or a government — being tacitly recognised by its partners as being the 'leader', responsible for the 'fixing' of price levels. This is most often the case for non-ferrous metals where examples of such procedures are numerous: cobalt supplies are controlled by three major firms and until 1978 the price was fixed exclusively by the world's foremost producer, Zaire, through a marketing agency, Sozacom. As a result of the Shaba War in that year, the initiative began to shift, on certain occasions, to the Zambians. Since the beginning of 1984, Zaire seems to have regained control of the market. This duopolistic situation also exists in a similar form for vanadium, the price of which is determined by the South African firm Highveld (Anglo-American Corporation), though not without taking into consideration the possible reactions of the powerful American company Union Carbide, second world producer. Another typical case was that of molybdenum, with a price which used to be fixed by the world's leading producer, the American firm Amax (its Climax division accounts for over fifty per cent of the world's production), but that stopped in the early eighties. Thanks to the creation of a futures market for nickel at the London Metal Exchange in March 1979, the price of this commodity ceased to be fixed by International Nickel (Inco-Canada) in the same period. The markets of a number of so-called 'minor metals' (dealings there concern metal rather than ore) exhibit the same characteristics: they are dominated by a few high technology firms, such as Indium Corporation of America for indium, Eagle Picher (United States) and Hoboken (Belgium) for germanium. . . This type of market is often complemented by an active free market or even a futures market, as is the case with the metals of the platinum group with the two South African firms Rustemburg and Impala (interlinked within the Johnson Matthey group and on a broader level within Anglo-American Corporation). Oligopolistic situations, where no one producer remains predominant for any length of time, are even more frequent. Cadmium for example is produced by most of the zinc producing firms and its price is fixed by the major companies such as St Joe (United States), the *Royale Asturienne des Mines* (Belgium) and Mitsui (Japan). The same goes for antimony, chrome, columbium (the market for which is determined by the processing capacities for lead and zinc). But for most of the foregoing products the notion of a producer price has lost almost all meaning.

Although it is true to say that producer markets frequently exist for ores and metals, we should point out that they increase in efficiency as we leave the market for ores and enter the market for metals. In fact, as in many other fields, the structure of international ore production has hardly been able to ride out the wave of decolonization and nationalization: at present almost no capital is expatriated via mining, (with the exception, however, of Brazil and in particular of Australia, whose governments are introducing increasingly stricter policies). For many other metals which are by-products of mining, the technical advantage held by the processor continues to operate to the detriment of the ore producers[4].

This is particularly evident in the case of titanium whose production is limited to six factories located in Western countries but whose market is dependent on whether or not the USSR is able to export.

As far as we can tell there is no producer market (government or firm) for agricultural products. In these sectors the profit to be derived from the technical know-how input is almost nil and the decolonization process has almost wiped out (at least in this form) the multinational production companies. Their last stronghold remains the banana trade but here all three dominant firms have realized a completely integrated chain all the way to the zones of consumption (furthermore, it is difficult to state that a world banana market effectively exists).

What is the behaviour ot the operators who dominate these producer markets? The fixing of the price by the market operators depends not only on where supply meets demand but also takes into account a certain number of elements:

– the cost price (when this can be calculated precisely: but one ought to reckon in terms of the marginal cost price of the last unit of capacity installed),

– the level of consumption: an excessively high price might trigger off the quest for substitutes; this often explains why producers often maintain low prices despite high prices on the free market,

– the possibility of a marginal supply from producers other than the members of the dominant oligopoly and notably from the socialist countries,

– the relationship between the national, regional and world prices (especially in the case of the United States' market).

2. *The consumer markets*:

Insofar as trading in ores is concerned, certain markets for metallic substances, as we have seen, are consumer markets. A consumer market is characterised by the dominant position of a few user and processing firms. In a market of this type, the primary product has no intrinsic value from the economic, technical and even from the marketing point of view unless it is processed into a finished product. This is the case for numerous ores which are totally valorized at the first and even at the second stage of processing: some of the tungsten ore consumers (the carburizers using scheelite) are grouped within the International Tungsten association (ITA) which publishes a *Users' Index,* a sort of *a posteriori* price calculated on the basis of the data sent in by the association's members to a firm of British chartered accountants. But we are a long way from a cartel of scheelite users! The case of manganese ore is somewhat peculiar: the main users of the ore are the iron and steel firms (production of ferro-manganese). They have had a tendency in the past to integrate manganese mines in their global process. They encountered little competition given the low intrinsic value of the untreated ore and the high freight costs involved. Around 1960, apart from Soviet production, almost all of the world production was integrated in this way[5]. The nationalization process was by no means total and today 15–20% of the world market (exports from Gabon and Brazil) are still constituted by tied sales. The market for iron ore is largely dominated by the American, European and Japanese iron and steel firms despite producers' attempts to organize themselves.

This pattern of domination which recurs in coal is particularly obvious in times of over-production. The same situation exists in connection with a certain number of agricultural products whose production consumers strove to integrate in colonial times: among the increasingly rare examples of this are the rubber tree plantations owned by the tyre firms and the oilseed plantations owned by Lesieur and Unilever. The local subsidiaries of the major tea firms on the other hand (Brooke Bond, Lyons, Lipton), formerly owners of tea gardens in India and Ceylon, were nationalized at the beginning of the seventies. But apart from these cases of tied sales, the majority of which are in the process of disappearing[6] and those of the primary ore markets dominated by the notion of technical advantage (see above), there are a number of products the consumers of which constitute a *de facto* oligopsony: the best example is tobacco, dominated by an oligopsony comprised of the seven cigarette and cigar multinationals the majority of which have, moreover, integrated much of the trade and which control almost 90% of trade in tobacco leaves. Here a technology-based profit definitely comes into play, but it is the marketing advantage which is decisive: the question arises as to whether it is the tobacco or the brand image of a cigarette which really matters. In a way, the

British tea blenders (Great Britain is the world's largest market) have a similar position in the London tea auctions. The buying of Brooke Bond by Unilever in October 1984, thus makes this firm the world's leading consumer.

Apart from the tied sales markets, there are therefore a number of consumer markets. It is worth remembering that they are mainly the result of an advantage held by the consumers: technology, know-how, marketing and even logistics. It is indeed possible that a product has no intrinsic value in the country of origin (therefore wasted there) and is gladly put at the disposal of the first organization capable of transporting, managing and distributing it. Although this is often done by the firms which are the direct consumers, it could also perhaps explain the strong position held by trading firms.

3. 'Arbitrage' markets:

We understand by 'arbitrage' markets those which are dominated by one or many trading firms which concentrate supply and demand at a given point in time and arbitrate between them: it is therefore the co-existence of an oligopoly and an oligopsony. Cases of this type are relatively rare since this sort of market presupposes a certain disinterest on the part of both producers and consumers: in general it occurs in the markets for by-products or for foodstuffs requiring a considerable logistic effort. A particularly graphic example is that of molasses. A by-product of sugar manufacture, molasses is both cumbersome and cheap. It can be put to many uses in the production of animal feed, in chemistry and in the production of alcohol. The United States is its major import market. Molasses is of little value to the sugar manufacturer and is, in addition, extremely bulky. For the consumer it constitutes, not infrequently, one of the important items on his supply list. International trade in the product is dominated by three or four trading firms equipped with storage facilities, ships and barges. They are the only ones in a position to make use of the surplus molasses, able to export and to stock it. The world price for molasses is nonetheless that of the main import market, and is fixed at the main US ports of entry by the American Department of Agriculture. But the traders controlling supply can have a marked influence on these prices. More or less the same occurs with alcohol and spices. Similarly the pepper market is dominated by a handful of traders in Singapore and Hong Kong.

This type of situation arises much less frequently with metals. True enough certain trading firms have integrated metal refining activities, thereby positioning themselves in a narrow but profitable market gap (e.g. Johnson Matthey in palladium). For the rest, there are no traders' markets in the true sense of the term. But the traders latter are of course very active on the competitive markets.

4. *The competitive markets*:

A competitive market is one in which no operator enjoys a predominant position: this type of market can cover all trade done in a given product (antimony, tungsten) or it could be residual, existing alongside a producer market[7]: the free market handles roughly 25% of all trade in molybdenum, 10% in cobalt and 20% in manganese. . . For many substances, it is impossible to get an exact idea of the proportion which passes through the free market.

As there is no futures market, the prices on the competitive markets are the result of compilations made by specialist bulletins: *Metal Bulletin* of London, *Metals Week* of New York, *Usine Nouvelle* in France. The prices of tungsten, antimony, cobalt are published in the *Metal Bulletin* and that of molybdenum in *Metals Week*. Unfortunately, such publications do not exist for agricultural products and it is difficult to get an idea of the day-to-day prices for meats, dairy products or alcohol.

A precise study of the running of these markets is extremely difficult mainly because of:

– the nature of supply: highly dispersed producers, the possible characterization of the substance as a by-product, the elasticity of supply (dependent on the degree of amortization of installations). . .

– the position of the socialist countries which almost always use the free markets but have a very peculiar interpretation of the concept of 'Act of God',

– the possible diversion towards the free market of certain tonnages coming from dominant producers practising an imposed price,

– the importance of the product for the consumer states and its possible inclusion in a strategic stock,

– the product's degree of purity, and the parallel position of the market for processing capacities (certain trading firms having semi-manufactures produced under contract or in their own factories),

– the moral rectitude of the operators on the market which is held to
be much less rigorous than when a futures market exists,

– in the case of agricultural produce, the length of time a product
can be stored (almost unlimited for pepper, but a maximum of 6–7
months for tea).

Finally, the free market is very often, though not always, a middleman's market: indeed most transactions in metals and certain
agricultural commodities are concluded directly between the producer
and the consumer, with the free market price serving in some cases as a
reference. As a matter of fact, the increasing presence of governmen-
tal or quasi-governmental structures at both ends of the chain (in
supply and in demand) could in the initial stages give precedence to
bilateral relations. Experience has shown, however, that it serves, on
the contrary to strengthen the role of the middlemen — traders and
brokers.

Yet there are a number of markets where direct negotiations take
place.

5. *The markets by private agreement*:

Instead of having a market in the real sense of the term, annual
negotiations bring together buyers and sellers who conclude yearly
supply contracts with each other. These markets are original in their
structure (they are bilateral oligopolies) and in that the negotiations
also fix the price which will be valid for the subsequent year[8]. In some
cases a parallel free market does not exist. The supply of phosphates is
thus concentrated in the hands of the American Exporters Association
(Phosrock), the *Office Chérifien des Phosphates* for Morocco and State
Boards for minor exporters such as the USSR, Togo, Jordan or
Nauru). Demand comes from the fertilizer industry which is highly
concentrated in the major developed agricultural countries (European
imports accounted for 63% of the world total in 1976). The one-year
delivery contracts are negotiated each year in November and December for the coming year, with each consumer requesting competitive
offers from the producers concerned. The duopoly relations between
Morocco and the United States are rather complex. In 1974 Morocco
initiated a price rise but it was the American producers who contri-
buted in 1977 to the drop in prices.

Another example of direct negotiations, this time with the existence of a parallel free market, is that of manganese: the annual contracts for this ore are generally negotiated in October–November. The iron market is even more obscure: long-term delivery contracts are negotiated between producers and steel manufacturers (the latter being in the dominant position). But the prices at which these contracts are concluded are kept in great secrecy making it difficult for the observer to get a precise idea of the real nature of these markets. The creation of an iron producers association, the *Association des Produc-teurs Exportateurs de Fer* (APEF), might, in the long-run, shift the balance of power. The auction system could, in some measure, be likened to a negotiation market: for tea, the sellers are most often government bodies (Tea Boards) which either organize their own auctions (Calcutta, Colombo, Mombasa. . .) or sell at the London auctions. The buyers are the great packaging and distribution firms.

• **Relations between supply and demand**, or rather between the various producer and consumer countries, are currently the subject of countless negotiations within the framework of GATT and UNCTAD (note, however, that the first international commodity agreement (sugar) dates from 1865).

The aim of a commodity agreement is to stablilize commodity prices by adjusting supply and demand. This can be done by means of:

– buffer stocks administered by a supra-national authority,
– production quota agreements,
– contracts guaranteeing sales and purchases at agreed prices,
– price brackets.

The problem lies in getting everyone to come to an agreement and, what is more important, to get all operators to participate in it. The refusals of the United States (cocoa–1976, sugar–1968, tin–1981); of the EEC (sugar–1977); of the USSR (wheat–1977), to participate in such agreements, and the flexibility demanded by the socialist countries (internal agreement between Cuba and the COMECON for sugar), has led to the breakdown of many an agreement.

The UNCTAD Integrated Programme (stemming from the famous resolution 96(IV) of UNCTAD (Nairobi, 1976) is at present running out of steam. One single new agreement has been signed — for rubber in 1980 (the jute and tropical timber agreements contain no economic clauses). In 1984 the negotiations on sugar and cocoa broke down. In

Table 3.5 An overview of international agreements

Cocoa	International Agreement	1986	Buffer stocks	The agreement of 1980 functioned without great success from 1982. New agreement negotiated since 1984. Not yet ratified in 1986. Non functioning since February 1986.
Coffee	International Agreement	1980	Export quotas	
Olive oil	International Agreement	1979	No economic clauses	
Sugar	International Agreement	1985	No economic clauses	
Tin	International Agreement	1981	Buffer stock	Total breakdown in October 1985.
Wheat	Extension protocol of the International Agreement	1971	No economic clauses (food aid)	Breakdown of negotiations in 1979.
Lead, zinc	International study group	since 1959		
Cotton	International Advisory Committee	since 1951		Six meetings held to pave the way for an agreement: failure.
Rubber	International Agreement	1979	Export quotas and buffer stocks	Functions since 1982. Negotiations under way.
Rice	FAO group		Non-binding directives	
Oilseeds and fats	FAO group			
Bananas	FAO group			
Tea	FAO group + UNCTAD			Failure of negotiations held towards an international agreement. Second UNCTAD 'window'.
Jute, kenaf, and related fibres	International Agreement	1982	No economic clause	
Hard fibres	FAO group + negotiations		Informal arrangement on the price of sisal (since 1976), and of abaca (1977)	Abaca arrangement suspended since 1979.
Meat	FAO group + International Meat Committee (GATT)	1980	No economic clause	
Wood	International Agreement	1983	No economic clause	Second UNCTAD 'window'.
Dairy products	International Milk Committee (GATT)	1980	Minimum export price	Not functioning anymore.

1985, the agreements on tin and coffee broke down. As a matter of fact, during 1986, only the agreement on rubber was performing somewhat satisfactorily. . .

• **Price variations on a market** are the most spectacular visible expression of the fluctuations possible between supply and demand, and of the incidence of speculation.

Globally speaking we could state that commodity prices vary more or less according to the *Kondratieff* cycle producing the following phases:

growth	1890-1920
trough	1920-1950
growth	1950-1974.

Paul Bairoch, in various writings, shows us here a theoretical curve highlighting the fact that each period of stagnation is followed by a period of great tension. This remains of course a very theoretical schema.

Roughly speaking, most commodity prices have followed this sort of curve and many still vividly recall the great price hike of 1972–74. But apart from these major evolutions, commodities are also subject to almost daily price fluctuations which can be of considerable magnitude. Whether some commodities can be said to be more unstable than others depends on when and where they are studied.

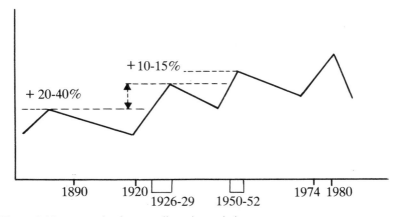

Figure 3.4 Long trends of commodity price variations.

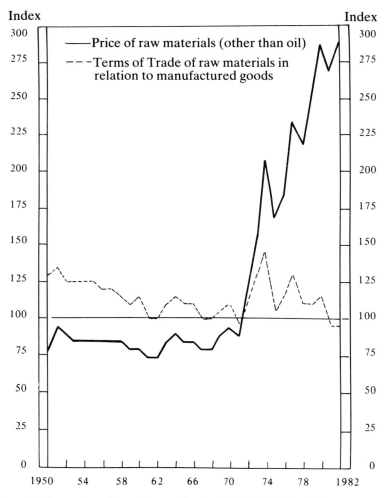

Figure 3.5 Commodity prices and terms of trade,1950–1982 (1972 = 100). Mineral fuels are not included.
Source: UNCTAD Secretariat calculations based on the UNCTAD commodity price index for 1960–1980; United Nations unit value price index (monthly statistical bulletin) and UNCTAD forecasts on stock prices.
(UNCTAD Document TD/B/863, p. 117).

Table 3.6 Analysis of price variations for some commodities.

	Mean price deviation of some raw materials computed on the basis of a moving average	Percentage variations of monthly prices *vis-à-vis* a linear trend	
	1955–76	1960–64	1967–70
+20		sugar tungsten	sugar
10 to 15	sisal, cocoa, zinc, copper	lead	copper
15 to 10	sugar, beef, rice wool, rubber, lead phosphates	copper, bananas,	pepper, rice, palm-oil, cocoa, tungsten, lead bananas, rubber copra
5 to 10	coffee, wheat, corn soya, jute, tin bauxite,iron manganese	cocoa, rubber, copra, coffee, groundnut-oil, copra-oil, tea, groundnuts, tin	coffee, groundnut-oil, coconuts, copra-oil groundnuts, hemp, tea, tin
0 to 5	tea, bananas, cotton	hemp, palm-oil	

Source: OSTERIETH, DECLEVE, *op. cit.*; HVEEM, in *Tiers Monde*, 1976, p. 490.
Note: the methods of calculation as well as the samples of raw materials are different. Any comparison would therefore be problematic.

Although it is difficult to come to global conclusions we could say that cocoa, sugar and copper tend to be unstable, whereas the markets for tea and tin are particularly calm. Futures markets do not seem to contribute in any great measure to instability.

There are however two factors which could cause some degree of instability:

– the freight market,
– the way in which the international monetary system functions, especially when 'investors' are replacing classical speculators.

It would be possible to engage in a lengthy discussion about the real efficiency of markets (widely diffused information, rational anticipation and behaviour patterns). In this sense no market is really efficient. It is really the posession of information (in the sale of US wheat to the USSR for example) that distinguishes one operator from the other.

The foregoing should help us to form a picture of the very diverse, unstable environment surrounding international commodity markets. We are clearly a long way from the relative calm of the managed economic zones of the colonial era. And it is this environment which, from 1950, gave birth to (or at least fostered the growth of) the major international trading firms which we shall finally proceed to discuss after this excessively long introduction (which we hope the reader will excuse!).

PART TWO

THE FUNCTIONING AND RATIONALE OF INTERNATIONAL COMMODITY TRADING FIRMS

D

Chapter 4

THE TRADER'S FUNCTION

Theoretical approach

What is an international commodity trader and what sets him apart from the trading companies described in the preceding pages?

The difference does not so much reside in his function itself — the purely trading function — as in the environment in which he exercises this function (briefly described in the preceeding chapters) and in the concentration of such activities at the world level.

By acting as principal in operations, whose physical and financial constraints he accepts, the international commodity trader brings together the supply and demand of a specific product from two zones which are separated both in time and in space. Such operations can take any one of the following forms:

– at time t, trader x purchases a cargo of merchandise in country A. It could be a purchase on f.o.b. terms pursuant to his having answered an invitation to tender made by a selling agency, or it could be a purchase made inside the country and transported to a f.o.b. position by the trader. The trader pays for the merchandise in local currency or, as is most often the case, in US dollars. Delivery is scheduled for the month $t + n$ and the trader has his bank take out a bid bond[1].

– at some point in time between t and $t + n$ ($t + m$ for example), x

resells all or part of the merchandise to a government or private body
in country B. He receives in payment a letter of credit issued by a
reliable banking establishment. The sale is made on a c.i.f. basis; x
takes responsibility for transporting the merchandise from A to B and
pays the shipping and insurance charges. This operation could also be
conceived the other way around and in fact traders generally prefer to
sell before buying.

In a stable economic climate such a simple double operation would
pose no major problems but since the middle of the nineteen sixties it
involves a high and varied number of risks:

– the possible price fluctuations between t and $t + m$ compounded
by the risk of not being able to find the equivalent amount of actuals on
the due date;

– the risk of fluctuations in the exchange rates of the various
working currencies and possibly in the interest rates on the financial
market;

– the very real risk of anticipating administrative decisions (estimat-
ing the size of EEC restitutions for example);

– the risk of fluctuations in shipping rates between A and B (or more
generally between A and any import destination) and to a lesser extent
in insurance conditions;

– the risk of one of the parties withdrawing from the contract;

– finally the day-to-day management and later the delivery of the
merchandise.

When he begins an operation, the trader does not know *a priori* how
it is going to end. He will therefore try to manage his risks:

– by hedging at the earliest opportunity on the futures markets of
the commodity;

– by doing the same on the financial markets (either directly or
through his banker) and possibly by hedging on the new American
financial futures markets;

– by holding a relatively large 'time charter' on the freight market;

– by using the available standard contracts (Grain and Feed Trade
Association (GAFTA) or other) in as restrictive a manner as possible
or by renegotiating them.

Risks aside, the profits from the operation will depend on:

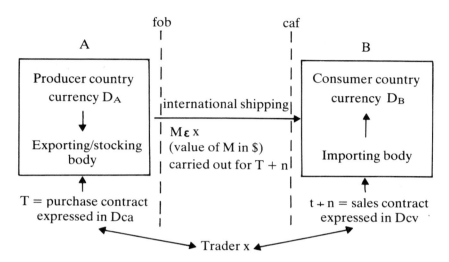

Figure 4.1 Flow chart of an operation in international trade (conceived by Danielle Salomon). Currencies: Dca used in the purchase contract (could be D_A, D_B, or others); Dcv used in the sale contract (could be D_A, D_B, or other).

– how accurately the trader can anticipate movements in the merchandise, both in terms of the basis and in relation to the level of the futures market;

– his evaluation of the freight market and its later evolution, and how efficiently he is able to manage delivery of the merchandise (no demurrage. . .);

– proper management of the financial aspect of the transaction;

– finally the way in which the hedging positions (for both merchandise and currency) will be opened and closed and the possible speculative expectations entertained by the dealer.

But in the interest of clarity and in order to bring this theoretical and therefore rather obscure explanation on to a more practical level, let us examine a life-size example.

A practical case: supplying wheat to Egypt[2]

● *Egypt*

Egypt is, as we know, a country with a deficit in grains for human consumption. With the growth of its great urban centres (especially Cairo), it is increasingly constrained to import food. This either takes the form of Western aid (especially since President Sadat's realignment) or of direct purchases on the international market. Since the Egyptian food problem is more a quantitative than a qualitative one (despite the development of local integrated breeding), the main foodstuff imported is wheat, basic element of the staple diet. The following shows the configuration of the Egyptian wheat balance:

Table 4.1 The Egyptian wheat balance sheet

(June to May)	1976–77	1977–78	1978–79	1979–80	1980–81 (estimated)
Production	1,960	1,872	1,933	2,070	2,000
Imports	2,810	4,100	3,850	3,510	4,200
among which:					
from the U.S.A.	1,540	1,495	1,505	1,230	1,000
from Canada	90	560	70	—	—
from Argentina	65	—	—	—	—
from the EEC	965	1,350	365	688	1,700
from Australia			1,250	1,492	1,500
Other sources	100	600	660	100	—

(in thousands of tonnes).

The area under cultivation varies little and yields have stabilized around the 35 quintal mark.

Of the 4.2 million tonnes of imports scheduled for 1980–81, 2.7 were to be covered by bilateral credits which therefore determined beforehand the origin of the imports:

– three-year agreement with Australia   1 million tonnes
– American P.L. 480 programme   1 million tonnes
– COFACE (France)   700,000 tonnes

That left 1.5 million tonnes to be imported by direct purchases on the world market.

● *The market*

In 1980 the world wheat market was influenced above all by the American embargo (4th January) on exports to the Soviet Union. Whereas the embargo was followed to a greater or lesser extent by the EEC countries, by Canada (until November), and by Australia, Argentina refused to follow suit. In fact thanks to Argentina and Turkey and owing to EEC export licences issued prior to January 4, 1980, the Russians had little difficulty procuring supplies on the world wheat market.

At the end of that year, the drought which plagued the southern hemisphere almost wiped out the Australian, Argentinian, and South African harvests. More than ever before was the United States the world's major wheat supplier; unable to be sold on the principal financially solvent market (the USSR), American wheats found themselves on the traditional markets of the Canadians and Australians (China) or of the Europeans (the Mediterranean).

In fact we could assume that there are two different wheat markets: that which is governed by food aid contracts between states (P.L. 480 and others) and the real market comprising financially solvent demand: the socialist countries, the richest countries of the Third World, Japan. . . During the summer of 1980, the FAO forecast the following for the year 1980–81:

Table 4.2 World wheat trade 1980–81 (FAO estimates in August 1980)

Exports		Imports	
United States	38.00	USSR	11.00
Canada	14.00	Latin America	12.00
Argentina	33.50	Brazil	(4.50)
EEC	10.50	Africa	8.50
Australia	14.00	Middle East	13.60
Other	3.00	Egypt	(5.20)
		Far East	27.00
		China	(9.50)
		Japan	(5.80)
		Western Europe	7.00
		Other	(4.90)
World Total	84.00	World Total	84.00
Developing Countries	(4.00)	Developing Countries	(55.00)
Developed Countries	80.00	Developed Countries	(29.00)

(in million tonnes).

- *The tender*

It was under these conditions that on December 1, 1980, a French trader received the following information from his agent in Cairo:

'The Egyptian government is inviting tenders for the delivery of 100,000 tonnes of 'optional' wheat on three dates: February, March and April, c.and f. any Egyptian port. Tenders should be in Cairo by 10 a.m. on December 6th and should remain valid until December 8th, 12 a.m. Paris time. If you are interested take out a bid bond.'

This meant that:

– the Egyptian government was buying 300,000 tonnes of wheat for delivery in three shipments of 100,000 tonnes each (in the months of February, March, and April 1981);

– the wheat was to be 'optional', in other words, the buyer had no preferences as to quality or origin. Since Egypt was paying from its own pocket, it was seeking above all a cheap grain;

– the wheat was to be delivered to an Egyptian port, with freight being payable by the seller. The buyer would bear the costs of insurance (a cost and freight contract);

– candidates would have to open an equivalent bid bond for their tenders to be examined.

The trader or the producer had six days in which to make a bid. His tender should include:

– the price of the merchandise calculated in dollars,
– the cost of freight.

Under the circumstances obtaining at the time, the trader had a choice between two sources of wheat (the United States and Europe) and between several qualities. In the United States:

– Hard Red Winter (HRW) wheat (of a relatively high density and a high protein content) from Kansas, Oklahoma, Texas. . ., loaded in general in the ports on the Gulf of Mexico,

– low density Soft Red Winter (SRW) wheat from the states of the Midwest, the Mississipi area and the Atlantic Coast,

– the White Wheat (used in confectionery) from the Pacific Coast, loaded in general in the ports of the same (98%).

The European wheats are basically divided into two types: milling wheats and wheats for animal feed. Note that the trader is obliged to consider a number of elements in respect of quality which would be appreciated to a greater or lesser extent by his clients: protein and gluten content, percentage of mould, density. . . In our case the Egyptian client made it known that the European wheat was worth $4 less per tonnne than the American ones for reasons of quality and moisture content.

The price of a specific type of wheat at a given moment can be broken down into two elements:

– the price on the futures market. For our purposes the dominant futures market is in Chicago, but we must also take into account that of Kansas City,

– the *basis* or difference between the forward and futures prices. Theoretically, it would not be incorrect to say that the basis is equal to the costs of freight and storage between futures markets' warehouses in Chicago or Kansas City and the silo where the merchandise is in fact stored (at an export port for example). In fact the basis corresponds to the difference between the price on the futures and forward markets.

Traders have gradually come to reckon exclusively in terms of the basis, which is the true factor of instability on the market. The price of futures is no longer mentioned: it constitutes merely a point of reference. There will be talk of 'X over' or 'Y under', meaning X above the price on the Chicago market or Y below the same. This was the situation on December 5th:

Closing price in	Chicago	Kansas City
March futures	5.18 1/4	4.99
May futures	5.27 3/4	5.09

(price expressed in dollars per bushel: a tonne is equivalent to 36.74 bushels)

Moreover the basis was the following:

delivery of actuals	SRW	HRW	WW	EEC	
February	+28	+55	−6.5	−1	on Chicago March
March	+34	+58	−2.5	+2	
April	+37	+50	−7¾	−4	on Chicago May

(basis in cents per bushel).

Conversion from bushels to tonnes gave the following prices:

in dollars per tonne	February	March	April
SRW based on Chicago	200.70	202.95	207.50
HRW based on Kansas City	203.55	204.65	205.40
WW based on Chicago	188.10	189.45	191.05
EEC based on Chicago	190.05	191.15	192.45

$(5.18\frac{1}{4} + 0.28)\ 36.74 = \$200.70$ per tonne.

To these prices must be added the freight charges for transporting the merchandise. We shall return at a later stage to the estimation of the freight risk. The freight department of our trader will produce the following estimates for Egypt (in US dollar per tonne):

	January	February	March	April
Gulf of Mexico	41.50	42.00	42.50	43.00
USA West Coast				
20–25,000 t.	50.00	50.00	51.50	52.00
35–40,000 t.	41.50	42.00	42.50	43.00
Rouen or Antwerp	41.50	42.00	42.50	43.00

The reader should not lose sight of the fact that these are personal estimates and therefore constitute a risk for the trader[3]. The person in charge of the freight department in the trader's firm will have to take other factors into consideration:

– how fast the ships can be loaded:
5,000 tonnes per day in the United States
4,000 in Europe;
– how fast they can be unloaded and the depth of the ports:
2,000 tonnes and 32 ft. in Alexandria
1,500 tonnes and 38 ft. in Port Said.

By December 5th the main elements needed for a calculation of costs and freight to an Egyptian port had been assembled:

	February	March	April
SRW	242.70	245.45	250.50
HRW	245.55	247.15	248.40
WW a	238.10	240.95	243.05
b	230.10	231.95	234.05
EEC	232.05	233.65	235.45

—

Table 4.3 Seasonal quarterly balances of the American and European markets

	HRW	SRW	WW	EEC
		(million bushels)		(million tonnes)
Carry-over stock				
at 1st June 1980	450	32	92	6.00
Production and Imports	1,105	383	276	49.40
Available in June	1,555	414	368	44.50
Used in June–Sept.:				
seeds	21	7	4	0.15
food industry	92	48	11	9.30
exports	158	78	45	2.70
animal feed	68	25		3.27
Total	339	158	60	15.42
Available 1st Oct. 1980	1,216	256	308	39.98
Used in Oct.–Dec.:				
seeds	21	7	7	0.60
food industry	71	32	8	6.50
exports	174	50	87	2.17
animal feed	(18)	(10)	4	2.26
Total	258	79	106	11.53
Available 1st Jan. 1981	958	177	202	28.45
Used in Jan.–March:				
food industry	63	31	7	7.00
exports	154	30	98	4.50
animal feed	65	1	10	2.13
Total	282	62	115	13.63
Available 1st April 1981	676	115	87	14.82
Used in April–May:				
seeds			2	
food industry	50	20	8	4.00
exports	86	20	28	2.13
animal feed	10	(4)		1.44
Total	146	36	38	7.57
Carry-over stocks				
at 1st June 1981	530	79	49	7.25

We are now in the realm of sure or at least relatively sure elements. In order to get the contract the trader has to attempt to feel the mood of the market and the direction in which it is likely to turn, especially as far as the basis is concerned.

He has a number of market forecasting intruments at his disposal, provided either by his own departments, or by national or international bodies (United States Department of Agriculture, CIA, the Landsat project for the observation by satellite of the progress of crops. . .). In this specific case and given the American position on the grain market, the trader will concentrate on the quarterly, seasonal balances of the European and American markets. On January 7, these balances stood as listed in Table 4.3.

The two final quarters are, of course, forecasts. The trader then has to compare the information provided in this table with the information available on the stocks carried over in preceding years:

	HRW	SRW (million bushels)	WW	EEC (million tonnes)
1976–77	605	72	93	6.70
1977–78	631	71	73	4.60
1978–79	420	27	68	6.90
1979–80	450	32	92	6.00

This analysis clearly shows that the White Wheat, whose prices are the lowest at that point in time, has the highest increment potential given the small quantities of stock expected to be carried over. Conversely, the EEC wheat whose estimated carry-over stock was forecast to be the highest in the past few years, had a strong potential to drop.

Our trader's analysis will naturally condition certain elements of his tender: if *a priori* the White Wheat was the most interesting at that very moment, it was quite probable, on the other hand, that the shipment would have to be filled with European wheats. The largest number of options therefore had to be made available to the seller.

The trader therefore submitted the following tender:

– United States grade No. 2 wheat (or, if the seller preferred, European wheat at $4 less per tonne) c. and f. Port Said:

	February	March	April
50,000 tonnes	230.10	231.95	234.05
or			
100,000 tonnes	231.10	233.25	236.05

The offer was restricted to a maximum of 150,000 tonnes, for risk and logistic reasons (the bid having been made on a weekend thus increasing the number of imponderables).

In order to land the contract the trader used as his basis the price of White Wheat loaded at ports on the Pacific Coast onto ships of 35–40,000 tonnes for delivery to Port Said, the deepest Egyptian port. The offer is limited to 50,000 tonnes at the most exact price, the market for White Wheat being particularly tight.

The tender does not specify the quality of wheat to be delivered (United States No. 2 is merely a general grade corresponding to the Chicago standard contract), nor the origin; this will be revealed, at the earliest, ten days before delivery.

After consideration our trader's tender, along with four others which were particularly competitive, were retained for a more detailed negotiation. In order to eliminate the competition, our trader was obliged to drop the prices even more and finally sold:

March   50,000 tonnes at 231.70
April   100,000 tonnes at 234.05

Were the price of freight to remain unchanged, the offer would be equal to an f.o.b. export price of:

March $231.70 - 42.50 = \$189.20$ per t. or \$5.15 per bushel
April $234.05 - 43.00 = \$191.05$ per t. or \$5.20 per bushel.

Note that the prices tendered by the trader are lower than the Chicago futures prices, with the result that his proposal is accepted by the Egyptian government.

If the trader were to deliver EEC wheat, taking into account the \$4 deduction per tonne compared to American wheats, the offer would stand at:

March $231.70 - 4 - 42.50 = \$185.20$ per t. or \$5.05 per bushel
April $234.05 - 4 - 43.00 = \$187.05$ per t. or \$5.09 per bushel.

Considering the futures prices in Chicago, there is thus a difference in value between the 'forward market basis' and the 'trader basis'[4] in March and April.

	Chicago futures $/bushel	'WW forward market' basis cents/bushel	'WW trader' basis cents/bushel	'EEC trader' basis cents/bushel
March	5.18¼	−2½	−3¼[1]	−14¼[3]
April	5.27¾	−7¾	−7¾[2]	−18¾[4]

(1) 5.18¼ − 5.15
(2) 5.27¾ − 5.20
(3) 5.18¼ − 5.04
(4) 5.27¾ − 5.09

This seemed a relatively appreciable sum inasmuch as there were no Russian or Chinese buying interests on the horizon. On the other hand the professionals were relatively surprised by the size of the Egyptian purchase: 575,000 tonnes (and not the scheduled 300,000) which risked creating a certain degree of tension on the market. The contract was drawn up on the model of a standard contract from the GAFTA in London providing for arbitration in the event of disputes (see below).

- *Hedging*

On the 8th December, our trader therefore sold 150,000 tonnes of wheat worth some $35 million. The risk of price fluctuations could be considerable in such a case where the trader has not yet bought the merchandise which he has contracted to deliver; moreover profit margins are small compared to the price fluctuations which can take place with commodities.

Considering the size of the sale and the non-determination of the origin of the wheat to be delivered, the trader chooses not to continue to hold an unhedged position. Finally, in order to reduce the commercial risk involved in selling at a fixed price merchandise which he has not yet purchased, the trader will have to hedge on the Chicago futures market: since he is selling actuals in March and April he will buy an equivalent amount of March and April futures in Chicago. When buying the physical commodity, he will sell an identical quantity on the futures market.

The trader is therefore going to take out an individual insurance policy, with speculators insuring the other side of his operation. The hedging operation may or may not, by itself, bring him a profit; but in the event of a loss, hedging will keep the latter at a minimum.

On the 8th of December the markets opened slightly lower, the session was calm and the volumes traded small. Our trader's correspondent on the Chicago market was able to buy at the opening price:

1,837 million bushels on March at 5.13½
3,674 million bushels on May at 5.23¾.

Prices were therefore lower than those of December 5th on which the calculation of the terms of the tender had been based.
From then on the situation was as follows:

	delivery in WW		delivery in SRW		delivery in EEC	
	March	April	March	April	March	April
Sales price	231.70	234.05	231.70	234.05	227.70	230.05
minus freight	47.50	43.00	47.50	43.00	47.50	43.00
f.o.b. price	189.20	191.05	198.20	185.20	185.20	187.05
futures hedge	5.13½	5.24¾	5.13½	5.24¾	5.13½	5.24¾
basis to be found						
(in cents/bushel)	+1½	−4¾	+1½1	−1½	−9½	−15¾

- *Procuring the merchandise*

From now on the entire reckoning will be done in terms of the basis. The problem is to know at what price one will be able to buy the basis, the equivalent of which has been sold. Between the tender and the hedge, the situation has already evolved rather favourably, though at this point the trader would lose were he to sell:

	WW		EEC	
	March	April	March	April
basis on 5 Dec. 'trader' basis	2½ − H	7¾ − K	2 + H	4 − K
from the transaction on 5 Dec. 'trader' basis from	3¼ − H	7¾ − K	14¼ − H	18¾ − K
the hedge on 8 Dec.	1½ + H	4¾ − K	9½ − H	15¾ − K

H: March futures
K: May futures

From the 8th to the 16th December prices on the market were generally depressed (reduction of the American prime rate) but there was also a great deal of fluctuation (uncertainty over Poland). The markets evolved as follows:

(in cents per bushel)	SRW	HRW	WW	EEC
March basis	36 + H	54 + H	2½ − H	0 + H
April basis	35 + K	56 + K	7½ − K	5½ − K
futures markets (in $US/bushel)	Chicago		Kansas City	
March	496½		481	
May	505½		491	

Seen in comparison with the 5th December the situation had already developed favourably for our trader. Although the White Wheat basis had increased slightly, the basis of the European wheat, on the other hand, had diminished appreciably. The idea of buying European wheat therefore seemed worth considering. Not having to specify the origin of the merchandise until January 31, the trader decided to await a strengthening of the trends which he had forecast.

During the month of December the trader's forecasting department up-dated its assessments of the quarterly balances. The following changes were recorded for the second quarter:

Exports Oct–Dec (million bushels)	HRW	166	instead of 174 expected
	SRW	57	550
	WW	101	87
(million tonnes)	EEC	1.89	2.17

This meant that White Wheat had already exceeded its normal export capacity and that exports would have to be curbed to avoid the risk of running out of stock. (It would therefore be practically impossible for our trader to fill his contract requirements in April with White Wheat). On the other hand the EEC wheat was selling badly and that meant that its basis would have to drop even more to allow it to 'get by': the EEC would clearly have to be even more generous with its export refunds.

On January 7, this is how the market stood:

	WW	EEC
March basis	3 + H	10 − H
April basis	1 + K	13 − K

The American freight rates had risen in comparison with European rates owing to the congestion of a number of American ports. Thus in European wheat we are approaching the point where our operation in terms of the basis is about to show positive returns. Let us take a look at the trader's global calculation:

	SRW		HRW		WW		EEC	
	March	April	March	April	March	April	March	April
Basis	36 + H	35 + K	60 + H	58 + K	3 + H	1 + K	10 − H	13 − K
Market	505½	513½	480½	488½	505½	513½	505½	513½
f.o.b. price	199.00	201.55	198.60	200.80	186.85	189.05	182.05	193.90
freight	44.50	45.00	44.50	45.00	40.00	40.50	38.00	38.50
c. and f.	234.50	246.55	243.10	245.80	226.85	229.55	220.05	222.40

From this point forward it becomes possible to carry out the operation using European wheat.

On January 7th the trader decides to execute the order scheduled for March by purchasing 50,000 tons of EEC wheat. He will therefore either purchase f.o.b. port of export or will buy inside the Common Market which would oblige him to stand the costs of transporting the wheat from an inland silo to a port silo.

Two new risks have to be assessed by the trader:

– he must anticipate the amounts he will be refunded when the 50,000 tons of wheat are exported;
– he must hedge against the exchange risk.

Since the price of wheat in the EEC is higher than the world price, the trader will be entitled to an export refund, in ECUs, the value of the ECU varying according to the value of the individual currencies comprising it; he also has to bear in mind the value of the European 'green' currencies since there could be discrepancies between the agricultural exchange rates and the money market exchange rates.

The trader will consequently have to take a hedge in foreign currency (dollars against the currencies comprising the ECU), it being always possible to unilaterally manipulate the 'green' currency of the country where he bought the wheat.

The purchase of European wheat can be made in two ways:

– at a price fixed in US dollars;

– in terms of the basis in relation to Chicago (generally the case in the United States, but less frequent in Europe).

Let us take the first case:

– price of French wheat on Jan. 8th $184.30

– price at the time on the Chicago

   Board of Trade (for the hedge) $5.15

The trader buys 50,000 tonnes of wheat f.o.b. at $184.30 and simultaneously resells his contracts on the futures market in Chicago at $5.15. Let us leave the question of freight aside for the moment. What is the global balance sheet of the operation?

It can be presented in two ways:

      a) 8th December   8th January

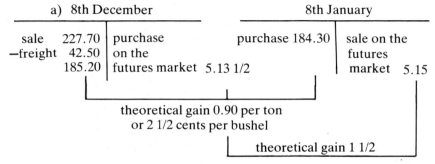

In other words a theoretical total profit of 4 cents per bushel. This is the way in which a hedging operation is usually presented. Note that owing to a favourable price evolution, the trader in this case wins on both accounts: in actuals and in futures.

But it is more likely that the trader will reckon in terms of the basis.

      b) 8th December   8th January

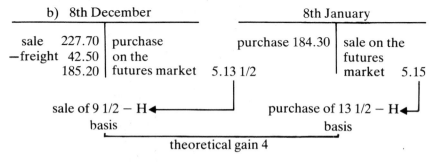

The outcome is the same but reckoning in terms of the basis gives a much clearer picture.

The entire operation will therefore result in a theoretical profit of 4 cents per bushel or, for 50,000 tonnes, a little over 70,000 dollars (more precisely: 73,490), that is 0.73% of the value of the f.o.b. contract. The entire risk assumed by the trader is limited in fact to his work on the basis and his accurate anticipation of its evolution. In our example the trader wins but it may very often occur that he loses on an operation. In most cases the recourse to hedging is systematic. In addition, the trader has to manage his own exchange rate risk and hope that the refund he receives from the EEC will be equivalent to the sums which he needs to make his operation a positive one.

The trader will also have to purchase freight and will therefore instruct his staff to buy freight for voyage from Europe to Egypt. Here are all of the elements which have been used in our calculations even though these are much less representative:

8 December	sale of March freight	42.50	
8 January	purchase of March freight	38	
	theoretical profit	4.50 (in $ per t.) or	
			11 cents per bushel

This could seem — and is in fact — rather expensive for a simple voyage from Europe to Egypt. But such variations over a month are quite frequent on longer distances (the Gulf to Japan for example).

The rest of the operation is relatively simple. The trader will inform his Egyptian client of the origin of the merchandise. His logistics department will then supervise the loading and unloading of the merchandise (checking the quality, waiting at the ports. . .) and his financial department will pay for them. We shall come back to these points at a later stage.

It is clear that this example has dealt exclusively with the problem of grain: the special methods required for different products vary considerably and the reasoning in terms of the basis which we have used here is essentially one for cereals.

The main sections of chapter 5 will deal in detail with a certain number of aspects concerning the running of a trading firm:

– the trader and the markets (actuals, chains, futures),
– the logistics of a trader's operations,

- the trader and the freight problem,
- the trader and the financial markets,
- the international legal problems of the trader,
- the organization of a trading firm.

Chapter 5

THE TRADER'S MANY JOBS

*'The trader needs a pencil. . .
with an eraser.'*
A trader

In the preceeding example we were able to see that a certain number of tasks organize themselves around a single trading operation. In the final analysis, each of these tasks represent totally separate professions in the eyes of the trader.

The administrative chart of a trading firm differs, of course, according to its size or the products in which it deals and even according to the strategy which the firm employs. On the next page can be found the 'active' administrative chart of the Louis Dreyfus company in Paris as it can be imagined on the basis of the preceeding case.

What do these structures tell us?

– on the one hand that a division exists between the operational departments which could be considered independent centres of profit, and management activities (the old distinction between 'staff' and 'line'); in Figure 5.1 the operational departments, or those which could be considered operational, are:

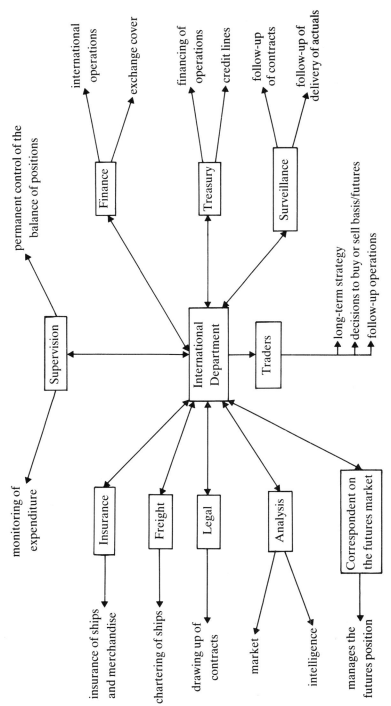

Figure 5.1 Flow Chart of an operation in international trade (designed by Danielle Salomon).

- the trading department which is the very centre of the firm towards which everything converges,
- the freight, insurance and finance departments which can, to a certain degree, work independently,
- the correspondent on the futures markets.

– on the other hand, it also makes clear that there is a distinction between functions: those which are predominantly financial (trading, finance, futures markets) and those which are predominantly concerned with merchandise (supervision, freight, legal questions. . .).

Let us take a closer look at some of these functions:

The trading department

The trading department is, without a doubt, the nerve centre of a trading firm. From a strictly material viewpoint it generally takes the form of an enormous open room in the 'open-plan' style, each trader having before him a number of telephones and video display units showing the prices on the major commodity futures markets and financial markets, as well as the dispatches of the news agencies (Reuter in general).

Such an office could house from one to a hundred traders, depending on the size of the firm and the scope of its activities. In general trading firms are located in a few of the strongholds of primary commodity trading (New York, London, Paris, Rotterdam, Rio, Buenos Aires, Tokyo. . .) or in countries which are sufficiently understanding in tax matters such as Switzerland (Geneva, Zug, Lausanne). Switzerland has moreover become one of the main centres of trade and in particular the preferred site for the establishment of the European headquarters of the major American traders (Tradax, Continental, Phibro. . .) thanks to the country's banking and commercial secrecy and the possibilities it offers for access to the Euro-currency markets. The location of a firm — in itself a relatively minor preoccupation given modern communications systems — will depend in fact on the product dealt in, on the the firm's standing in the profession and on the importance accorded to maintaining contacts with the local environment.

Practically, we could compare the trader's profession, in certain aspects, to that of the exchange broker. It requires a remarkable mental agility to assimilate at the same time a large number of parameters and to juxtapose long-term strategy analyses with short-term decisions. Traditionally, the trader was trained on the job: he joined the firm at the age of 18 and spent his first years cutting out the press dispatches before gradually working his way up the hierarchy. Today an increasing number of young traders are university graduates although, to our knowledge, there is no specific training which can prepare one for the trading profession, the few possibilities offered in this domain seeming more or less doomed to failure.

In general traders are young: it is rare to find in the rooms of the trading department men who are much older than forty. Trading is a profession which burns people out, both physically and nervously. It is also a profession which ignores any concept of time and demands total availability both day and night: for example the working timetables of the trader in the case previously described, working in Paris, are more or less 8 a.m. to 1 p.m. and from 2 p.m. to 9 p.m., the important hours of the day being 4 p.m. to 9 p.m., the opening times of the Chicago Board of Trade. On the other hand the real trader travels little and for only short periods. In fact he hardly knows the persons with whom he deals, and never sees the merchandise in which he deals. He is physically totally isolated. Of course the high salaries earned by such men compensate for this workload[1]. The psychological balance of the trader, whatever post he might occupy in the firm, is paramount. This point was dramatically illustrated in 1977, with the disastrous results of a large firm which specialized in trading and in the processing of agricultural products: the director of the trading department had been abandoned by his wife! Such cases can take an even more tragic turn as in August 1982 when the President of the New York Cotton Exchange committed suicide at a time when the cotton market was particularly depressed.

All of these details might well seem anecdotal, but it should not be forgotten that the capital of a trading firm is the men which comprise it, their expertise, their knowledge, their luck and at times their loyalty too. In most of the trading firms the spirit of enterprise and teamwork is highly developed. It is poorly thought of for a trader to switch firms and most often a person will begin and end his career in one and the same firm. The enticing away of employees is only practised at the highest levels. Very often, moreover, once the teams are made up they hardly ever dissolve and even survive the firms which employ them.

Thus in grain a part of the team from the Goldschmidt firm which went out of business in 1968 reformed until 1977 as the European arm of Cook Europe and, since the bankruptcy of the latter, forms the core of Tradimer. The problem moreover of a company trying to break into the trade of a specific commodity is less a problem of money than one of finding the necessary competent staff. Note that most of the directors of trading firms are former dealers: from the late Maurice Varsano (*Sucres et Denrés*) to Marc Rich or David Tendler (Phibro). The grafting of outside elements has hardly proved successful and remains an exception.

The trading department can therefore be limited — and is indeed sometimes limited — to one man, one telephone, a telex and of course a certain degree of financial and professional credibility. The last point is particularly important in so far as all transactions and agreements are made by telephone and are immediately binding on the firm. (Very often the operation is already executed even before the contract documents change hands). It is obvious that any firm which were to default would be immediately put outside the pale of the profession.

The trader carries out two types of activities:

– those which effectively correspond to physical operations and therefore comprise the purchase or the sale of a commodity with a view to delivering it,
– those which entail taking positions on the markets as a result of the economic climate in order to make a profit.

Of course the limit between both varies according to the commodity, the country and the market techniques. A distinction must be made between:

– those markets which correspond to our preceding example where there is a real basis market (essentially the market for grain);
– those market equipped with a futures market but on which reckoning on the basis is not common (grain in Europe even today);
– those markets which have no dominant futures markets.

The techniques used on the latter are so special as to require separate treatment. For the first two it is really a question of the different methods employed:

– in the first case the trader works on a single market, that of the basis (he is a 'premium trader'). He is often totally ignorant of the futures markets on which the firm also operates:

$$\text{end price} \; = \; \text{premium or basis} \; + \; \text{futures markets price}$$
$$\text{[premium trader]} \; + \; \text{[futures trader]}$$

– in the second case the trader works at the same time on two markets: the forward and the futures markets.

Let us go back to the activities of the trader. In order to be able to effectively carry out a transaction in actuals, the trading firm must constantly carry a certain number of open positions on paper. As soon as he feels the market move in one direction or another, the trader will take out a short or long position, depending on whether he expects prices to rise or fall. This position is hardly ever taken on the futures market itself since it is extremely dangerous for a trader to hold a position on 'paper'. As is said in the profession: 'one always ends up being wrong'. The position will essentially be taken on the level of the basis or its equivalent. The trader will constantly buy and resell the basis according to how he assesses the market. When a basis system does not exist, the operation is more complicated: contracts corresponding to physical quantities to be delivered are exchanged and, when necessary, the trader hedges simultaneously on the futures markets. Let us take the example of the grain market within the European Community. The absolute price of wheat can only vary between the threshold price and the intervention price (that is a maximum variation of 25%). In order to remain in position, the traders exchange with each other contracts called 'fob CREIL' (the zone in the EEC with the highest surplus). In this case hedging in Chicago is not a must. Since the contract often changes hands, a chain is gradually formed and at liquidation time it is retraced from the initial buyer to the final seller (the number of intermediaries could be very high) and the differences between each phase are merely offset. It is a relatively cumbersome system, the basis system being far more practical. This system of chains is moreover the only one to exist when there is no futures market (we are here in a forward market): this is the case for the Rotterdam oil and oilseeds market. It stands to reason that the risks in such markets are much higher.

On the basis market, as on the forward or futures market, the trader can also take positions when he believes that there is an imbalance in the market. He could thus paradoxically take the position of the opposite dealer in speculative operations when these are becoming far too abnormal for his liking. He could, if he considers the difference between two prices too wide, buy on one contract to be able to sell on the other (making a spread); he could repeat the operation between two markets or between two commodities (soya oil, seeds, and cakes, for example).

The trader must constantly seek to flow with the market, to make the little difference which will help fill the till at the end of the period. Note, moreover, that a certain number of trading firms deal exclusively in 'paper', either because they do not want to go any further, or because they observe the market carefully before dealing in actuals.

These paper trades, accompanied or not by connected operations on the futures markets, deal with huge quantities which are out of all proportion to the quantities of actuals which change hands. For example the Louis Dreyfus wheat desk in Paris (two dealers) executed 240 transactions with a total amount of some 10 million tonnes from the 1st of January to 15th September 1980 (remember that the international wheat trade handles approximately 90 million tonnes). The figure is particularly high in this case, inasmuch as a firm which is very active on the forward market needs to be constantly in position and therefore works according to a substitution principle.

How much independence does a trader enjoy within his firm and how is the trading risk managed?

The amount of freedom enjoyed by a trader varies according to the firm, according to the experience of the individual trader and the economic circumstances obtaining at the time. We could generally assume that the age of the adventurers has given way to that of the managers.

Roughly, before 1970 firms were inclined to leave a rather large margin of freedom to their agencies and within the latter to the traders: these were in the habit of 'pulling off stunts' but they dealt in small quantities in a relatively stable climate and therefore did not excessively endanger the existence of their respective firms.

Since 1970, and especially after the frenzied period from 1972–75, most firms have strived to formalize their management structures and to place the activities of their traders and subsidiaries under stricter control.

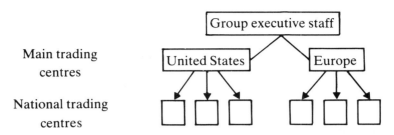

Main trading
centres

National trading
centres

Figure 5.2 The standard structure of a trading firm

There are, in fact, two types of stuctures:

– those which are extremely centralized and leave practically no
autonomy to the various subsidiaries, where almost every hour of
every day the central management must be apprised of the group's
position on the international level. The upshot of such a system is that
the different offices have extremely little autonomy. So it is with the
grain trading firms like Cargill or Louis Dreyfus. In this type of firm the
traders are gradually subordinated to 'managers', to Harvard MBAs.
Generally speaking, there has been a premium on this type of structure
in recent times;

– the more decentralized structures where each office enjoys a
certain degree of autonomy, a quota of open positions, the ability to
bind the firm on contracts involving a certain sum. This is to some
extent the old method conserved by a number of firms as long as
business is running smoothly. In times of crisis (like since 1976) there
is, however, a general trend towards increased supervision and centralization. Under such circumstances, certain firms like Philip Bros used
to leave a large amount of room for manoeuvre to their national
offices.

In any event the dominant feature of risk management in
trading appears to be a trend towards more precise and exacting
techniques. Trading today is also characterized by an almost systematic recourse to hedging. Here there is a difference of opinion between
those firms which claim to hedge almost their entire position on the
international level every day (not including the in-house hedging

possibilities), and those which believe that a hedge can be spread over a rather long period of time (1 month), as long as one is always ready and able to hedge or reverse one's position when necessary.

Risk management finally boils down to the problem of constantly having to steer a course between the speculative temptation to believe that one is right and the conservative temptation not to take any risks. According to circumstances and the skills of the men involved, one of these inclinations will take precedence over the other.

Table 5.1 Some of the international commodity trading firms which have gone bankrupt in the last years

	trader	product	reason
1963–64	Julio Lobo	sugar	position taken against the market
1968	Goldschmidt	grain cocoa	management problems
1977	Cook Industries	grain	speculation
1979	GIE *Union Française des Céréales*	grains	
1981	Sasetru (Argentina)	oilseeds	
	ACLI	coffee	speculation

But even when the first temptation is confirmed by the prospect of spectacular profits and success, the trader will never be able to shrug off the spectre of the numerous 'corpses' which punctuate the history of international commodity trading or the losses suffered by such and such a trading giant often over long periods of time. We shall return at a later stage to the profit structures of trading firms but we can already introduce the reader to a few of these 'corpses' (Table 5.1) and analyse the reasons for their collapse.

The Cook case is interesting enough to be recounted in full.

The ups and downs of trading: the Cook case[2]

The Cook Company was founded in Memphis in 1918 by Everett Cook, former American aviation ace in Europe. A brokerage and trading firm on the internal American cotton market, it was sufficiently prosperous for Everett's son, Edward ('Ned') to receive the best

possible education: Hotchkiss and Yale. After having served as a pilot
in Europe during the Second World War (and not in the secret service
as some are wont to say, confusing all too readily the grain trade and
the CIA), he joined his father in Memphis. But the post-war period
was not a good one for cotton, undermined as it was by surpluses and
by competition from synthetic fibres. In 1961 Ned began to look
elsewhere and decided to try his hand at grains and oilseeds, activities
which he carried out on a small scale until 1967 when his father passed
away.

He then decided to invest the entire family fortune in developing the
firm's grain operations. He had come to understand that if he wanted
to be taken seriously he would have to be more than an armchair
trader. He decided to commission the construction of an export
elevator in Reserve (Louisiana) at the mouth of the Mississipi river
(some 50 kms from New Orleans) for a total investment of $12 million.
This was an exorbitantly large elevator which considerably exceeded
the capacity and needs of the firm. It meant on the one hand that
capital had to be found fast, and on the other that operations had to
grow at least enough to be able to fill the elevator. The first problem
was solved in a rather curious way: Cook succeeded in merging with a
Memphis firm, which was then struggling to recover from a scandal
over the appropriation of funds by one of its directors. This firm, E.L.
Bruce and Co, manufacturer of floors and floorings, was worth three
times as much as Cook and had much greater liquidity at its disposal.
The new firm was called *Cook Industries* and profited in the event from
Bruce's quotation on the American Stock Exchange. Ned Cook had
solved his financial problems by going public (an element which is not
without its importance since this was going to constrain the firm to
publish its results and accounts, something which the other traders, all
private companies, are not obliged to do). Cook subsequently continued to buy up other firms though with little success; he gradually
came to acquire:

– Bruce and Co mentioned above,

– 95% of Riverside Chemical Co, a distributor of chemical products
used in agriculture (fertilizers, pesticides. . .) and which was his only
successful venture (December 1969),

– two insurance firms: C.I.P. and C.T.H.,

– a distributor of anti-termite products: Terminix International Inc.
(April 1974).

But this was negligible compared to the development experienced in the grain trade. The firm's international activity really took off with the recruiting of the former Goldschmidt team (after that firm collapsed in 1968), under the direction of Gerard Emler. From Paris, where Cook International was based, operations extended to Europe, Eastern Europe, the Middle East, Africa, China and Australia. From Memphis, Japan and South America were tackled. The results, nevertheless, bear testimony to the fact that at the beginning the outlook was less than rosy:

1970   − $1.7 million
1971   + $9 million.

The company was just beginning to gather momentum, when, emulating the executive vice-president Philip Mac Caull, almost all of the management staff of the grain sector left Cook to join the New York headquarters of Louis Dreyfus which was making a comeback in the sector at that time. 'Traders' hopscotch' is a well-known fact in the business, but seeing it happen on the level of an entire team was, nonetheless, a rare occurrence!

Then came the great opportunity for Cook. In July 1972, a Russian mission arrived in New York for the purpose of buying grain. And the miracle took place: Ned Cook's display of charisma and gift of speech were so impressive that he was admitted to deal on a par with the majors. At that time no one imagined the magnitude of the intended Soviet purchases, not only in grain but also in soya. In July and August Cook managed to land the contract to supply 600,000 tonnes of wheat and 1,000,000 tonnes of soybeans to the Soviet Union. William Sparks, who succeeded MacCaull, estimated that the contract, whose total value amounted to $133 million, put Cook in such a strong position on the market thereafter because of its new hedging power, that the firm earned over $10 million!

The company's profits were certainly affected:

1972 $4 million
1973 $40 million.

From 1972 to 1976 Cook Industries was to experience a phenomenal growth in the field of grains and oilseeds which was to make it the world's third largest trader. The firm proceeded to expand its facilities. In addition to its elevator in Reserve it owned:

– a soya crushing plant in Marks (Mississipi) with an annual capacity
of 16 million bushels and another in Europia (Kansas) with an annual
capacity of 12 million bushels,

– an oil refinery with a capacity of 72,000 pounds per day (in Marks),

– three cotton grinding plants (with a total capacity of 155,000
tonnes per year),

– inland silos (18 along the Mississipi) with a total capacity amounting to 33 million bushels (a single silo had a capacity of 21.5 million
bushels),

– a new elevator constructed in Galveston (Texas) with a capacity of
4.5 million bushels and another in Portland (Oregon) with a capacity of
1.5 million bushels,

– 1,700 leased freight cars and 212 barges, 31 of which were owned in
full, the others chartered.

The book value of the investments made by Cook Industries rose
from $32 million in 1970 to $113 million in 1976.

The item which interests us most at this point is the margin made on
commodity trading (grain, cotton). The latter culminated in 1974 with
a total of over $100 million. It subsequently levelled off to around $75
million. If we were to separate grain from cotton we would obtain the
margins displayed in Table 5.2.

The position of the firm in grain trading began to deteriorate in 1974
but was compensated, it is true, by improved results in cotton. On the
market, Cook had a reputation for being a highly speculative firm. In
the grain sector up to 25% of its activities were dedicated to trade
inside America and the rest to international trade. In 1976 the USSR
accounted for 20.5% of the total activites in grains. But since the
margin did not include the financial charges, it is interesting to see that
the short-term borrowed capital increased considerably:

    1973 $152 million
    1974 $225 million
    1975 $373 million
    1976 $353 million.

The financial situation of the company on 31 May, 1976 was mediocre: the assets' liquidity ratio had dropped from 16.41% in 1975 to
10.27 % in 1976 and the firm's indebtedness was clearly on the
increase. It has now come to light that after 1976 the firm's directors

Table 5.2 The Cook Accounts (*Moody's Industrial Manual*, 1977) (in $ 000)

	1976	1975	1974	1973	1972	1971	1970
Total sales	408,830	433,593	353,784	220,745	163,785	128,054	108,374
Margins on commodity deals	73,630	76,964	101,827	60,221	13,913	20,733	8,527
Other earnings	5,403	9,296	4,900	3,935	2,606	3,171	4,461
Total earnings	487,863	519,853	460,511	284,901	180,304	151,958	121,362
Net company profits	22,215	21,810	46,226	22,729	3,585	2,271	544

Table 5.3 Cook's margins (in $ 000)

	1976	1975	1974	1973
grain margin	51,683	62,971	91,094	56,836
cotton margin	22,054	14,136	10,936	3,379

Source: *Cook Annual Report*, 1977.

increased their speculative activities in an attempt to maintain its growth rate in a rather depressed market. The year beginning on 1st June, 1976 was to mark the beginning of the decline for Cook. Losses first struck in soybeans in the autumn of 1976: the company's directors were convinced that soybean prices, which then stood at $6.50 per bushel, would fall. They therefore sold, in the hope of being able to buy back their contracts at around $5 per bushel. Alas, unexpected droughts and an increase in consumption made prices escalate to over $7 per bushel. Losses were considerable:

1st quarter 76–77 — $13.5 million
2nd quarter 76–77 — $0.7 million
3rd quarter 76–77 — $13 million

amounting to, on 28 February 1977, accumulated losses of $27 million. The company's directors then decided to make up their losses by playing double or quits (the story now belongs to the realm of pure speculation and no longer in that of trading). In January–February of the same year, soybean prices stood at $7.50 per bushel. The Brazilian harvest was expected to be a good one and logically prices were expected to fall back to where they had been in November (when the

E

Figure 5.3 Caricature of Bunker Hunt published in the *Financial Times* on 25 June, 1977. (From the French edition of this book)

American harvest came on the markets). They therefore decided to make a spread:

– selling short of June-July contracts
– buying long of November contracts.

Theoretically Cook was covered and should have made a huge profit if, as its directors expected, the difference between the two quotations had narrowed. But this was not to be:

	Quotations May and July	Quotations November
February	7.50	5
April	10.50	6

(Average quotations in dollars per bushel)

Cook had taken out a huge short position (there is talk of over 20 million bushels), but — though no one knew this at the time — it was exactly the moment chosen by the Hunt family (Texan oil billionaires) to try to corner the soybean market[3]! The Hunts had bought May and July contracts for even more fantastic amounts: 22 million bushels, without anyone apparently having noticed their move. Moreover the exceptional Brazilian harvest expected by Cook turned out to be so mediocre that the Brazilian government was forced to take a number of measures which were tantamount to an embargo on exports. On the other hand the November price evolved little given the forecasts of a bumper American harvest.

It meant a fortune for the Hunts (they made over $100 million) and ruin for Cook. The directors sought in vain to bring the question of the Hunt family's manipulations before the CFTC (Comodities Futures Trading Commisssion), the body which controls the running of the American futures markets[4]. It was in any case too late for them. True enough, intervention on the part of the CFTC forced the prices down somewhat on 21 April and on subsequent days, but they soon rose again rapidly. About this time the Chicago Board of Trade began to be concerned about Cook's position and doubled and later tripled the firm's deposit and the corresponding margin calls. It was then that Cook's bankers became aware of the gravity of the situation.

According to Dan Morgan, Ned Cook was not aware of the magnitude of the crisis until 20 May, 1977. There is reason for scepticism here. At the end of May the banks obliged Cook to liquidate its position. The losses were, as was to be expected, enormous. (If Cook had had the financial means to hold on for another 15 days, the forecasts of his directors concerning the drop in prices would have been realized: but the banking consortium led by Chase Manhattan refused to wait, deeming the risk too high).

Cook was forced to sell off, bit by bit, a number of its assets in order to hold onto its position. All the same, the results of the fourth quarter were disastrous: a loss of $53 million. The general results for the year were no less disastrous:

total losses (in $ 000)	90,306
of which losses on trading and crushing operations	91,526
margin on the grain trade	−39,543
margin on cotton	+18,644

But the losses on soya were entered under the heading:

'Loss from continuing operations' − $ 81,893,000

amounting indeed to an average loss of $4 per bushel, on a total of some 20 million bushels or more.

The firm was forced to sell other assets:

− almost all of its inland silos (including the one in Saginaw with a capacity of 21 million bushels),
− the soya crushing facilities and refinery in Marks (Mississipi),
− the cotton crushing plant and a number of cotton warehouses,

for a total of approximately $21 million.

The two directors of trading, Willard R. Sparks and C.R. Parrott resigned. Ned Cook adduced that he had not been informed of the firm's positions, which appeared, to say the least, surprising, and declared that he intended to make a reshuffle of his entire staff.

But the firm's position was irreparably compromised. In July Cook reached an agreement with the consortium of bankers led by Chase Manhattan which stipulated the terms under which a short-term loan of a total of $310 million would be made available, but with a number of conditions: the supervision of Cook's undertakings in trading and a mortgage on its assets notably on Riverside Chemical (which was sold off before long).

The firm resumed activities and even in August, Cook announced sales to the USSR (500,000 tonnes of wheat and 250,000 tonnes of maize), the first for the year. The USSR maintained its confidence in Cook even as the bankers were losing theirs. But this did nothing to improve the situation:

Table 5.4 Cook's last results

	Results for 6 months ending	
	30 November, 1977	30 November, 1976
Total profits	+ $14,520,000	− $14,176,000
Trading sector and agricultural products	− $3,978,000	− $11,367,000

In January the bankers abandoned Cook and he was forced to sell the rest of his assets. The third largest grain trader in the world had been wiped out in six months.

The Cook case provides a perfect illustration of the speculation risk inherent to the trading risk; as one trader told us: 'any trader who earns money on the basis of luck alone constitutes a danger for his firm, because one day his luck will run out'. Without generalizing unduly, it would be in order to claim that such cases are no rare occurrence. Some of the most recent include: the $32 million lost in the winter of 1981 by Farmers Export (the trading arm of a number of American grain cooperatives) and the losses (estimated at $60 to $80 million) incurred in the same period by the ACLI group, foremost world coffee trader (and which resulted in the latter's acquisition by the Wall Street firm Donaldson, Lufkin and Jeanrette, and later by Cargill).

Another danger is posed by the trader, whatever his position in the hierarchy, who 'falls in love' with his position (this is what had happened to Sparks in the Cook example). We have been told of traders keeping contracts in their drawers and not divulging them, convinced that they were going to be right in the long term. This brings us back to what we were discussing before: the need for a very stringent control of the trader's activities. (Michel Goldschmidt, president of J.A. Goldschmidt, a company which disappeared from the trading scene in 1969, attributed the firm's failure, *inter alia,* to the 'betrayal' of one of his directors and in particular to the adoption of data processing facilities, which required a six-month trial period during which it was practically impossible to have up-to-date information on the firm's position).

Let us recapitulate this essential point — the function of the trading department which is, of course, the cornerstone of the firm's activity. As we have said, it generally enjoys little independence, being either strictly supervised by a financial department, or having to carry out decisions taken at a higher level in the firm (the problem often being to know if the directors have retained a trader's mentality or if they themselves have become essentially managers). Its profits or losses derive, on the one hand, from commercial activities *stricto sensu* (but such cases are rare unless there are no hedging possibilities), on the other hand from speculative activities of greater or lesser magnitude, characterized by the taking of positions. The profit-making capacity of the firm depends not only on the skill and the competence of its men but also on the possession and accurate interpretation of information.

Information

Information is certainly the key to the power wielded by the trading firms. The markets are constantly moving on the basis of rumours which are, to a greater or lesser extent, founded in truth: harvests, floods, coups. So whoever knows the truth — and knows how to interpret it — possesses a great deal of power. But there are many types and therefore many qualities of information:

– there is first of all 'general' information available to any operator in return for a consideration, supplied by the news agencies and the specialized newspapers. Among them Reuter with an almost total monopoly, and Unicom News. As a rule this very rapid but disjointed information (the client has to know how to analyse it) arrives after the event. For each product there is, in addition, one or more specialized statistical agencies which are authorities in the field of forecasting: F.O. Licht for sugar, Lesly (and the USDA) for American grain, Oil World for oilseeds, Gill and Duffus for cocoa. . . Some of these firms also operate as traders, a situation which can, at times, lead to confusion;

– the special information provided by private agencies and the traders themselves. In this case it is less important to find out what is happening than what is about to happen. In general the trading firms have their own information networks and make their own forecasts (see the preceeding case). The facts they possess are identical to those already known to the public but they are supplemented by the assessment reports supplied by the firm's representatives on the spot. The British firm Gill and Duffus, the world's leading cocoa trader, employs teams of 'pod counters' whose task is to do an on-the-spot evaluation of the potential size of the next cocoa harvest. More sophisticated measures go as far as the use of satellites to assess grain harvests (the American Government's LASIE programme is available to the largest trading firms).

Most trading firms have communication systems which are as sophisticated as those of the Japanese *sogo shosa*. Henry Rothschild, executive vice-president of Philip Brothers, declared in December 1981 to the *Institutional Investor*: 'Our communications system is, in all likelihood, the most sophisticated in the world with the exception, perhaps, of the Defense Department and the CIA. I can't imagine a single place on this earth which produces a commodity we deal in, where Philip Bros does not have an informant'. David Tendler, president of Philip Bros adds: 'Our tentacles reach everywhere'.

In fact, the trading firms are not only users but also providers of information. Each firm publishes its forecasts on the market or at least passes them on to a few correspondents. Consequently, the trader can use his special information either for his own account or, by diffusing all or part of it, employ it as a means of directing the market to suit his own purposes. This sort of manoeuvre is very tricky since it should in no way undermine the credibility of the firm. The only firm which plays the dual role of trader and statistician is Gill and Duffus, the world's leading firm in the cocoa trade whose forecasts constitute the authority as against those of the international cocoa organization (ICCO) or the USDA[5]. But even without this exceptional case it is posssible to affirm that the research and processing of information is one of the basic constraints of international traders. Most of the large firms have set up data-banks which are constantly being up-dated and relayed to most corners of the globe. Cargill, to give an example, receives over 14,000 messages per day in its Minneapolis office[6].

But information is one thing, and 'contacts' is another. The trader has to maintain contacts in all places where his interests call for more or less interested 'relations'. He has to strive to infiltrate 'soft' structures such as those of government bodies either by gaining a political foothold, or by generously bribing those in charge. To the trading firm time is a form of capital on which it depends for its very survival. It is paramount for the the trading firm to be apprised of the changes to be introduced by political or administrative decisions before its competitors; it must also be able to influence these decisions as far as possible. It is perhaps the great paradox of international traders that they are, in a capitalist world, the entities which depend most on the decisions made by the public sector. All the more reason for them to want to infiltrate the government apparatus.

This infiltration can be effected at many levels. One possibility is the use of the classical bribing techniques, which in certain countries of the world are the natural concommitant of every transaction of a commercial nature. Among the great grain traders, Cargill and Cook have had to confess to the existence of a secret fund earmarked for 'special payments'. In 1976 Cargill allegedly spent $5 million on payments of this kind. But in the final analysis there is really nothing new about such payments. It is in the interest of the trader to maintain the best possible contacts with the decision-maker even if he is honest (which is, after all, most often the case).

Of course it would be even more interesting to make the decisions oneself and this is why trading firms often hire former senior civil servants or, notably in the United States, former traders become part of the administration. The Department of Agriculture under Nixon provides us with a suitable example:

– Clarence Palmby: Assistant Secretary for International Affairs with the USDA, formerly of the U.S. Feed Grain Council, took over the vice-presidency of Continental in 1972;
– Carroll Brunthaver: successor of Palmby in 1972, formerly of Cook Industries;
– William Pearce: Special Deputy trade representative to the White House, vice-president of Cargill.

There remains no doubt that the grain traders exert a powerful influence on the decisions made by the American administration in this field (notably in the negotiations which culminated in the International Agreement). Although this influence varies according to the party in power, and was very limited under Carter who imposed the embargo, it remains a major factor. It is usually exercised either directly, as we have seen, or through pressure groups or lobbies such as the National Grain Trade Council and the National Grain and Feed Association[7]. Examples of such a strategy outside the United States are Continental's hiring of Olivier Wormser, former governor of the *Banque de France*, and the recruiting of the former French minister Paul Dijoud by *Sucres et Denrées*.

This development has led us rather far away from the strict control of information. It is however the logical consequence thereof and it is from this arrangement that the companies draw most of their strength.

In fact it is probably in this sector of information and contacts that economies of scale play their most important role. To clinch one deal or to clinch one hundred, requires the same infrastructure of offices and agencies the world over (on average the major trading firms are present in some thirty countries). The American economist Richard Caves estimates that one of the reasons for the concentration of the grain trade in the United States lies in the economies of scale realized

Figure 5.4 The relationship between the US Administration and the grain trading firms as seen by a left-wing organization. 'US Grain Arsenal', *Nacla's Latin American Report*, vol.IX, no. 7, October 1975. (From the French edition of this book)

in the gathering and processing of information. In his reasoning, information becomes a productive asset[8]:

– the fixed costs of obtaining information can be spread among a variable volume of transactions. Information requirements can therefore bring increasing returns;

– being active in trade implies being able to engage in arbitrage dealings (between market-places) and consequently being adequately familiar with the market-conditions obtaining on each one, hence incurring the expenses involved in gathering information. The covering of one additional market-place (market $n + 1$) gives the trader n additional possibilities of operation. If the cost of gathering supplementary information is kept within 'normal bounds', economies of scale are possible;

– finally since information is a highly perishable good in the short term, it will go to waste if a company is not constantly in position on the market. This explains the need — at least in the grain trade — to be permanently active on the market[9].

Caves concludes with the following theorem: 'The average productivity of commercial information increases with the volume of information collected, the volume of transactions carried out on the basis of each element of information, or according to both'[10].

Thus — and we fully share this opinion — constant access to information is one of the incentives to the concentration of firms in international commodity trading, and most probably constitutes one of the main 'barriers' to entry into the 'club'.

The other barrier is the capacity to manage the logistic aspect of the transactions in actuals.

The physical management of operations

The role of the trader is to ensure the transfer of goods from one place to another. This implies:

– storing the commodity at the point of origin and taking care of intermediary warehousing if necessary,
– packaging and/or a certain degree of processing,
– transport within the national territory,
– international transport,

and last but not least, the manual handling of the merchandise at various stages. This is of course a very complex set-up but the degree of complexity also depends on the nature of the products handled. Theoretically, all these tasks could be carried out and managed without any logistic infrastructure: the trader would rent or charter the necessary storage and transport, and employ sub-contractors. His would then be merely a coordinating and supervising role. This would afford him both advantages and disadvantages; on the one hand he could get by with a light infrastructure and need not compromise his future, on the other, he would remain exposed to the economic vicissitudes governing the markets on which he has to contract the services he requires. This is why a certain number of firms have been led to integrate some of these services or at least to ensure a presence on their markets in an attempt to shield themselves from adverse developments in the economic situation.

Let us go back to the case of grain. In theory the grain trader does not need to own the infrastructures required for transactions in actuals. He can buy merchandise on a f.o.b. basis and rent or use the services of a public grain elevator; he can then charter a ship to transport the goods, delivering c.i.f. He will only need a representative in the loading port to supervise and speed up the operations, a team familiar with the shipping market (we shall come back to this at a later stage), a representative in the port of destination to avoid, as far as possible, disputes upon delivery. A great many firms are content to rely on this sort of arrangement and even entrust representation in certain ports to specialized firms.

The larger firms have come to realize, however, that this method of operation leaves one exposed to the vagaries of the economic situation and that any firm which owns its own elevator has a considerable differential advantage over its competitors. True enough, this would be superfluous in a period of normalcy, but in periods of congestion its ships would not have to wait in the same queues. The generalization of this reasoning has led the majority of the main firms to buy-out export elevators in the United States and at present there is no truly important firm which does not own one in the Gulf of Mexico (remember the Cook example). Outside the United States traders own elevators in Canada, in Argentina and in Europe. . . Similarly the cooperatives, wishing to ensure a presence on the world markets, have acquired control of port elevators. The history of the construction of export

elevators in Canada is rather interesting. Canada's main problem lies
in transporting its grain harvests from the Great Plains to the export
ports in the east and in the west of the country: to date, Canada has
suffered considerably under a less than efficient transport system and a
lack of storage capacity in the ports. As a result, in the autumn of 1980,
the government commissioned the construction of a vast complex at
Prince Rupert in British Colombia. Financed in part by the state of
Alberta, it is administered by a consortium of the three 'Wheat Pools'
of Alberta, Manitoba and Saskatchewan and three trading firms
(Cargill, Pioneer and a cooperative, United Grain Growers). The
entire project's cost is estimated at over $200 million. This team-work
between state-controlled bodies, cooperatives and traders, shows
quite well that the latter hope to gain, in return for their cooperation,
some logistic advantage (or political leverage with the Canadian
authorities). The ticket to becoming a successful grain trader therefore
seems to be owning an export elevator in the United States. From this
point of view, it is interesting to see who gained control of the Cook
assets in 1977–78:

– the Japanese *sogo shosa,* newcomers to the trade (Mitsui and
Sumitumo),
– the American cooperatives (Farmers Export, Farmaco, Gold
Kist),
– other traders (Bunge).

But the traders — especially in the United States — have also come
to realize that it is more profitable to seek the merchandise as near as
possible to its site of production. They consequently acquired control
of an ever-growing storage capacity along the great communication
routes and even in the collection areas. It is rather difficult to make a
quantitative analysis of this trend since the only truly reliable data at
our disposal is that provided by Ray Goldberg for the wheat, soya and
orange-juice chains in the United States in 1963. At that time the
international traders controlled 10% of the 'local' silos for wheat and
5% for soya as well as 25% of the wheat and soya silos located along
the main routes. We could assume that since then the concentration
has increased, either to the benefit of the cooperatives which have
strengthened their structures or to that of the most important traders.
In 1978 Cargill had a world storage capacity of 8.8 million tonnes (90%
of which was in the United States)[11]. In 1976 the capacities of the silos

owned or used by Cargill, in terminals accessible to ships of 35,000 dwt, in the main exporting countries stood at: 740,000 tonnes in Canada, 3,324,000 tonnes in the United States, 260,000 tonnes in Brazil or 41.7%, 63.9% and 49%, respectively, of the total storage capacity of each of these countries[12].

This trend was logically complemented by the taking over of the inland means of transport (barges, trucks, freight cars). Depending on the sophistication of the market, these transport facilities were either totally integrated (that is the case in Europe) or were governed by the domestic freight market: the market for barges on the Mississipi for example. In the latter case, the grain traders which owned barges gradually began to manage them separately (as they did in the case of ships for transport on the open sea). In the United States Cargill owns 5,000 freight cars and 500 barges, Continental has a specialized subsidiary (Conti Carriers and Terminals), Cook, at the time of its collapse, either owned or leased 1,700 freight cars and 212 barges. In France, Cargill owns freight cars (as does the group *Transcéréales* set up by the cooperatives).

The same evolution can be observed everywhere: the necessary investment made in connection with the logistics of the firm's operations is at first managed from the trading sector; it then acquires the status of a special centre of profit, even independent from the rest of the group. The same reasoning could apply to a processing operation such as soya or oilseed crushing (then again, the preparation of a shipment of grain is in itself a processing operation). We shall see that this type of reasoning explains to a great extent the degree of vertical diversification practiced by the grain trading firms.

How does this compare with the situation outside the grain trade? We could draw a distinction at least between those commodities which absolutely require the material control of the logistic facilities and those for which it is only accessory.

• One of the best examples of the first case is international trade in molasses. Molasses, a by-product of sugar production which takes the form of a viscous mass, is used primarily in the manufacture of feedstock and alcohol. It has a very low unit value[13] and is very cumbersome to store and transport. It is of little value to the sugar producer who seeks above all to get rid of it. The international molasses traders must therefore own their own storage and handling installations both in the production and in the consumption centres. Let us take the case of the leading firm in the sector, United Molasses, subsidiary of the British sugar company Tate and Lyle, which accounts for about 40% of the world trade in molasses. United Molasses is present in 33 countries and controls storage capacities of some 1.3 million cubic meters in 60 installations around the world, fleets of road-tankers, etc. In the consumer countries, it controls distribution subsidiaries which distribute the commodity to the end user[14]. The whole operation is totally integrated (since there is no intermediary market in any case). Later on United Molasses decided to develop the services sector by controlling the storage installations for fluids (such as hydrocarbons). A similar situation exists in the banana trade where the three 'majors' control warehouses, banana ships and ripening facilities.

• But most other commodities do not present the same logistic constraints in the initial stages. For some of them the transport and storage factor is of secondary importance, being a negligible part of the cost of the commodity (coffee, cocoa, metals. . .). For others, the structures of production and consumption are powerful enough to take charge of these operations. The trader will then adopt a policy consistent with his long-term strategy[15]:

– sugar does not call for investment in logistics. Yet, the world's leading trader in this commodity, *Sucres et Denrées,* decided in 1978 to commission the construction of a 50,000 tonnes export terminal for white sugar in Dunkirk — but this project, carried out in association with a number of French firms, was designed to promote European exports of white sugar. Furthermore the sugar trader, S. and W. Berisford, bought the only British beet sugar producer, the British Sugar Corporation in 1980 (in time, this was to prove a too heavy investment for the trading company).

– for coffee and cocoa, as for a certain number of metals, no investment in storage is necessary or even desirable. On the other hand, it could prove profitable to control one or the other processing stage (the grinding of cocoa beans, the roasting of coffee, the refining or the reprocessing of certain metals). Thus the majority of the cocoa traders (Gill and Duffus, S. and W. Berisford, *Sucres et Denrées)* are also grinders (there are in fact practically no independent cocoa grinders left).

Intervention in the storage or processing stage is therefore, with the exception of a few special cases (molasses, bananas) and that of grains, limited to the appreciation of the strategic choice of a firm and depends on its evolution (see below). A company like Philip Bros has always sought to avoid such investments.

Whether it is the owner of the installations it uses or not, the international trading firm will always have a department to supervise the physical management of transactions.

As a rule each transaction in actuals concluded by the trader is accompanied by the signing of a contract of purchase or sale containing very precise stipulations governing the terms of the transaction. As often as not this contract is merely an adaptation of one of the standard contracts published by any of the main trading associations: the GAFTA (Grain and Feed Trade Association which is the authority in all that concerns grains, oilseeds and coffee) and *Synacomex* (for grain in France). According to the terms agreed on, (f.o.b., c.i.f., etc. . .) these contracts generally provide for the standard qualities to be delivered (bearing in mind the level of impurities, dusts, broken grains in the case of cereals, mould, deadlines and probable penalties. Disputes are brought before a court of arbitration (International Chamber of Commerce, GAFTA, *Chambre Arbitrale* in Paris. . .)[16]. It is very important that a trader respect a contract to its very letter, including, in a shipment of grain for example, the allowed percentage of dusts and impurities (not more but by no means less).

Frauds in both directions can never be avoided even though they can seriously jeopardize the reputation of a firm. The greatest fraud ever discovered concerned grain consignments from American ports in the Gulf of Mexico. The cargoes had been checked by private inspectors, holders of a federal licence. It was they who certified the quantities effectively loaded onto the ships and the precise quality of the grain. In 1975 and 1976 FBI investigations revealed that a certain number of trading firms had bribed some inspectors to cover-up fraudulent activities: prior washing of the grain samples, and even outright falsification of the latter, entries of ficticious deliveries onto phantom barges to prove that actuals had effectively changed hands. The major names in the business were implicated: Adnac (association of Archer Daniel Midlands and Garnac-André), Continental, Feruzzi and especially Cook. In the case of Cook, instructions from the highest levels of the company (Ned Cook and his executive director Philip Mac Caull) stipulated that the margins of error for consignments destined for modern, well-equipped ports (such as Hamburg and Rotterdam) be limited to 0.125% but that, in the case of badly equipped ports (for example those of the Indian sub-continent), this margin could range from 1.5% to even 3%[17]. Of greater gravity was the revelation by the enquiry that such practices were current in the ports of the Gulf of Mexico.

Complaints about the quality and quantity of the commodities traded are therefore numerous. In general they are settled by means of arbitration even though, if one of the parties happens to be a public stucture, it often refuses to submit to an external court of arbitration. The other great difficulty in managing actuals transactions is keeping one's deadlines (not being too early or too late) and in particular avoiding bottlenecks which could result not only in a specific product, but what is worse, in a ship, a barge or a silo being blocked. Here the management of internal transport is just as important as the coordination of loading and unloading operations (which could become more expensive as a result of the expenses involved in keeping ships immobilized).

But beyond this aspect, the most important point of course remains the management of the transport risk and in particular the management of the freight risk[18].

The freight risk

Most primary commodities in international trade are transported by sea and there are a variety of shipping contracts which charterers can choose from, depending on the commodities to be transported and the tonnages involved:

– the regular liners, characterized by a steadily increasing use of containers. Tariffs are established by shipping conferences grouping the ship-owners servicing the same route. Commodities lifted by shipping conferences are generally small, with an unit value which is high enough to render the cost of transport unimportant. On the regular lines we also find ships working outside the conference lines and often charging about 20% less. They are, however, reputed to be less reliable. Commodities such as coffee, cocoa, rubber, certain metals and in fact all shipments of under 500 tonnes travel on regular lines;

– tramps: these carriers have no fixed itinerary but go wherever shippers desire. They offer two types of freight contracts: the voyage charter, under which the ship-owner places his ship or cargo-space therein at the disposal of the shipper for the duration of a particular voyage (payment is per tonne transported or at a fixed rate of hire), and the time-charter whereby the ship-owner places his ship and crew at the disposal of the shipper for an agreed period of time (payment per tonne of dead-weight capacity for the duration of the contract but variable costs must be met by the charterer)[19].

– the contract of affreightment, or charter-party, is generally modelled on a standard contract similar to those drawn up for merchandise[20].

Almost all of the major primary commodities are carried by tramps and constitute the majority of all seaborne tonnages. The distribution between time and voyage charters depends on the commodities and the time of year (95% of all iron ore shipped is lifted in time-chartered vessels, as against 40% in voyage-chartered vessels and 60% on time-charter terms for grains[21]. All in all, the voyage charter market is a relatively marginal one except in the case of grains: 8.7% for coal, 4.1% for ores, 4.2% for other types of merchandise and a maximum of 15% for oil).

Table 5.5 Raw materials in international shipping (millions of tonnes)

1982:	World shipping trade			3,648
	of which	oil	1,803	
	solid cargo			1,845
	of which	iron ore	375	
		coal	276	
		grain (and protein bearing commodities)	283	
		phosphates	52	
		bauxite and alumina	50	
		sugar	29	
		resinous woods	39	
		manganese	4	

The freight market functions like any other market according to the law of supply (the ship-owners) and demand (the shippers). None of the freight exchanges has a particularly privileged position among

dealers: in London many dealers meet at the Baltic Exchange between
1 p.m. and 2 p.m. but this is no more than a meeting place. The main
market-places are New York, London, Tokyo for shippers, Bergen,
Oslo, Athens for ship-owners.

Quotations are listed *a posteriori* by brokers or specialized agencies[22]. The freight market is often prey to fluctuations within very wide
limits and its cycle, which is akin to that of the mining or plantation
economies, generally lasts from 5 to 7 years. According to the figures
for solid cargoes published by the *Norwegian Shipping News* after a
boom in 1973–74 during which the index rose from 110 to 240 at the
beginning of 1974 for voyage charters, (base year 1971) and from 150
to 330 for time charters (base year July 1965–June 1966), freight rates
levelled off at around 130–140 for the voyage charters and 150–180 for
time charters. In 1979 the market began an upward swing which
culminated in June 1980 with prices of 226 for voyage charters and 420
for time charters before falling back to previous levels.

For the trader, the freight problem is double-sided: on the one hand
he has to be in a position to secure the shipping tonnages required, but
most of all (as we saw in the Egyptian wheat example) he must be able
to make accurate assessments of how freight rates are likely to evolve
so as to make relatively exact forecasts. The problem faced by the
trader is that no immediate risk coverage for freights is available[23]. He
is therefore constrained to anticipate the evolution of the market as
accurately as possible and to bear the consequences of any errors of
judgement on his part. There is no possibility of hedging one's risks on
a particular operation, but possibilities of doing so are available on the
medium and long term:

– on the medium term by taking out positions on the market and by
switching from voyage charter to time charter,
– on the long term by owning one's own fleet.

Let us take a look at those two possibilities. In general each trading
firm has a shipping department which is relatively highly developed.
Run by specialists, its role is to provide the trader with estimates and,
often at a much later stage, to purchase the necessary fixtures. To this
end the trading firm generally employs a shipping broker (see above).
Of course in up-dating his forecasts, the trader will have assimilated a
whole series of data concerning either the ships (congestion ports, new
contruction work), or the commodities (growth of a country's imports

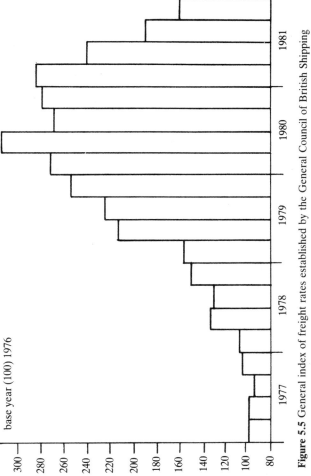

Figure 5.5 General index of freight rates established by the General Council of British Shipping

(Source: *Public Ledger's Commodity Yearbook*)

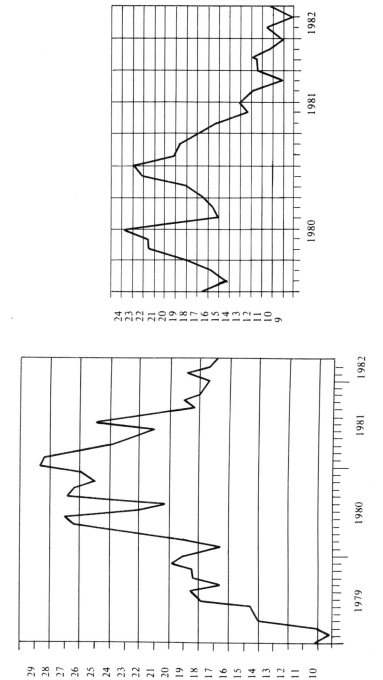

Figures 5.6 and 5.7 Two average indices: grain: Gulf of Mexico – Rotterdam; coal: Hampton Roads (USA) – Japan.
(Source: *Public Ledger's Commodity Yearbook*, 1982).

or exports, links between tankers and dry cargo carriers). But his judgement might not always be correct. His only possible guarantee against an error on his part would be to be present on the market and to hedge time charters against voyage charters. If we go back to the example on Egyptian wheat, his theoretical reasoning might be the following:

– on the 5th December the freight department is asked for a price for Egypt March (voyage US – Gulf – Egyptian port). The department gives its estimate assuming a greater or lesser degree of risk (open (tramp) fixture or other);

– on the 7th January the freight department receives instructions to contract freight. There are two possibilities: either the rate is in line with or less than the forecasts, in which case there is no problem, or it is higher, causing a corresponding reduction in the operation's potential margin. The only protective measure open to the trader would have been to simultaneously hold a long position on the time charter market: this implies that the freight department would have — in one of the cyclical periods of depressed prices — chartered a number of ships which it subsequently would have used to meet its own needs and, what is more important, would have managed as a shipowner, chartering them to others on voyage terms. Having chartered on the long or short term and sub-chartered on a voyage basis he would be in a reversed position on the market in relation to another trader who is seeking fixtures to fill a precise need. His risk will thus have been minimised:

	trader	freight department
time t	sale of a voyage charter for $t+n$ at an intended rate of x	time fixture at a rate corresponding to a voyage rate of x
time $t+n-1$	voyage chartering of a vessel at a·rate of $x + a$	chartering of the vessel by a third party at a voyage rate of $x + a$
	loss of a	theoretical gain: a

This example is of course purely theoretical since it is practically impossible for the operations to be executed with such simultaneity. But it is the principle of the mechanism which is important here. By the very complexity of its operations we see that the shipping department of a trading firm must be extremely competent, if it is to be in a position to minimize its risks. It must constantly switch between the roles of charterer and ship-owner managing a number of ships. Anyone who is aware of the costs involved in tying up a ship for a single day will readily understand the importance of the operation.

But in the even longer term the 'complete' (but not necessarily the best) hedge would be to purchase one's own fleet and a number of trading firms have done so. There are diverse reasons behind this move, a number of which go back to the reconstitution of the world fleet after 1945. Some traders were able to buy up liberty-ships and most often — given the general paucity of unfixed cargoes — used them for their own trades before hiring them out to third parties at a later stage. At present, outside certain specific ships which are rarely available on the charter market (banana boats, timber ships. . .), most traders manage their fleets (tankers and dry bulk vessels) totally independently. The long-term strategy of the group is usually the following:

– when the freight markets are depressed, the fleet will lose money but the trader will be confident of having sufficient carriers for his tonnages,
– when freight rates are high, the fleet will make a profit even though the trader will have to pay more to lift his cargoes.

Though not a very elaborate reasoning, it can, on the long run, prove to be accurate. It presupposes, however, that the trader controls a sufficiently large fleet to make the operation efficient and to avoid the consequences of isolated and unexpected events: in the field of shipping it does not pay to be an amateur. This fact was brought home strongly to the directors of the Tate and Lyle group which had bought the leading world molasses trader, United Molasses, in 1965. Since 1925 United Molasses had gradually built up its own fleet of molasses tankers and had given its molasses transport operations a greater degree of independence, expanding into the shipping of other liquid cargoes, notably oils and petroleum (Athel Line). It had also participated in the creation of a company of 'parcel tankers' (for liquids in small quantities) (Anco Line). Moreover, since the beginning of the fifties Tate and Lyle had practically integrated the transport of West Indian sugar into its British refinery operations (with a fleet of small bulk carriers, the Sugar Line). In the early seventies Tate and Lyle owned a somewhat heterogeneous fleet with a cargo capacity of 630,000 tonnes (dwt). In the aftermath of the freight market crisis in 1975, Tate and Lyle began to disengage itself from its shipping operations feeling that it had too little capital to devote to this sector. At the end of 1980 this policy concluded with the sale of the last ships: since then its molasses is transported in chartered vessels (apart from two small tramps which the company still owns in the West Indies).

Table 5.6 A list of capacities owned by trading firms

Grain:	Cargill Inc.	Total tonnage of the fleet controlled: Tradax Export SA: fleet of 444,279 dwt controlled 1,700,000 dwt. under the Liberian flag.
	Louis Dreyfus	Fleet of 437,000 dwt and control of fleets with a capacity of over 650,000 dwt (see CETAMAR, Sanagra). Buries Marke Ltd: 250,000 dwt and 54,142 dwt.
	Toppfer	14 vessels
	André	12 vessels (500,000 dwt).
Oil:	Philip Bros	Oil-tanker fleet purchased from 1978, liquidated in 1982.

(These figures cannot be directly compared with each other since deadweight tonnages tend to have totally different meanings in different places)

There are however, still a number of integrated (or semi-integrated) fleets in the fuel and mineral trades: most of the oil giants have their own fleets of tankers (and are engaging more and more in trading activities): Philip Bros, the leading private oil trader, had its own fleet from 1978 to 1982. When the fleet was first acquired, a particularly interesting reasoning was presented in the annual report: 'These new activities dovetail with our traditional business, constitute a hedge against fluctuations in ocean freights and provide Phibro with a new source of profits'[24]. But in 1982 Philip Bros liquidated both its fleet and the rest of its fixed investments. . .

In 1980 the Phibro-controlled fleet comprised almost 40 bulk-carriers. In the coal trade, the only French importer, ATIC (which also engages in trading) has its own fleet. An estimated 3% of the world iron ore tonnage is carried in fleets owned directly by the iron and steel firms[25]; the three aluminium 'giants' own small mineral fleets[26].

But by far the most outstanding sector where traders have direct ownership in shipping is the grain trade. It is in fact the only commodity transported in bulk whose unit value is sufficiently low for the cost of freight to be an important factor. Most of the grain traders run their own fleets but these are managed in a totally autonomous way. 'My wheat requires the cheapest freight possible', observes one trader, 'and my ships the highest. We can't seem to get along'. The most active trading firm in this sector is Louis Dreyfus (whose international network has been built up since the end of the 19th century): the first ship commissioned by Louis Dreyfus was built in 1903 and in the Thirties the firm invested in a fleet of specialized cargo-ships for the transport of grain (the Louis Dreyfus fleet as such was first run under the French flag, then under the British flag from 1938 through a subsidiary, Buries Marke Ltd., finally under the Argentinian flag from 1947). The fleet owned or managed by Louis Dreyfus in 1980 had a tonnage in the region of 2 million dwt. The other grain shippers, Cargill, Topffer and André also own the ships they use.

There now remains no doubt that direct ownership of ships is only rarely inspired by a logistic need (the final example being the banana ships and the refrigerated carriers). It is more a question of a global hedging of the freight risk on the group level and as good a means as any other to invest profits. In any event most trading firms are present on the shipping market where they operate as independent agents through their specialized subsidiaries (like Ralli Bros through its subsidiary, Duncan Fox Oil, Ship and Insurance Brokers Ltd, and ACLI Marine).

As we can see, the 'freight' risk is one of the most fundamental which a trader has to assume. When one considers that in 1983 Philip Bros chartered more than 1,500 ships, it is easy to grasp its importance.

The financial management of operations

Having taken a look at the greater part of the activities involved in trading (trading itself, the management of logistics, freight) it remains for us to tackle the financial side of the operations. For a trader the relations with his banker are extremely important: the size of his operations will directly depend on the confidence placed in him by his bankers. The confidence which a banker exhibits in a trader is rarely ever to be explained rationally: in fact the banker cannot acquire confidence in a trader on the basis of the value of the latter's physical assets, because he very often has none. Only some ten firms can effectively offer industrial-type guarantees and the financing of this type of firm (the largest and the 'most reliable') is the object of intense competition among the major banks. In general the banker will base his confidence on the trustworthiness and the experience of the individual, on his reputation as a potential speculator, on his popularity on the market[27]. This would allow him to modulate his intervention according to his evaluation of the 'country risk' according to the destinations envisaged. As a French banker, H. de la Mettrie, once wrote: 'The risk posed by a client cannot be studied in the same way as that posed by a multinational with an industrial added value, and it is in such circumstances that the appreciation of the technical risk, in other words, the capacity of the trading group to honour to perfection all of its contractual obligations (other than the financial ones), the fulfillment of which is also guaranteed by the banker, takes on its full significance: our analysis, which is in essence a financial one, must be supplemented by an evaluation of the trader's administrative and commercial skills, of his negotiating capacity and his ability to intervene on the markets, his relational assets and the like[28].

The American banks were the first to specialize in financing the exchange of commodities. From the end of the sixties, Bankers Trust and Chemical Bank had 'commodities' departments. We should also mention Chase, Morgan Guaranty, Citibank. . . Towards the end of the seventies, the French banks also began to take an interest in such activities: *Crédit Lyonnais, Banque Nationale de Paris, Banque Vernes, Indo-Suez,* and more recently the *Crédit Commercial de France,* the *Crédit Agricole,* the *Société Générale.* Paradoxically, the British banks (with the exception of Barclays) are all absent, but some banks of other nationalities have ensured for themselves a slice of the business: the Austrian *Kredit Anstalt,* and the Dutch bank Mees and Hope.

When he makes a tender the trader asks his bank to open a bid bond which generally amounts to 5–20% of the estimated value of the contract. If the trader is not among the successful tenderers it is automatically cancelled, otherwise it is converted into a performance bond[29]. Later on, the banker who has been entrusted with the oper-

ation follows the classical documentary circuit (accelerating as much as
possible the circulation of the documents). In general moreover, the
banker would have been consulted beforehand, usually during the
negotiation of the commercial contract, and the trader would have
received advice on a number of elements, notably on how to handle
cases of deferred payments:

– $x\%$ on delivery or on order,
– a maximum of x months credit from the delivery date, payable in x
instalments,
– $x\%$ over the LIBOR (London Interbank Offered Rate) on the
settlement currency.

Much more important, from the point of view of the trader, are the
financial facilities which his banker can grant him: the trader is in fact
obliged to finance his operations on the forward and futures markets
himself. Deposits and margin calls can assume considerable proportions if the hedge is placed against the flow of the market, in which case
the financial charges on the margin calls alone might be enough to turn
an apparently profitable operation into a losing one. Although the
clearing bodies of some futures markets readily accept sureties from
national banks, the American futures markets require accounts to be
settled immediately in cash. There too, the trader will have to play off
his bankers against one another and choose the one which will offer
him the closest rate — in Europe for example — to the LIBOR. On the
forward market operations mentioned above, bankers generally prefer to operate on a 'case-by-case' basis, but a trader might be fortunate
enough to obtain a stand-by credit, a sum which is constantly at his
disposal and which he can use without having to give an explanation[30].
The banking facilities which a trader can obtain depend in fact on the
relationship which he has with his banker and in general this poses no
insurmountable problem for the giants in the profession (the Antwerp
subsidiary of one of the grain majors had a stand-by credit of over $100
million a few years ago).

The trader also has to seek, with or without the assistance of his
banker, to minimize and even to eliminate his financial risks. These
can be of three types: the exchange risk, the interest rate risk and
finally what is increasingly known as the 'dollar commodities' risk.

The exchange risk is a classical one and is handled by the banking
system. Any operation which at some point in time involves the

exchange of goods from one currency to another, whether this is done on the spot or on the futures market, is exposed to the exchange risk[31]: a French company selling grain expressed in dollars at a time t, with payment scheduled for $t + 3$ will have to hedge immediately against the risk of fluctuations in the exchange rate of the dollar (possibly, to make matters more complicated, in relation to the ECU, that is, to a basket of currencies). Here too, the trading firm generally manages its foreign currency positions in a global fashion at a given moment in time. But this foreign exchange risk is hardly different from that which constantly confronts the treasurer of a multinational corporation (and even here there is the possibility of converting it into a source of profit). The 'dollar commodities' risk is rather similar: it concerns the risk of fluctuations in prices, expressed in national currency, of a commodity quoted in dollars. If a trader buys soybeans in Deutsch Marks or in Dutch guilders he is exposed to a double risk: the fluctuation of the soya futures market prices in Chicago and the fluctuation of the DM in relation to the dollar. He would therefore have to hedge against the second risk.

Finally the trader is exposed to a risk of variations in interest rates: if he is paid in x days after receipt of the bill of lading he will have to hedge against the risk of variations in interest rates during the waiting period. This can be done on the financial markets in Chicago and now in London (the hedging process is therefore no different from that of merchandise).

In evaluating his financial risks, the trader must weigh all those elements in his position which are likely to vary, to analyse his risks and hedge accordingly.

In the French case such hedges would have been impossible — or at least difficult given the existence of very strict exchange controls. This is why most most French trading firms used to base their operations outside the French borders.

In 1978 the *Banque de France* established a special agreement on international trade permitting traders to hold open exchange positions but obliging them, in return, to make all of their operations accesible to the *Banque de France* for supervision. It was this agreement which permitted *Sucres et Denrées* to repatriate its operations from Switzerland to Paris.

On this level, as on that of the physical management of operations, the problem arises as to how profitable it is to directly control one's own banking facilities. We shall limit our analysis, first to the two main French trading firms Louis Dreyfus and *Sucres et Denrées.*

Louis Dreyfus created its own bank at the beginning of the 20th century to facilitate its operations in grain (it was at first run by Robert Louis-Dreyfus, son of the founder). Since then the Louis Dreyfus bank has grown considerably in the field of banking and is now counted among the largest commercial banks in Paris. Its operations are totally divorced from those of the trading section.

The approach adopted by *Sucres et Denrées* was quite different. Around 1965–1970 its directors came to the conclusion that no French bank possessed enough experience in the financing of commodity trade. They therefore proceeded to create two banks, the BDEI (*Banque pour le Développement des Echanges Internationaux*) with headquarters in Paris and *Compafina* based in Geneva. These two banks further developed their activities in the field of trade financing and notably built up solid teams of specialized bankers. But the banking context also evolved, many French banks subsequently created specialized departments and the need for a group bank became less of a priority. At the end of 1980 *Sucres et Denrées* ceded 35% of its banks' capital to the *Crédit Lyonnais*. Similarly Philip Bros controls the *Phibrobank A.G.* based in Zug in Switzerland with a branch in London. *Phibrobank* constitutes above all a financial partner for countries or firms with which the group works. We should also mention Craneheath Securities Ltd, member of the S. and W. Berisford group.

All in all it could be assumed that when the banking network is large enough there is no need for the trader to develop his own network. On the other hand, a host of trading firms which have their own brokerage activities on the futures markets have — especially since 1973 — begun to engage in activites as financial middlemen similar to those of the commission houses.

In fact we have seen above that most of the trading firms have their 'headquarters' on the futures markets where they deal. This, moreover, constitutes one of the few cases of practically automatic vertical integration (for basic considerations of discretion). In some cases the brokerage activity existed prior to the trading activity as such (notably for commodities such as sugar, coffee and cocoa). These subsidiaries also offer their services on occasion to third parties and especially to private clients (whether institutional investors or private individuals). Since the growth phase experienced from 1973 by futures markets, trading firms have expanded their services to be present on financial futures markets, as well as to include the management of commodity funds and investment counselling. The margin of influence which traders have on the market has therefore been incremented by the volumes handled by brokerage subsidiaries which could, in turn, directly or indirectly influence the decisions of their clients. During the Seventies, most big American traders opened a commission-house branch: Conti Commodities Inc., Cargill Investor Services, ACLI. . . Most of those encountered problems in the early eighties and sold off these ventures (e.g. Conti Commodities sold to Refco[32]). There was a move of the same nature made in Britain, with Ed. and F. Man. Similarly we find many trading firms on the precious metals markets, where they are newcomers, next to the more traditional financial agents. As a result, most of the major traders are members of the Chicago and London gold futures market.

The security of operations and their legal environment

We should now turn our attention to this corollary of the financially successful trading operation — the security measures which the trader has to take. These are of two types: transport insurance and the negotiation of the terms of contracts with the possible recourse to arbitration.

The first point is of relatively minor importance: the trader must insure his shipments. In general he does this through specialized brokerage houses but a certain number of firms have created their own brokerage subsidiaries for insurance, at the outset as an integrated department (ACLI), and then later as an independent center of profit (the same approach as above). We may not forget Gill and Duffus, whose subsidiary Gillbrooke Insurance (founded on parity with the agro-food group Brooke Bond Liebig with Gill and Duffus resuming total control of the former at the beginning of 1982), recorded £16 million in brokerage fees in 1981 for a profit of £2.1 million. There are also S. and W. Berisford and its subsidiary Berisford Mocatta, Cargill with its subsidiaries Horizon Insurance (commercial) and Summit National Life Insurance, Tate and Lyle. . . The interest shown by trading firms for insurance can also be explained by the fact that they can utilize the funds collected by the insurance companies to finance or at least to guarantee the firm's trading activities.

On the other hand, the legal environment surrounding trading contracts is much more complex. We have seen that most contracts are based on standard contracts drawn up by commercial associations such as the GAFTA. These make provisions for most of the likely causes of dispute and try to eliminate them beforehand.

The very drawing up of the contract is a particularly delicate matter, especially as it concerns the terms of payment (credibility of the other parties to the contract, the problem of exporting foreign currency) and the cancellation clauses (*force majeure* etc.). The affair is particularly complex when one is dealing with a public entity and when there might be collusion between it and the local authorities without there being, from the legal point of view, any link whatsoever.

In any event, most contracts contain an arbitration clause and not one which refers the matter to a state court. In the words of one of the major French experts in the field, Mr. Jean Robert, lawyer[33]:

'As regards international trade in general and trade in commodities in particular, referral to a court of arbitration instead of state jurisdictions is, practically without exception, the rule. Essentially, the reason lies as much in the peculiarity of a set of international regulations with which the practitioners are much more familiar than are the state jurisdictions, as in the desire to eschew the application of foreign national laws unknown to the contracting parties and therefore implying an additional risk. Arbitration is hence characterized as a procedure of a contractual nature according to which, by the express desire of the parties, the dispute will be judged by private persons designated directly or by means of recourse to specialized organizations.'

The main conflicts arise from the application of the clauses of acceptance of the merchandise, financing, and finally — and these are the most spectacular — those governing cases of *force majeure*. We shall not deal here with the first two types, which in the final analysis are relatively current in commercial transactions (problems of quality, measurement, settlement delays). The problem of the *force majeure* (or fortuitous event) can prove to be much more serious for a trader especially — as we have already said — when the other party involved is a public structure (and, as the reader will recall, the latter are becoming increasingly widespread in commodity trading). The conditions necessary for a declaration of *force majeure* are the following:

– the event invoked must be outside the control of the parties – it must be unforseeable
– it must be unavoidable.

Now in the case of public structures, the first of these conditions might not be so easy to determine: a government can declare an export embargo on a commodity but to what extent can the state-controlled company, responsible for the exports, invoke this as an excuse for not meeting its committments?

Two *causes célèbres* help to explain this quandary:

– at the begining of 1974 *Sucres et Denrées* bought 250,000 tonnes of white sugar from *Rolimpex,* the Polish state body and sold them in Africa. The year 1974 was the year of the great crisis on the world sugar market: from 15 cents per pound at the end of 1973, prices rose to 65.5 cents in mid-November before collapsing. The Russian harvests had been particularly bad and Moscow turned to its Comecon neighbours (Cuba had also had a bad harvest that year). Poland first had to supply the USSR and decided to cancel its export contracts by declaring an embargo. *Rolimpex* claimed *force majeure. Sucres et Denrées* then had to resort to the world market — where in the interval prices had risen by ten cents or more — to procure the 250,000 tonnes needed to fulfill its contract, since the latter did not specify the origin of the sugar to be supplied. Before the court of arbitration, the Poles successfully adduced that a difference existed between the Polish state and the private law entity — *Rolimpex.* A specious argument it is true, but one which 'held water' from the legal point of view and which cost the French trading firm several million dollars;

– in 1973–74 a number of grain trading firms sold 500,000 tonnes of wheat to *Topakofis,* the Turkish government's import agency. Some months later there was a change of government in Turkey. In the meantime, the price of wheat had dropped considerably. The new government refused to honour the commitments of its predecessors and *Topakofis* declared a case of *force majeure* when the Ministry of Finance refused to grant a foreign currency export licence. Continental was particularly affected since it had sold no less than 350,000 of the 500,000 tonnes. The court of arbitration and later the British jurisdictions (as high up as the House of Lords) delivered a sentence against the Turks, deeming that the Turkish decision had been motivated by a variation in the prices of wheat and was therefore a 'self-induced frustration'[sic]. In addition, a clause in the contract had provided that the foreign currency export licences would be guaranteed by the buyer. But the Turks stubbornly refused to pay the damages due. Continental was forced to lobby actively in Washington, basing its case on a law, until then relegated to oblivion, stipulating that the United

States was not allowed to provide aid to a country having outstanding debts with an American citizen. Finally Continental received a cargo of wheat which, in the words of its directors, compensated amply.

Two examples which are similar in substance but whose outcomes were — as we have seen — diametrically opposed.

Trading firms are constantly increasing the number of precautions they take when dealing with states which are known to be untrustworthy. Thus in December 1978, Louis Dreyfus seized 70,000 tonnes of wheat already loaded for delivery to Iran fearing that its client would default (this took place one month before the abdication of the Shah). Another case will illustrate the need for the performance bond. At the end of 1980 Ed. and F. Man had bought 200,000 tonnes of sugar to be delivered in instalments from January to June, 1981 to the State Trading Corporation of India. The performance bond for the STCI had been given by the State Bank of India. In February 1981 the Indian government declared an embargo on the export of sugar. Ed. and F. Man took its case to the courts of arbitration going as far as the House of Lords, won it (sentence by Lord Denning on 17th July 1981), and was able to collect the performance bond of some £1.3 million!

At the end of 1983 the Indian government once again blocked the export of 300,000 bales of cotton sold to European traders by a state monopoly, *Mahfed.*

Such conflicts are, however, not limited to public entities alone and a host of legal problems arose in 1973 among the trading firms themselves in the aftermath of the Mississipi floods and the soya embargo decreed by the American government: where did *force majeure* begin and where did it end?

Clearly the legal climate and the security of contracts is not something to be taken lightly by the trading firms.

The financial management of the firm

We have very little information on which to base an analysis of the financial structure and management of trading firms. In the absence of a detailed analysis we could attempt, nevertheless, to present a few general characteristics:

– a low level of capital funds in relation to turnover (with few exceptions): the pre-tax cash-flow easily amounts to one fifth or one quarter of the owners' equity;

– few and often self-financed fixed assets, implying, here too, a low level of medium and long-term indebtedness. Most borrowing is done on a short term basis and financial charges are one of the biggest items on the trading account;

– little or nothing for depreciation (unless the group has an industrial base);

– a ratio of pre-tax cash-flow to turnover which never rises above 5% and in general oscillates between 1% and 2%.

It is extremely difficult to go any further than these rather general facts. The accounts of the major trading firms consolidate the industrial, trading and even banking activities.

Table 5.7 A few significant ratios occuring in trading firms

		Pre-tax cash-flow	Pre-tax cash-flow
		Turnover	Equity
Groups' consolidated accounts			
Phibro-Salomon	1982	1.4	20
(Phibro 1980)			(37)
Cargill	1983	1.6	20
Continental Grain	1982	1.7	10.1
Sucres et Denrées	1982	0.6	15
Hochschild	1982	0.7	2.6
Gill and Duffus	1980		25
S. and W. Berisford	1980		16
Commercial Metals	1981		5
Amalgamated Metal	1979		7
Safic Alcan	1981		49
Companies' accounts (non-consolidated)			
Marc Rich A.G.	1982	2.3	23
Bunge Corp., USA	1982	2.9	22
Louis Dreyfus France	1982	1.5	11.2

In fact one could try to encapsulate the financial management of the trading firm in the words of a trader who once said:

'At the beginning of the year, I know what my company is going to cost me in overheads and variable costs (excluding financial charges). I therefore have to make sure I earn at least enough to come out even at the end of the year: everything I earn in excess will be my profit.'

Simple but effective!

The legal position of the trading firm

As regards their legal status, most trading companies are private companies, still owned by the founding families and/or executives. Some have had a Stock Market quotation, but this seems to represent a problem for them: a public company has the obligatin to publish quarterly reports and accounts, and it is known that traders' results can vary very much even from year to year. Philip Brothers, S. and W. Berisford, Gill and Duffus and of course Cook Industries have all suffered from their public company status. In 1985–86 people such as David Tendler at Phibro, and Ephraim Margulies at Berisford have tried to take their company back towards a private identity: 'In privacy they thrive.'

Chapter 6

CLASSIFICATION AND EVOLUTION OF TRADING

The reader is now more or less familiar with the main characteristics and functions of the international trader in commodities. It remains doubtful, however, whether it is feasible in such a constantly changing and so varied a context to contend that such a thing as a precise model of the international trader exists, to affirm that copper traders and pepper traders have something in common and that the major firms whose turnovers lie in the region of $30 billion and the traders who operate in two-room appartments have traits in common! And yet there are a host of similarities among the markets themselves (the major difference being whether they they are equipped with futures markets or not), among the strategies peculiar to traders of all types (buying a commodity with a view to re-selling it more or less in the original form), and among the stages in the very evolution of these firms in the course of their history, especially since 1945.

But before moving on to the internal evolution of the trading firms, we shall attempt to classify them according to a specific set of criteria (size, product(s) handled, origin. . .) all of which should facilitate our endeavour to situate in its context, a set-up which at first sight appears somewhat heterogeneous.

An attempt at classification

We are immediately confronted with our first problem: how many international commodity traders do in fact exist? And on this first point we must confess our total ignorance. It is practically impossible to estimate the number of companies in the world which either constantly or sporadically deal in commodities[1]. We could simplify the problem somewhat by contemplating the size factor which will allow us to assess the importance of the main structures.

A. Analysis according to size

Having reached this far, one must decide on the criterion to determine the size of a firm: is it to be the turnover, the volumes traded or the size of its network?

Most classifications of multinational corporations are based on turnover: admittedly, it constitutes one of the rare criteria common to all accounting structures all over the world, which in all other aspects vary considerably from one country to another. But the use of this criterion is extremely questionable, especially when different sectors of activity are being compared, in which case it is far more instructive to compare concepts such as added value or owners's equity.

In the case of trading firms, classification by turnover poses an additional problem in that most traders are not constrained to publish their accounts unless they are public companies. Most companies are in fact still in private hands and jealously guard their accounting secrets. Furthermore it is worthwhile to consider carefully on what basis these turnovers are calculated: whether all operations are included (even those which are merely 'paper' operations), or whether are considered only operations in actuals, or the recorded margins, etc. Here evaluations are apt to vary from firm to firm and often depend on the accounting customs prevailing in the country of origin[2].

The following 'classification by turnover' is therefore to be treated with extreme caution and should only be seen to offer some idea of the size of the company in question (see Table 6.1).

The figures presented are more or less consolidated group turnovers and therefore include industrial activities. In most cases it would be impossible to go into greater detail.

Moreover, we are not familiar with the turnover of groups as important as ACLI, Ed. and F. Man, Czarnikow. . .

Table 6.1 A few known turnovers of trading firms

	(source)	Firm's total turnover	(unit)	Year
• Over $10 billion turnover				
Phibro–Salomon	AR	29,757	($m)	1983
Cargill	P	25,375	($m)	1983
Continental Grain		14,000	($m)	1982
Marc Rich	est.	10,000	($m)	1982
Bunge and Born	est.	10,000	($m)	1979
• From $5 to $10 billion turnover				
Metallgesellschaft	AR	11,00	(DM m)	1981
Louis Dreyfus	est.	20,000	(FF m)	1976–77
• From $1 to $5 billion turnover				
Toppfer International	est.	10,000	(DM m)	1982
Tate and Lyle	AR	1,420	(£m)	1980
Amalgamated Metal Corp.	AR	1,197	(£m)	1979
Noga	est.	4,500	($m)	1983
Feruzzi	est.	4,000	($m)	1981
S. and W. Berisford	AR	2,729	(£m)	1982
Sucre et Denrées	AR	19,641	(FF m)	1983
Gill and Duffus	AR	1,250	(£m)	1983
Johnson Matthey	AR	901	(£m)	1980
Volkart Brothers	est.	3,000	(SwF m)	1981
Interbras	P	2,500	($m)	1981
André	est.	9,800	(SwF m)	1982
Lee Rubber	est	1,000	($m)	1983
• Some firms with a turnover of less than $1 billion				
Ralli Brothers	P	400	(£m)	1980
Safic Alcan	AR	2,695	(FF m)	1983
Bernard Rothfos	Ar	1,500	(DM m)	1980

Sources: AR: Annual Reports; P: press; est.: author's estimate

Table 6.2 Classification of trading firms according to the size of their equity (value of the firm, in $ million)

Over $1 billion		
	Cargill	2,600
	Phibro	1,800
	Bunge and Born	over 1,000
From $500 million to $1 billion		
	Marc Rich	800
	Continental Grain	500
From $100 million to $500 million		
	Hochschild	380
	Louis Dreyfus (trade only)	400
	S. and W. Berisford	317 (£m)
	Gill and Duffus	84 (£m)
Less than $100 million		
	Sucres et Denrées	638 (FF m)
	Toppfer International	138 (DM m)

In any event the two top firms in this classification (which also ...cludes the oil companies which count as trading firms) would rank among the first thirty industrial firms in the world.

In terms of the 'value' of trading firms the picture would of course be a different one: only three firms exceed the $1 billion mark. But many of the 'majors' are worth over $100 million (*Sucres et Denrées*, Toppfer. . .).

What conclusions can be drawn from this initial classification, limited to those companies which file their accounts (or at least for which it has been possible to provide an estimate)? It would seem that the figure of $1 billion constitutes a barrier between the multinational corporations and those firms whose activities are still restricted to a national territory. We have compiled a list of 15 firms whose turnovers are above this threshold figure. We deem it necessary to add to this a similar number to cover those firms on which we have no data. This would give us a first bracket of some thirty firms characteristic of international trade in commodities in the true sense of the term. Next in line are a certain number of firms of secondary importance, devoid of industrial infrastructures and trading only on a national basis. It is difficult to give an estimate of their numbers; their influence, in real terms, on the international level is, however, a negligible one.

This brings us to a second approach based on the organization and geographical scope of the firm's activity. The classification devised by

Charles Michalet for the multinational corporations[3]: 'ethnocentric' firms (centered around a national territory of origin), 'polycentric' firms (around national host territories) and 'geocentric' (global strategy) can be used to advantage here. There remains no doubt that the distinctive characteristic of the international trader is its stateless nature and its global conception of development in an international setting. This, of course, goes hand in hand with a presence in all production, trading and consumer centres of a given product all over the globe. There are some fifty firms (if not more) which are organized along 'geocentric' lines and have a network which spans the globe (this clearly widens somewhat the category of firms having a turnover of over $1 billion). Then come the 'ethnocentric' firms (there are no 'polycentric' firms in the field of trade): these are the national traders, operating especially in the export trade and carrying out, from time to time, operations among third countries (the Japanese *sogo shosas* fall into this category). 'Ethnocentric' firms can, moreover, exhibit the beginnings of an international infrastructure.

These two approaches (turnover and geographical conception) form part of a third criterion which can be more easily evaluated: the physical quantities of a product effectively traded (excluding, therefore, the paper operations). A product by product analysis considering only the largest firms would give the table 6.3.

Although not by any means an exhaustive one, this list contains, all the same, no less than 35 names. For each of the products we could add a certain number of the ethnocentric firms mentioned above:

Grain:	Cremer, Kampfmeyer (Federal Republic of Germany), Feruzzi (Italy), *Compagnie Grainière, G. et P. Levy,* Soufflet, CAM (France), Peabody (G.B.), Granaria, Schouten (Netherlands), Intercorn (Belgium), Agro (Canada).
Oilseeds:	Sime Darby (Malaysia), Alimenta (Switzerland), Nidera (Argentina), *Frahuiles* (France), Interco (Malaysia).
Sugar:	Czarnikow (G.B.), Czarnikow-Rionda (U.S.A.), Woodhouse Drake and Carey (G.B.).
Coffee:	American Coffee and Folger (U.S.A.), Unidaf (France).

Table 6.3 Major trading firms classified according to the product handled

Product	Firm	% of world trade	quantity of actuals traded
Grain and	Cargill	17 to 28	50 m. t.
proteo-seeds	Continental Grain	17 to 25	50 m. t.
	Louis Dreyfus	13 to 15	25 m. t.
	Bunge and Born	8 to 12	
	André	8 to 10	
	Toppfer	8 to 10	
Oilseeds	Cargill	10 to 20	
	Continental Grain	10 to 15	
	Bunge and Born		
	Noga		
Sugar	Ed. and F. Man	15	2.5 m. t.
	Sucre et Denrées	20	
	Tate and Lyle		
Cocoa	Philipp Brothers–Cocoa Merchants		200 to 300,000 t.
	Gill and Duffus–Pacol		200 to 300,000 t.
	S. and W. Berisford–Rayner		200 to 300,000 t.
	Merkuria–Sucre et Denrées–Touton		160,000 t.
Coffee	Rothfos	10	
	ACLI–Cargill	10	
	Volkart	5	
Cotton	Cargill–Ralli		
	Volkart		
	McFadden–Valmac		
	W.B. Dunavant		
	Bunge and Born		
Tobacco	Universal Leaf		
Alcohol	Louis Dreyfus		
Molasses	Tate and Lyle		
	Sucre et Denrées		
	Van Ginniken		
Crude oil	Philipp Brothers		
	Marc Rich		
Non-ferrous	Philipp Brothers		
metals	Marc Rich		
	Asoma		
	Commercial Metals		
	Preussag–AMC		
	Metallgesellschaft		
Rubber	*Lee*		
	Safic Alcan		

| Cocoa: | General Cocoa (U.S.A. and the Netherlands), Moutafian (G.B.), Tardivat (France). |
| Non-ferrous metals: | Boliden (Sweden), *Comptoir Lyon Allemand Loyot* (France), Gerald Metals (U.S.A.). . . |

Using a graphic demonstration, one would obtain the following diagram:

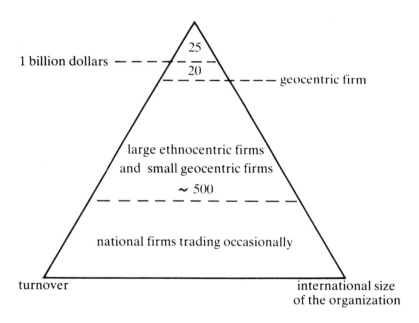

Figure 6.1 The 'trading pyramid'

B. Analysis as per origin

The way in which a firm operates also depends on its origins: whether it has sprung from the ranks of the traders, the producers or the consumers.

- *The trading community*

By far the largest number of firms originated in the trading community. These are unquestionably the oldest of the lot and include the ancient national traders, the brokerage firms, the international trading companies. Few firms engaged in international trading activities from the very start, and in general the trading firms are of most recent creation. Before 1945 there were no international commodity traders as we know them today, save for a few exceptions, the most notable of which are the grain traders such as Louis Dreyfus or Bunge and Born, and a few cotton traders (Ralli Bros). Even after 1945 the *ex nihilo* creation of such firms was also rare: *Sucres et Denrées* in 1954, a certain number of small structures generally centered around one man (*Tradigrains, Interagra* for example) and then the exceptional case of Marc Rich founded in 1974.

It should be noted that an exception of another type, that of the international molasses trade (United Molasses, 1926), is the result of logistic considerations. Far more numerous are the firms whose past is rooted in the field of international brokerage and which were most often created around the middle of the 19th century: for agricultural produce, Goldschmidt (1866), Continental owned by the Fribourgs (1813), Czarnikow (1861), Woodhouse, Drake and Carey (end of the 19th century), for metals Philipp Brothers (created at the end of the 19th century by the Philipp brothers, Hamburg brokers who moved to London in 1913 and later to the United States). For these firms, the transition from brokerage to trading took place rather smoothly at the beginning of the fifties.

At the outset, however, many firms combined international brokerage with harbour trading, a situation which might make our distiction appear fallacious: at the origin of *Safic Alcan*, we find the firm *Hecht Frères et Compagnie* founded in 1847 as a trader for tropical products. But unlike firms such as Louis Dreyfus or Ralli, their dealings took the form of a minor harbour trade, very similar in fact to brokerage. It was also the case of ACLI (founded in 1898 in New Orleans under the name of *Leon Israel and Bros, coffee importer*). Similarly, Woodhouse was a merchant importer before specializing in brokerage around the middle of the 19th century. The Bunge family were merchant importers of tropical fruit in Amsterdam from 1818 before becoming involved in the grain trade in Antwerp and Buenos

Aires. Before moving on to the sugar trade in London in 1908, Golodetz had been a timber trader in Russia as early as the the mid-19th century.

Around 1950, a certain number of trading firms, whose activities had until then been restricted to the national territory, began to tackle the international market: such was the case with Cargill (founded in 1854, international trader from 1954), Toppfer in Hamburg, S. and W. Berisford (until that time domestic trader in British sugar since its foundation in Manchester in 1850), and from 1970 onwards a certain number of European grain merchants which have nevertherless remained very Eurocentric (Soufflet, Granaria, Peter Cremer. . .). In fact this category is evolving rapidly, with the largest firms prudently turning their attention to international trade: this is also particularly true of the traders hitherto based essentially in the United States (metals, cotton . . .)[4]. There are also a number of very ethnocentric firms such as McFaden–Valmac, W.B. Dunavan for cotton, Lee of Singapore for rubber, the major Japanese firms. . .

Finally, a number of international trading companies have gradually turned their attention to commodity trading, at the outset with the aim of supplying the domestic market (the *sogo shosa* of Japan for cotton at first and in the past few years for grains: Mitsui and Sumitumo in particular), then with a view to participating in international trade (the Dutch firm Internatio from 1955, and more recently Jardine and Matheson). Conversely, the French international trading companies (e.g. SCOA) are practically absent from commodity trading. Worthy of mention in this context are the Australian and New Zealand subsidiaries of the Dalgety group which became traders for wool and meats after having been responsible for organizing the auctions for these products. To a lesser extent Volkart had followed the same path starting off as an import-export company dealing with India and Ceylon.

Most of the international commodity trading firms with a commercial background go back a long way. Their longevity is, moreover, not infrequently a guarantee of the competence of their managers, of their 'seriousness' and many firms are at least one hundred years old. By contrast, in recent years, the *ex nihilo* creation of trading firms has become relatively rare. It has taken place either immediately following the Second World War when it became necessary to fill the 'gaps' in international trade (this is notably the case of *Sucres et Denrées*) or in

Table 6.4 Classification of trading firms according to origin

	Date of creation	Date on which commodity trading was initiated	Product handled
1. Commercial circles			
– international commodity trade			
Louis Dreyfus	1850	1850	grains
Bunge and Born	1818	1876	grains
Ralli Brothers	1818		cotton
Sucres et Denrées	1955	1955	sugar
Tradimer	1978	1978	grains
Marc Rich	1974	1974	oil
United Molasses (Tate and Lyle)	1926	1926	molasses
Ed. and F. Man	1783		sugar
– brokerage			
Goldschmidt	1866	1953–1968	grains
Continental Grain	*ca.* 1850	1921	grains
Czarnikow	1861		sugar
Woodhouse, Drake and Carey	end 18th c.	1950	sugar
Philipp Brothers	end 19th c.	1920	metals
– import trade			
Raoul Duval	1826		coffee
ACLI	1898	1913	coffee
Safic Alcan	1847		rubber
Gill and Duffus	1907	1929	cocoa
André	1877	1930	grains
– national traders			
Cargill	1854	1954	grains
Toppfer	1919		grains
S. and W. Berisford	1850	1950	various products
McFadden Valmac			cotton
W.B. Dunavant			cotton
Lee			rubber
– international trading firms			
Internatio	1868–1959		coffee, cocoa
Mitsui	1868–1959		cotton, grains
Sumitumo	1928–1962		
Marubeni			grains
Mitsubishi	1868–1954		grains
C. Itoh	1949		palm, cotton
Jardine Matheson	1832		sugar
Dalgety	1845		wool, meat
Volkart	1851		cotton, coffee, cocoa

Table 6.4 continued

	Original sector of activity	Date of entry into trading	Activity
2. Circles upstream of trade			
– farming cooperatives			
United States and Europe	nationwide grain cooperatives	1978	50% participation in Toppfer
Farmers Export	six US regional cooperatives	1968	International grains
Socopa International	cooperative union		meat
– state bodies			
Interbras	subsidiary of *Petrobras* (oil)		soya cakes. . .
Cobec	ditto		metals, grains
– intergovernmental firms			
Café Mundial			coffee
Pancafé S.A.	countries of Bogota Group	Feb-Aug 1980	coffee
Communbana S.A.	countries of UPEB	1977	bananas
– plantation firms			
Sime Darby	acquisition of Faure Fairclough and development of trade	1970	oilseeds
– industrial firms			
Anglo-American	28% of Philipp Bros. Johnson Mathey		metals
Noranda	50% of Rudolf Wolff and Co. Ltd.		metals
Amalgamated Metal Corporation	Patino mining group (at present subsidiary of Preussag A.G.)		tin and other metals

UPEB:Union of Banana Exporting Countries

Table 6.4 continued

	Original sector of activity	Date of entry into trading	Activity
3. Downstream trading circles			
– agro-food firms			
Tate and Lyle	sugar refining	1965	sugar, molasses, coffee
Pillsbury	milling	1975	grain
Central Soya	soya grinding		grain, proteo-seeds
Archer Daniel Midlands	soya grinding	1982	acquisition of 50% of Toppfer Interantional
Anderson Clayton	groceries and grinding		oilseeds, coffee
Unilever	soap, margarine: special subsidiary: Tropical Sales Products		oilseeds
Dalgety–Spillers	milling: 66% of *Lecureur Frères*		grains
Rothfos	roasting		coffee
Interfood	chocolate products		cocoa
British American Tobacco	Export Leaf		tobacco
Imperial Tobacco	Kulenkampf and A.C. Monk		tobacco
– metallurgical firms			
Preussag	controls AMC		non-ferrous metals

the seventies when financial capital was attracted to markets on which large profits were apparently to be made, or when new markets were liberated (Marc Rich on the oil market for example). At that time, capital from the upstream or downstream sectors of trade also came into play.

- *The upstream trading circles*

Upstream of trade, agricultural and mining products go their separate ways.

To the agricultural producer, international trade has often seemed to be a mirage whose secret had to be penetrated at all costs: is not the mission of agricultural cooperation by its very presence on a market, a stabilizing one? Of course, we could doubt the advantages for the agricultural producer of seeing the product of this cooperation — the cooperative — participate in international trading (with the attending risks) beyond the bare act of exporting. We should point out before going any further, that on the whole these endeavours have been failures or, at best, half-successes. They have generally been the product of:

- cooperative associations
- government structures.

The most advanced strategy employed by the cooperatives was in grain and seeds. Both in the United States and in Europe the large cooperatives attempted to put paid to the 'monopoly' held by the five major shippers. So as to be constantly 'on the market' they were obliged to go beyond their export activities and become traders themselves. They went about this in two ways. Most of the big grain cooperative unions, the European (e.g. UNCAC, France) and American groups which were well into the regrouping and concentration phase at the end of the seventies (Farm Export, which from 1968 regrouped six regional cooperatives, Farm Bureau of Indiana, Goldkist, Farmland), strove to acquire the means, and to pursue the activities, of genuine traders (dealing consequently in products other than their own)[5]. At the same time, the cooperatives sought to unite their efforts: at the end of the sixties with Eurograins functioning as an international broker (UNCAC France, CEBECO Netherlands, DRWZ Germany. . .), but especially at the end of 1978 when a group of American cooperatives (Goldkist, Farm Bureau of Indiana, Land O'Lakes) together with a group of European cooperatives (UNCAC,

CEBECO, DRWZ) bought 50% of the trading firm, Toppfer International (excluding industrial assets). After having contemplated the possibility of creating their own trading company, the cooperatives had in fact chosen to associate with an existing structure. After some fruitless contacts with Louis Dreyfus and André, they approached Toppfer, then the seventh largest grain trader in the world and going through a rough period. Relations between Toppfer and the shareholding cooperatives have remained informal. It is certain that Toppfer has frequently been able to become the main trading partner of one or the other cooperative as a result of this arrangement. The latter on the other hand have benefitted from Toppfer's international experience.

The balance of the operation seems to be an altogether positive one. Toppfer has been able to improve its position and now trades volumes more or less comparable in size to those of Bunge or Louis Dreyfus. Certain cooperatives such as UNCAC from France have been able to increment their activities on the international level. In 1983, the soya crusher Archer Daniel Midlands (first producer of corn–gluten–feed in the United States) bought 45% of the Toppfer capital, thereby increasing even further the scope of the shareholders.

Conversely, an association between Louis Dreyfus and the other French grain cooperative group, UGCAF, which had led to the creation of the *Union Française des Céréales* (using the legal status of *Groupe d'Intéret Economique*, an *ad hoc* association of companies which otherwise retain their individual identity, legal and otherwise) resulted in a definitive failure and the dissolution in 1979 of the *Union Française des Céréales*. The association of Brazilian soyabean producer cooperatives (Bantrade) also carries out similar activities.

Despite all of these developments, the impact of the cooperatives on the grain trade remains at present very limited. The same holds true for sugar (notwithstanding the presence of the French cooperative group, *Sucre Union*, which, not unlike its Brazilian counterpart, *Coper Sucar*, has remained essentially an exporter. On the other hand some of the structures set up by cooperatives have been able to ensure niches for themselves on the less structured markets such as those for meat (the French firm *Socopa International*) or for dairy products.

Finally a word about the projects for international cooperative trading companies put forward by the late Jean-Baptiste Doumeng and agreed to in principle by the *Alliance Coopérative Internationale*. There is reason enough to be sceptical about the entire affair, all the

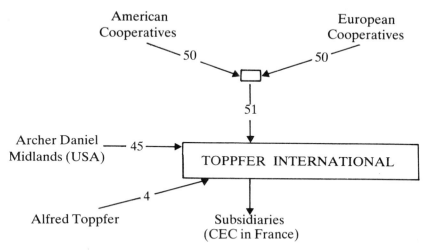

Figure 6.2 The capital structure of Toppfer International

more since the proposed integration into this cooperative network of the state 'cooperative' bodies of the socialist countries leads one to question the real motive behind this manoeuvre[6].

In any event, it is difficult to see how the cooperatives could really benefit from participation in the international trade of their products unless they see it as a means of finding new outlets. In most other cases, the risks outweigh the inferred strategic benefits to be gained[7].

Alongside the cooperative groups, a number of other groups, created by governments to represent the interest of producing countries, have gradually been attracted towards international trade: the Brazilian companies *Interbras* (subsidiary of the Brazilian national oil firm *Petrobras* and present notably in the market for soya cakes, coffee and cocoa) and *Cobec* (grains and metals). These are still rare examples insofar as governments generally prefer to try and avoid the middlemen in trade[8]. We must relegate to a different plane the attempts to create interstate trading companies responsible for marketing the produce of the members of a cartel-like association[9]. Most often than not they have not been very successful. In coffee there was

Café Mundial, then *Pan-Café* (1980), the arm of the Bogota group. *Comunbanana*, founded by the members of the Union of Banana Exporting Countries to resist the ascendancy of the large banana companies, had an export turnover of $40 million (from the six member countries) in 1981.

A few plantation firms also carry out trading activities: Sime Darby (Malaysia) for oilseeds, Lonrho (Great Britain) for sugar and, of course, the large banana companies.

Finally many mining groups have become interested in trading. It would be safe to affirm that most of the large mining multinational corporations (*Péchiney*, *Imétal* in France, RTZ, Alcan. . .)[10] have their international trading subsidiaries whose activities often differ from (and at times clash with) those of the parent company. We shall spare the reader an exhaustive list of these companies all the more since it is often difficult to really appreciate their importance. The Anglo-American group, a large South African mining concern (gold, diamonds. . .) indirectly controlled 27.3% of the capital of Philipp Bros before its acquisition of Salomon Brothers and also owns shares in Johnson Mathey. The case of *Péchiney* is particularly instructive: its trading subsidiary *Brandeis-Intsel* has become one of the world's leading traders in non-ferrous metals.

Similarly, the Canadian mining firm Noranda owned 50% of the capital of the British broker and trader Rudolf Wolff and Co., but sold it after the 1985 London Metal Exchange tin crash to the Australian conglomerate, Elders. Finally, the Patino group (tin) gave birth to one of the leading metal traders, Amalgamated Metal Corporation, bought a few years ago by the German group Preussag which controls 79.3% of the shares.

For some time now, the state-owned firms of the Third World have also been showing an interest in trade: in 1983 and in 1984, respectively, the Malaysian Mining Corporation and the Zambian Mining Corporation bought seats on the London Metal Exchange[11].

- *The downstream trading circles*

Agro-food companies have always been highly tempted to integrate trading activites. As a matter of fact, their strategy has generally been directed, in the first instance towards controlling the sources of supply and therefore towards integrating the elements of their chains. From the sixties onwards a certain number of them began to show an interest in trade. Very often this interest was merely incidental, but at times it reached such proportions that industrial firms were transformed into trading firms. The most striking example of this evolution, taken to an extreme, is the British sugar refiner Tate and Lyle which bought the world's leading molasses trader, United Molasses, in 1965 and proceeded thereafter to make a name for itself in the sugar, alcohol (Unalco), oils, and fats (Berger and Plate, Faure Fairclough. . .), and coffee trades. In grains, the leading American miller, Pillsbury, is now present on the world markets (after all but succeeding in buying out all the Cook assets in 1977). No such list would be complete without the British millers Spillers (now a member of the Dalgety group), and Rank Hovis and Mac Dougall. Spillers controls the French trader Lecureur, while the parent company Dalgety has owned the trading and brokerage firm Goldschmidt and Charteris since June 1979[12], and the cocoa trader Gill and Duffus since October 1985. Present are also a number of soya crushing firms such as Central Soya, Archer Daniel Midlands (through its participation in Toppfer) or more diversified firms such as Anderson Clayton (groceries and soya crushing), present through its Swiss subsidiary in the oilseeds and coffee trades. In the field of oilseeds we cannot fail to mention Unilever (present both as commodity producer and as processor) which controls a specialized trading subsidiary, Tropical Sales Products, and owns the journal, *Oil World*, which is in some measure the official mouthpiece of the oilseeds trading community. Similarly, a certain number of coffee roasters are very actively involved in trade: the German firm Rothfos is also the world's leading trader. The same pattern can be observed with Douwe Egberts (Netherlands) and the Jacobs-Interfood group (Switzerland, Federal Republic of Germany). Most cigarette manufacturers also procure their leaf tobacco through their own subsidiaries: British American Tobacco (Export Leaf) and Imperial Tobacco (Kulenkampf and A.C. Monk). This list is, of course, by no means an exhaustive one.

Also very prominent in the ore and metal trades are groups specialized in metallurgy (especially in non-ferrous metals) which very often operate both upstream and downstream of trade, as consumers of ores, metals and even of semi-products: Preussag, the *Metallgesellschaft*, Hoboken (Belgium), to name but a few. Finally, most of the oil companies are involved in free trading (*Elf Aquitaine*. . .). In December 1980, for example, the firms Premier Consolidated Oil Fields, a

small independent British oil company and the trading firm Ed. and F.
Man announced the creation of a new firm: Premier Man.

A final point must be made concerning the ethnic origin of international commodity traders. The need of trust and confidence in the
young trader had induced companies to develop and to recruit into
family and circles of relatives at home and abroad. Among Western
companies, the most numerous are Jews and Protestants (the André
family are darbyist). But there are many other origins to be found: in
Africa, the Syro-lebanese and the Indians, in the Middle East, the
Lebanese of course and families from the Gulf, in Asia, the Chinese.
Among Arabian traders one can mention Yusuf bin Ahmed Kanoo
(estimated trunover in 1983–84: $500 to $700 million) in Bahrain, the
Bahwans from Muscat and the Fullaims from Dubai; in Saudi Arabia
the Juffalis (turnover: $1 billion). . . In English speaking Africa
Indians and Lebanese are most active. In Nigeria for example, vegetable oil supplies were realized by Nessim Gaon with his Noga company
based in Geneva, and sugar and rice came through Esal Commodities,
owned by Rajendra Sethia — now in jail in Dehli following what is
known as the world's biggest bankruptcy ($170 million).

In Asia, Chinese trading groups are extremely powerful but difficult
to classify as their trading, banking and manufacturing activities are
very tied together. Founded by Lee Kong Chian, the Lee group is
known as the world's biggest rubber trader, with at least 500,000
tonnes per year. But it also owns about 100,000 acres of rubber and
palm estates, and controls the Overseas Chinese Banking Corporation. This family network was recently reckoned to be worth $1.4
billion! The Kuok group dominates the sugar trade in Asia and owns
estates in Malaysia, as well as flour mills, ships, hotels. . .: net worth
$2.1 billion. Last but not least, Liem Sioe Liong based in Jakarta
(where he is known as 'President Suharto's Chinese') dominates the
grain trade in Indonesia, owns the dutch coffee trader Hagemeyer, as
well as banks in Asia and in the U.S.A. The group's turnover was
estimated in 1983 at well in excess of $1 billion per annum.

In fact, all over the world rather 'informal' types of trading groups
survive and even develop to a considerable size. They are not the true
subject of this book, but one should always remember that international traders are now doing in a 'modern' way what they have done
for centuries with a pen and an abacus.

C. Analysis by products handled

In the 19th century there was no very clear specialization as to the products handled by import or brokerage firms. Around the year 1830 Ralli Bros, for example, dealt in silk, grains, cotton fabrics, metals, indigo, tallow. . . In 1860 Woodhouse was trading in sugar, rum, saltpetre, rice and pepper. Gradually, however, specialization began to take place first in grain, metals, and tropical produce (beginning of the 20th century) and subsequently the vast range of tropical products split up into so many different trades and professions.

By 1950 most traders were specialized in a single product but around the late sixties a certain number of firms (usually the largest) began to adopt a 'multiproduct' approach and, as can be seen from the numerous examples at hand, the phenomenon caught on and spread rapidly from 1975 onwards. In some cases this move constituted a natural extension towards related products: grain merchants extending their activities to oilseeds for example (Cargill, Continental. . .), coffee traders turning to cocoa, and vice versa. But more often than not, there was a desire to extend to other products an expertise acquired on a specific market. Thus Philipp Bros sought, though with little success, to expand from metals and oil to sugar, grain and more recently, to cocoa and rubber. Cargill extended its activities through its subsidiaries in cotton (Hohenberg, Ralli since 1981), metals (C. Tennant), sugar (Pan Am, but this was a failure), molasses, coffee (purchase of ACLI in 1984).

The problem was generally approached in one of two ways:

– a company would buy out an already existing firm (thus acquiring a name but above all a team). The annals of trade contain many such examples: the acquisition of Pacol by Gill and Duffus in 1962 and therewith its ticket to the coffee and rubber trades, the buying of the four previously mentioned firms by Cargill, and of Cocoa Merchants by Philipp Brothers (end of 1981). Another possibility open to the interested firms is to buy out firms in serious difficulty (*Sucres et Denrées*'s take-over of the cocoa trader *Touton* and later of the cocoa grinder *Cacao Barry*, Tardivat's take-over of the Goldschmidt cocoa team);

– the second possibility is to embark on a new field of activity using an already existing logistic base: Philipp Brothers moved from metals

to sugar (1976) then to grain (1978). Since 1975 Gill and Duffus and
Jardine and Matheson have been acting jointly in sugar. Embarking on
the market in this way generally proves to be a costly manoeuvre since
the newcomer is obliged to over-bid in order to gain acceptance and to
build up a reputation. The following is the *Institutional Investor*'s
description of Philipp Brothers's strategy (December 1981):

'They study the market carefully often for a number of months. Unless there is laready
someone competent on their staff, they employ the services of top traders from firms
which are already established, but the former are constantly supervised by one of
Phibro's top executives. After a few trials they make their way onto the market in search
of big deals at very competitive prices with the largest producers and consumers.'

But such a strategy does not always pay and Phibro allegedly lost
heavily on the sugar market in 1980[13].

Table 6.5 The inter-product diversification of trading firms

Firms	Original product	Diversification and date
Philipp Brothers	metals	oil (1968), sugar (1976), grains (1978), cocoa (1981), rubber (1981)
Cargill	grains	cotton, metals, sugar, coffee (1984)
Sucre et Denrées	sugar	meat (1976), milk (1970), cocoa (1975), precious metals, coffee (1976)
Louis Dreyfus	grains	meat, alcohol
Goldschmidt	grains	sugar (1964), meat (1960), coffee, cocoa
Gill and Duffus	cocoa, nuts and spices	coffee (1962), tea, rubber (1962), sugar (1975), metals
Marc Rich	oil	metals (1975), grains (1981)
Cook	cotton	grains (1967)
Ralli Bros.	cotton	jute (1969), coffee (1970), rubber (1970), hard fibres (1971)

Nevertheless the trend at present seems to be towards the creation
of a small number of very large 'multiproduct' firms, although, to our
mind, no more than ten firms are capable of making such a switch.

This leads us to the question of a trading firm's evolution and place in
history.

The internal evolution of trading firms

This 'industry', which we know as international commodity trading, is one of the least static in existence. It evolves with incredible speed; its situation is that of the 'Tarpeian Cliff on the Capitoline Hill'. It took Cook a bare ten years to become the third largest grain trader in the world; his downfall did not even take a year. A study of the evolution of a number of firms could lead us to certain conclusions and to an outline of the beginnings of a theory. We have been able to discern six stages in the evolution of a trading firm[14].

The first stage is that of the local or even nationally-based trader operating in a clearly defined territory (grain and non-ferrous metal traders, reprocessors). Also in this category, but operating in a totally different environment, is the international trader 'on paper' who never operates in actuals and does not have the logistic facilities to do so. There are countless examples of these two types of firms. The latter often rapidly move on to the second stage.

This second stage is generally characterized by the control of a number of physical facilities, if needed for the product dealt in (transport, storage, etc.). On this level we find the import or export traders, whose activities are restricted to bilateral operations carried out from the national territory of origin (the ethnocentric firms such as the Japanese *sogo shosa* ensuring supplies of grain to Japan), or a 'paper' trader dealing for the first time in actuals (initially through a c.i.f. purchase) and not intending to make a regular activity of it. Such firms are already less numerous. The first case is closely linked to a country's external trade framework which is often directed preferably towards its former colonial dependencies, whereas the second is still a transition stage even though many firms do not go beyond this type of activity and deal only occasionally on the international market[15].

At the third stage we find the international trader, the 'shipper' in the real sense of the term; these firms carry out operations among third countries by means of an international network of offices and agents, and very often have a material infrastructure at their disposal. This category comprises most of the trading firms which have been mentioned in the previous pages. Before long these companies are forced to deal with the problem of reinvesting the profits garnered in the trade sector. Since the structure of most such firms does not call for a considerable immobilization of fixed assets, their taxable profits,

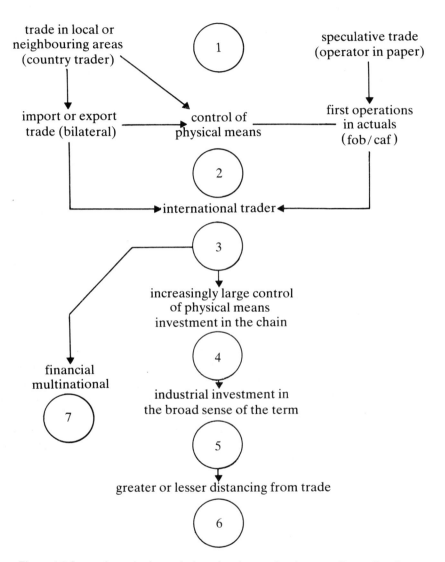

Figure 6.3 Some phases in the evolution of an international commodity trading firm

despite their countless tax evasion schemes[16], remain considerable, as they have practically nothing to show for depreciation. A trader's first investment will be in the logistics of trade: for a grain merchant that would mean an export elevator, freight cars, barges. . . He will then turn his attention to the nearest upstream or downstream activities. He will do this not only for strategic reasons, to establish privileged ties with the production or processing sectors, but also because these are

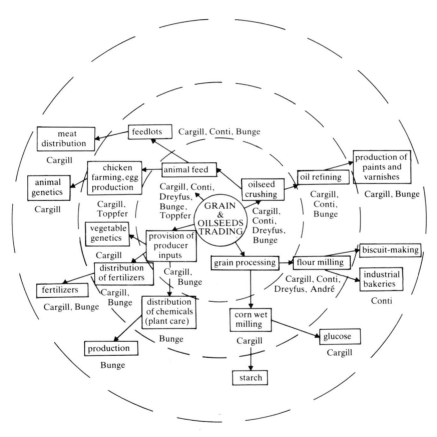

Figure 6.4 Diagram of the most frequently encountered patterns of diversification within the grain chain

the fields which he knows best, being, as a trader, all too familiar with
their strengths and weaknesses.

The trading firm in the fourth stage of development proceeds little
by little to invest the whole chain of the product or products which it
handles, whereupon the size factor becomes decisive: the firm constitutes an essential element ensuring the cohesion of the product-system
on the international level: from an operator buffeted by the whims of
the market, it has been transformed into one of the latter's primary
elements. Although it remains difficult and risky to make any sort of
conjecture in connection with these sectors, we believe that, having
reached this stage, a firm should be in a position to avoid being ruined
by the errors most widely committed in trading (Cook had almost
reached this stage before its collapse in 1977). Let us take a quick look
at the most common investments made within a given product chain.
The grain trade (grain and oilseeds) is a peculiar one insofar as the five
'majors' have, to an astonishing degree, implemented a policy of
vertical diversification based on this same principle of investing in
sectors with which they are relatively familiar and which are related in
some way to trading (Figure 6.5). For non-ferrous metals, the situation
is complicated by the often complex relations existing among traders,
industrialists and mining concerns, to such an extent that it is often
difficult to know with what type of firm one is dealing (the *Metallgesellschaft* is a case in point).

The other commodities display a common tendency for trading firms
to try to get a foothold in the first processing stage, in cases where the

Table 6.6 Some of the diversifications realized by trading firms within their product-
system

Product	Investment upstream	Investment downstream
Sugar	production (S. and W. Berisford)	
Coffee	processing (ACLI)	
Cocoa		grinding and semi-products (*Sucres et Denrées*, Gill and Duffus, Berisford)
Non-ferrous metals	production (Phibro, Japanese firms)	refining, specialized productions
Rubber		rubber products (*Safic Alcan*)

latter is likely to be taken over by the producing country: most of the cocoa traders have consequently set up bean grinding facilities and have developed the production of semi-finished products such as butter, powder and cakes.

The general order of preferences for diversification activities is therefore: first of all the logistic requirements (storage, insurance, financing, and possibly transport), followed by the structural connections both up and downstream, and finally the whole product-system.

It is also possible to complement this policy of investing within a chain, with a more general industrial diversifiction based either on a firm's familiarity with a country (the grain merchants which have considerable investments in South America ranging from hotels to ranches: Bunge and Born is thus the top-ranking agro-food firm in Argentina), or simply on considerations of convenience (coal represents, for Cargill, a return freight for its grain barges).

In this way the firm gradually acquires an industrial base and should its directors decide to continue along this path, it would lose all resemblance to a trading firm. In fact the logic of the classical manager does not allow for a coexistence with that of the trader: the firm's ability to assume risk will diminish and it will be forced to reduce its dependence on its trading activities. Such an 'exit' remains for most firms a remote possibility but a few — Bunge and Born, Toppfer, Louis Dreyfus, *Sucres et Denrées*, Berisford — are probably no longer very far from this stage. This would be, to a certain extent, the ultimate stage in the evolution of a trading firm: its transformation into an industrial group — and in the grain-processing sector which we shall mention again, the traders have become essential factors (Figure 6.4).

It would seem, however, that some firms do not evolve in the direction of a classical industrial multinational but are gradually transformed into financial multinational corporations. This point, to which the attention of the reader has already been drawn, is illustrated by the different manoeuvres which took place in the course of 1981:

Philipp Brothers	→	Salomon Brothers
ACLI	←	Donaldson Lufkin and Jenrette
Jack Aron	←	Goldman Sachs
Safic Alcan	←	the financial interests of the Agnelli family

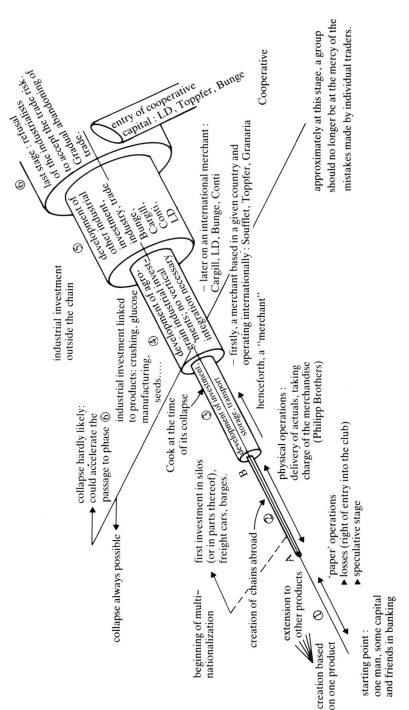

Figure 6.5 Theoretical and academic diagram of a trading company in the grain and oilseeds business

But on this level, the trader gives precedence to the 'commission house': the technical know-how brought by the trader is employed on the futures markets and not for actuals. The problems which attended the Phibro–Salomon association in 1983 clearly demonstrate the many difficulties inherent to this type of union.

In the final analysis, money constitutes the ultimate commodity and it is therefore logical to expect the traders to try to get closer to its source. A tissue of connections is therefore woven among traders, international bankers, commission houses. . . The stakes are nothing less than the financial domination of world trade. Owing to their 'stateless' and geocentric character, the commodity traders are particularly well placed to play this role.

Or at least some of them are! In fact, the last characteristic of the evolution of the commodity trade which we would like to stress, is the trend towards concentration — regardless of the product traded — around a small number of firms. We have already discussed the tendency of firms to move from one product to another: in fact such operations have permitted a certain number of firms to extricate themselves from their environment and they are now in the process of creating a trading oligopoly for all commodities: unless the present rules of the game are modified, the advent of new operators will remain an exceptional feat, if not practically impossible[17]

Thus concentration, industrial vertical diversification and financial growth seem to be the three main characteristics of the evolution of the commodity trading firms. We shall now take a more detailed look at these points by analysing some sectors and firms.

PART THREE

THE MAJOR TRADING FIRMS AND THEIR ENVIRONMENT

Introductory Note:

Part three of this book comprises a certain number of sector analyses in which we have inserted the monographs of the most important companies. We shall refrain, however, from delving into the major macro-economic balances of the markets of the products under study.

Chapter 7

THE GRAIN TRADE

In this study we have already quoted abundantly the example of the grain trade and the main firms involved in it. We shall not proceed to repeat in detail what we have said in the previous pages but shall seek to extend the scope of our study to embrace the grain trade in its entirety.

It must be noted that the American term 'grains' designates, not only grain for human consumption, but also all products destined to complement those grains in the feeding of livestock: protein cakes, fish or meat meal, manioc. By extension, this group must be widened to include oilseeds and vegetable oils (oilseed cakes were considered in the past to be merely a by-product), at least those which gravitate around soya. The grains economy is in fact based on the wheat–maize–soya trilogy, its nerve centre being in the Chicago Board of Trade on which these products are quoted[1].

An 'American' centre of gravity

The essential characteristic of the international grains trade is the dominant position occupied in it by North America in general and the U.S.A. in particular.

G

Figures show the U.S.A. to be the world's main exporter of wheat, soya, and even of rice.

But that country's domination of the trade is ensured not only by its huge exports but also by a number of other factors:

Table 7.1 The principal grain exporters

Wheat	U.S.A., Canada, EEC, Australia, Argentina
Maize	U.S.A., Argentina
Barley	Canada, EEC
Soya	U.S.A., Brazil, Argentina
Manioc	Thailand
Grain by-products (corngluten feed)	U.S.A.
Rice	U.S.A.,Thailand

– the futures markets on which the trading operations hinge are American markets (the Chicago Board of Trade for wheat, maize and soya along with those of Kansas City, Minneapolis. . .). The price in Chicago, accepted in international trade as the world price (the price on which the basis will be calculated), reacts essentially to variations on the American market;

– the U.S.A. (28% of the world grain production) can afford to let land lie fallow, thus substantially reducing production, or at least grant their farmers storage possibilities by means of deficiency payments (influence of the PIK programme in 1983);

– the U.S.A. is the leading foodstuffs exporter in its categories: studies have shown that the price variations in maize and wheat were closely tied to one another, especially for the period 1960–64 and since 1970. Since then, the rice market has also closely followed the lead of the wheat market. The preponderance of soya in the oilseeds trade is indisputable: all vegetable oils fluctuate closely in line with soya oil. As regards cakes and fish-meal, here too soya pulls the market behind it, with the exception perhaps of groundnut cakes whose variations are more erratic. Although it does not account for more than 30% of world exports in oilseeds, the U.S.A. manages to dominate the markets through its clout in soya;

– finally the American authorities support their export activities by large food-aid programmes known under the name of the law which authorizes them, P.L. 480, passed in 1954.

After a relative eclipse during the seventies, export assistance programmes took on a new lease of life from 1980 and especially from 1982. Thus at the end of January 1984, after a tour of the Maghreb by the American Secretary of Agriculture, John Block, almost 4 million tonnes of wheat and flour were sold on very concessionary terms to those countries. Since then, a major trade war has erupted between the United States and its main competitors, especially the EEC. This has resulted in declining prices and rising export bonuses almost everywhere.

The international grain market is nevertheless still an American market. Under these circumstances it should come as no surprise that all of the major trading companies have centered at least a part of their activities around the U.S.A., not hesitating to go all the way to the producer himself.

The other export centres are of lesser importance and, as we have seen, are most often regulated by quasi-governmental intervention bodies: the Canadian and Australian Wheat Boards, the Commission of the European Communities. . .

The import markets are dominated in the West by two centres (the EEC and Japan) and in the East by two socialist centres (the USSR and China). Most of the countries in the Third World are the beneficiaries of one of the food-aid programmes set up by the exporting countries (essentially for wheat and rice). On the user side it is interesting to note the duality between grain for human and for animal consumption.

Today, the international grain market is almost a direct reflection of the requirements of livestock breeding. Outside the wheat market which is dominated by food-aid quotas, all other markets, including those of oilseeds, move in accordance with the requirements of industry and of livestock breeding. This constitutes, in our view, the most prominent feature of the change which took place during the sixties and which has been characterized by a phenomenal development in the trading of coarse grains (equivalent to 60% of the wheat trade in the fifties, 115% today) and more or less processed oilseeds. The upshot of these events was the transformation of the profession of the trader who has extended the range of products which he handles to fish and meat meal, and even to molasses and manioc. . .

It would be no exaggeration to say that today's grain market is, above all else, an animal feed market.

The major traders

Grain traders can be divided into several categories: on the one hand, the 'world' traders whom we find in all production and consumption centres, in most of the invitations for tenders, and on the other, the major bilateral traders (or those who specialize in a given zone) who are marked by their geographical origins, and finally the national traders who are only present in the import-export trade on an intermittent basis.

Table 7.2 The major grain traders

The 'worldwide traders'		
Cargill	United States	17–28%
Continental	United States	17–25%
Louis Dreyfus	France	13–15%
Bunge and Born	Argentina	8–12%
André	Switzerland	8–10%
Toppfer	West Germany	8–10%
and		
Philip Brothers	United States	
Tradigrains	Switzerland	
Richco Grain	Switzerland–Netherlands	
The major bilateral firms		
United States	Farmers Export	
Italy	Feruzzi, Pagnani	
France	Soufflet, *Compagnie Grainière,* CAM, *G. et P. Levy*	
Japan	Mitsubishi, C. Itoh, Marubeni, Mitsui	
West Germany	Peter Cremer, Kampfmeyer	
Brazil	Interbras, Cobec	
Canada	Pioneer	
South America	Esteve	
Specialization in certain products		
Rice	*Action* (France), Connell Rice (US), *Riz et Denrées* (France), Cargill (US)	
Manioc	Topffer (F.R.G.), Krohm (F.R.G.), Peter Kremer (F.R.G.)	
Oilseeds	Noga (Switzerland) + the 'worldwide ones' + Tropical Sales Products (Unilever)	
Sunflower	Nidera (Argentina)	
Groundnuts	*Frahuiles* (France)	
Palm-oil	C. Itoh (Japan), Sime Darby (Malaysia)	

The members of the last two categories are in any case left to scramble for the crumbs of an international trade dominated by six firms transacting some 70% of international business.

Around 1975, these six majors accounted for 96% of exports in American wheat (95% in corn), 80% of the exports of Argentinian wheat, and 90% of the European exports of wheat and maize.

A measure of how concentrated the grain trade has become, can be given by the number of fixtures contracted on the voyage charter freight market by the large companies (Table 7.3).

Cargill, Continental Grain, Louis Dreyfus, Bunge and Born, and to a lesser extent André, and Toppfer, are, by virtue of their ramifications, their networks, and their interests, not only the main actors in the grains trade, but also in international commerce as a whole. The activities of these companies — more than of any others in commodity trade — are shrouded in the most total silence. They are all private companies, and as such are not constrained to publish their balance sheets, a fact which makes it no easy task to attempt to piece together the puzzle of their empires[2].

- *Cargill*

'Cargill wants to be the General Motors of Agriculture'
(*Business Week*, 14 September 1981).

What can be said about the number one firm in the world grain trade except that it controls an empire which, though it has undergone an extreme diversification, remains predominantly based on the grain trade.

William Cargill, a presbyterian Scotsman, emigrated around 1830 to the North of the U.S.A. where he became a captain in the merchant navy. In 1857, he settled in Winsconsin. In 1865, his oldest son, Will, bought a first silo in Conover, Iowa, then shares in silos being built along the new rail routes. Will, assisted by two of his brothers, began to have silos built almost everywhere on the Great Plains, with the help of Robert Elliot, a Millwaukee banker. By 1880 Cargill controlled practically the entire grain trade in five States (North and South Dakota, Iowa, Wisconsin, Minnesota). After having barely escaped bankruptcy in 1906, the company was taken over by John Mac Millan who had married a Cargill in 1895 and in 1914 the firm moved to Minneapolis.

Table 7.3 Voyage charters contracted by the major grain houses from September 1982 to June 1983 (in thousands of dwt)

Cargill–Tradax	6,800
Continental Grain	4,217
Toppfer International	2,760
Bunge and Born	2,678
Louis Dreyfus	2,648
Richco Grain	1,451
Japanese traders	4,123
Total charters for the period	47,502

Source: *Drewry* monthly report. These figures are merely indicative. Many traders sell on f.o.b. terms (to the USSR for example) or do not charter directly. Note that André–Garnac is missing from the list.

From 1865 to 1954, Cargill developed exclusively on American soil gradually setting up a grain collection and transport network covering the entire American territory. With the beginning of the forties came the development of activities in supplies, animal feed, processing and packaging of agricultural produce.

At that time, Cargill already dominated the grain trade, not only in its region of origin but also, from 1935 onwards, around Chicago. During the Second World War, federal government aid permitted it to complete its storage infrastructure for next to nothing. Cargill gradually secured its predominance in domestic river and rail transport (barges from 1958), where its 'clout' as a transporter enables it to wrangle favourable conditions from the railway companies[3]. Even now, Cargill invests $150 million per year to improve its logistics network, which includes 430 barges, 23 ships and 340 elevators.

Cargill's international expansion really dates back to the beginning of the fifties. The firm's international trade department goes back to 1954 with the founding of Tradax International in Panama (for tax reasons), the nerve centre being first in Montreal and from 1956 in Geneva (the *Crédit Suisse* holds 30% of the capital of Tradax–Switzerland). Since that time expansion has taken place both on the international level, first in grain, then in other primary commodities, but also upstream and downstream of the grain–oilseeds–meat line:

– 1954: debut in international trade on a large scale; purchase of an ocean-going fleet, and of salt mines (providing return freight along the Mississipi);

– from 1960: development of oilseed crushing and refining outside the U.S.A., animal feedstocks, processing of corn by-products (corn wet milling) in the U.S.A.;

– from 1970: flour-milling in the U.S.A.; production and marketing of meat, poultry and eggs; iron and steel, barge-building, coal mines (return freight on the Mississipi).

Cargill's strategy in the recent past seems to have led to an increment in purchases and investments both in the U.S.A. and in Europe, in five main sectors:

– glucose and starch production and the remarkable development of isoglucose. In the U.S.A., Cargill owns four factories. In Europe, the company bought out the almost insolvent factories of the Dutch firm KSH in 1978 (isoglucose plants in Great Britain (Albion Sugars) and in Holland), began construction of a factory to process corn by-products in Bergen Op Zoom, Netherlands (capacity: 200,000 tonnes), and purchased the German firm, *Dufrit* (potato starch). In the U.S.A., Cargill launched a research programme with Miles Laboratories and set up new production units in Memphis (Tennessee) and in Dayton (Ohio). Without a doubt, the firm wants to ensure for itself a predominant position in this sector which is now in full boom.

– similarly, the acquisition of the milling activities of Seaboard Allied Milling, at the beginning of 1982 made Cargill the third biggest American miller with 15% of that country's total capacity;

– the poultry and egg production sector, through a series of takeovers in the U.S.A., which made Cargill the first American egg producer;

– meat production and marketing: after investing in feedlots, the purchase of MBPLX Corps, second meat packer in the U.S.A. (turnover: $1 billion), for $75 million in November 1978 and construction of new abattoirs in Kansas in 1982 ($30 million). There has also been a net reinforcement in this sector as a result of numerous purchases effected by the US animal feed subsidiary of the Nutrena firm. It must be pointed out that a very important role is played by Brazil and Argentina in these investments;

– finally the crushing of oilseeds, a sector where Cargill has strengthened its European position (Great Britain in 1984).

Since 1981, Cargill has reinvested 87% of its cash-flow, with $463 million allocated to capital investment in 1984.

Confronted with this essentially industrial strategy, we are forced to consider what position trade still has in all this. Trade (through the Swiss firm Tradax) apparently still plays a preponderant role in the strategy of the firm although it represents, at present, only one-third of its activities.

Outside the grain chain, Cargill has attempted to diversify into trade in other primary commodities: the most important development in this field was the purchase in 1981 of the world's leading cotton trader, Ralli Bros, of Liverpool, subsidiary of the Bowater group, for £15 million. Cargill, whose subsidiary Hohenberg was already present on the cotton market, thus reinforced its position on this new market. In May 1984, Cargill bought the trading department of the ACLI group for an estimated $80 million. This purchase should permit the company to increase its presence in cocoa and coffee. Cargill is also present, albeit to a lesser extent, in sugar, molasses, metals and oil[4].

Finally this company accounts for almost one quarter of the world grain trade and can exert a considerable influence on the market (not least through graft which is estimated to have cost the firm $5 million between 1971 and 1977). In 1974, its share of the grain exports of the U.S.A. was as follows:

barley	42%
oats	32%
wheat	9%
sorghum	22%
soya	28%
maize	16%

In 1974, Cargill gained a foothold in Canada by purchasing the National Grain Company which controlled inland and harbour silos as well as animal feed plants.

On the whole, the company employs 42,000 people in 52 countries.

Since it is a private firm we have very little information on its financial results. The figures which we present here (turnover and profits) are not very significant since the turnover does not stipulate the

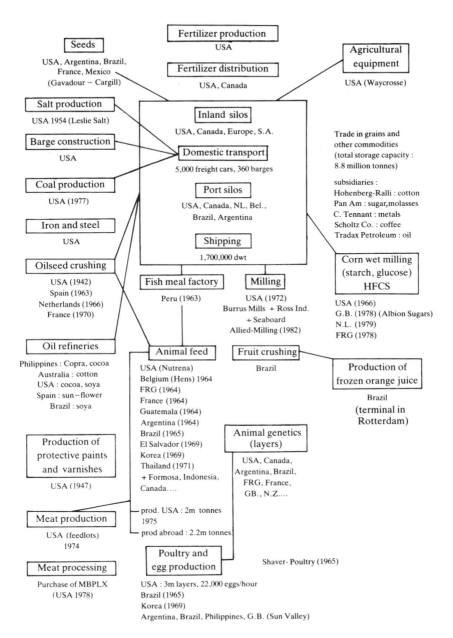

Figure 7.1 The Cargill empire

Note: the links we demonstrate here are those of a logical process. They by no means imply an attempt at vertical integration.

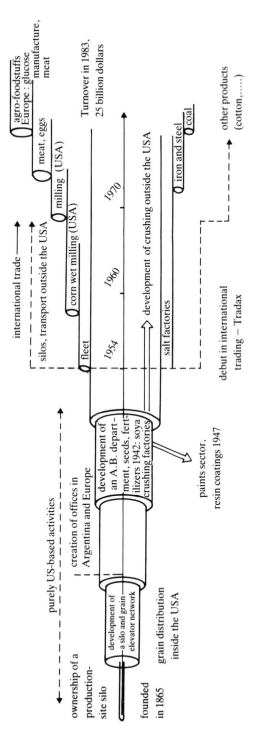

Figure 7.2 The development of Cargill

It is impossible to define precisely the share of the different activities. Trading nevertheless remains, according to us, the driving force of the group.

effective margin made either in grains or in oilseeds, and for a firm like
Cargill the profits do not mean a thing if we have no idea of the cash
flow generated[5]. It is obvious, nevertheless, that the firm was at its
most prosperous around 1974 as a result of the grain boom and that
growth since then has been increasingly confined to the industrial
sector.

The majority of the capital is still controlled by the Cargill and Mac
Millan families and by the Cargill foundation (a total of 33 shareholders).

Table 7.4 The Cargill 'accounts' (at least those few rare figures published during
take-over bids or during official hearings)

	1973–74	1974–75	1975–75	1976–77	1977–78	1978–79	1982–83
Turnover ($ billion)	9.10	10.90	10.80	10.90	11.30	12.60	25.30
Profits ($ million)	212.50	218.40	179.00	110.00	120.00	150.00	137.00
Ratio (%)	2.34	2.00	1.66	1.00	1.06	1.19	0.54

(for 1978–79: *Business Week*, 16 April 1979).
(fiscal year beginning on June 1st).

Slowly but surely the group's centre of gravity has shifted towards
industrial operations which currently represent almost 60% of its
turnover (if we consider this criterion to be meaningful), as against
40% around 1970. From 1972 to 1979, Cargill spent over $1 billion in
industrial investments.

Is it possible to speak of vertical integration in the case of Cargill?
Apparently, yes, and this is the thesis defended by quite a number of
observers[6]. There remains no doubt that the Cargill investments since
1945 were made upstream and downstream of its trading activities in
sectors where the technical and economic know-how of the Cargill
men were a guarantee of success. Moreover, it is certain that on the
level of the firm's global strategy, its position in various points of the
chain allows it to hedge profitably and to create new markets. There
seems to be no integrated management, each centre of profit being
considered independently: Cargill corn will not necessarily go to the
glucose plants of the firm. The old notions of vertical integration are
largely outmoded.

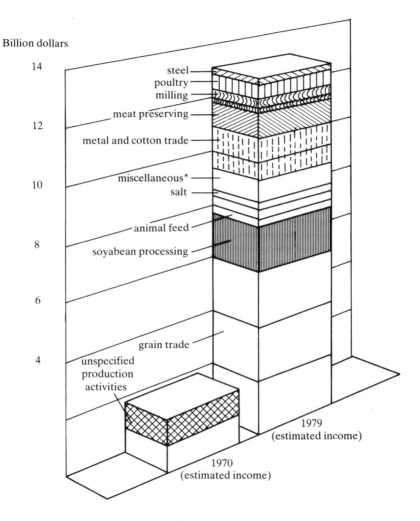

* chemicals, coal, oilseeds and insurance

Figure 7.3 Cargill: estimated income in 1979
Source: *Business Week*, 16 April 1979

What constitutes the strength of the firm, is its ability to be present at all the stages of grain processing and trade, seeking at all times to maximise profits on each level. Has it any other powers? Is it the *deus ex machina* of the grains economy? Such an assumption would most likely be an over-simplification of the facts.

Relying on the efficiency of its grains logistics, Cargill was able to take full advantage of the boom years of the grains market (1972–1974) and to build up a new empire in the agro-foodstuffs sector. And over the years, the logic of the enterprise has become an industrial one, illustrating this last phase of the evolution of the trading firm mentioned above[7].

● *Continental Grain*

The more we know about Cargill, in general due to its preeminence, its purchases of companies quoted on the Stock Exchange and various Congressional enquiries, the more it seems that the Continental Grain group remains shrouded, if not in mystery, then at least in ignorance.

The second world trader in grains was set up in Belgium in 1813 by the Fribourg family which still controls 90% of its capital. Until 1939, it was run from Paris. The German invasion convinced the Fribourgs to move to New York. At present the firm is run in a very personal and apparently autocratic manner by Michel Fribourg[8].

Continental Grain's share of the world grain trade is estimated at 20% and its turnover in 1983 was $12 billion. The company owed a substantial proportion of its growth to its excellent relations at the beginning of the seventies with the USSR: in 1972 for example, 'Conti' — as it is known — sold some 7 million tonnes of wheat and corn to the USSR.

Table 7.5 Continental Grain's accounts (various sources)

	1974	1975	1981	1983
Turnover ($ billion)	7.20	9.40	14.30	12.00
Net profits ($ million)	101.00	51.00	73.00	36.30

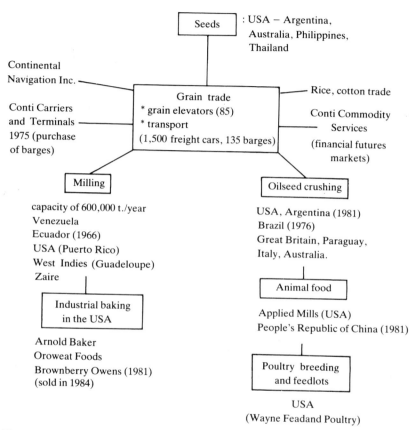

Figure 7.4 The vertical diversification of the Continental Grain group
(Note that we have even less information on this group than on Cargill).

On the other hand, the industrial diversification of Continental Grain is much less advanced, and it is estimated that a mere 15% of its turnover comes from industry (notably from the processing of grain: milling, industrial baking (turnover in 1981, $330 million), crushing operations, animal feedstocks. . .)[9].

It would seem moreover, that after losses sustained in trading and on the futures markets, 'Conti' was forced to disinvest: in May 1984, it sold its entire industrial baking interests to General Foods and a soya crushing plant to Archer Daniel Midlands. Its Liverpool operation was also sold in 1985 to Cargill. It is possible that this move was made in response to the desire expressed by the Fribourgs to maintain the accent on trade.

Continental has, furthermore, profited phenomenally from the development of the futures markets. Having started from scratch in 1970, its subsidiary, Conti Commodity Services Inc., received over $100 million in brokerage and portfolio (commodity funds. . .) management commissions in 1980. One of the star managers was Richard Sandor, former professor at the University of Berkeley, 'inventor' of the futures markets in financial instruments. However, in 1981, Conti was one of the major commission houses (along with ACLI and Bache) whose existence was threatened during the silver market debacle (after the Hunt affair). Michel Fribourg allegedly reinjected $81 million into the subsidiary at the time, but had to sell it in 1985 to Refco.

All in all, notwithstanding its size (18,500 employees), Continental has, in essence, remained a trading firm, which in 1986 does not look at its best.

● *Louis Dreyfus*

We have already related at length the history of this trading firm founded in Basel by Leopold Dreyfus in 1850 and which was one of the first truly international trading firms before 1945[10]. At present, the visible part of the Louis Dreyfus firm, still controlled by the family and directed by Gérard Louis-Dreyfus, great-grandson of Léopold (assisted by a former senior civil servant Jean Pinchon), centres around three elements: the trading company, the fleet, the bank.

The shipping company and the bank, 50% of which is controlled by the Bruxelles-Lambert group, are managed independently and only partially contribute to the total effect of trade. In grains, Dreyfus accounts for 10 to 15% of world trade. Although the headquarters of the company are located in Paris, the nerve centre of the firm is in New York[11] and, historically, the group's interests have given it strong positions in South America (Argentina and Brazil); after a prolonged absence from trade on a large scale (until 1965), Louis Dreyfus began

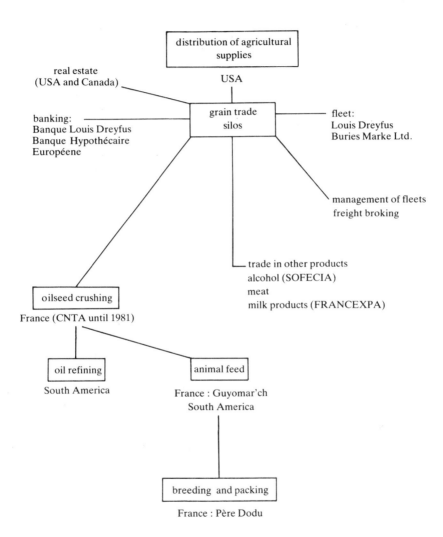

Figure 7.5 The diversification of the Louis Dreyfus group (Here, too, a very incomplete picture. . .)

to rebuild its teams (especially in the United States) in 1970 (buying out notably a large part of the Cook team). For a long time, the firm was associated in France with one of the major French grain cooperative groups (*UGCAF* – *La Fayette*) within the *Union Française de Céréales* (UFC) which was engaged in the French export trade; as a result of bad management, the UFC was obliged to close down, apparently without any great loss to Louis Dreyfus (1976). Similarly, in 1981, Louis Dreyfus severed its ties with another group of French cooperative background, the CNTA (*Comptoir National Technique Agricole*) specialized in the crushing of oilseeds, through their joint subsidiary *Oléafin* (which controlled notably the Bordeaux soya crushing plant with *Elf-Aquitaine*)[12].

In France, Louis Dreyfus controls one of the leading livestock feed producers, *Guyomar'ch*[13], which has integrated its product-chain rather far upstream (*Père Dodu* turkey-based products). In South America, Louis Dreyfus is present in the crushing and refining of oilseeds, animal feed etc.

Outside the grain chain, the firm's activities are far from negligible. It engages in trade in other products: alcohol, where its subsidiary SOFECIA accounts for 70% of world trade, dairy products, where an associated company, FRANCEXPA, is also on top of the international list (turnover in 1983, 1.6 billion francs), meat and meat-products (turnover in 1978 for meat, 1 billion francs), cotton (Allenberg, bought out in 1981), sugar for which Louis Dreyfus created a subsidiary in 1984, the Louis Dreyfus Sugar Corporation.

The group's other industrial assets are more difficult to identify as such: estimates in 1977 put the turnovers of the Louis Dreyfus subsidiaries in South America at between 800 and 900 million francs in sectors as different as glass (Santa Cristal in Argentina), chipboard, water meters, hotels. . . But it is perhaps in the real-estate business that the firm's diversification has been the greatest: in North America the family owns the best hotel in Washington, the *Four Seasons*, valued at $60 million, office buildings in New York, Buffalo, Toronto and Montreal[14].

Around 1978, the group as a whole (fleet and bank excluded) was estimated to be worth some 300 million francs with a turnover which supposedly exceeded 20 billion francs[15].

Much less 'world-oriented' than its predecessors, Louis Dreyfus remains marked by its French and South American background. This is also the case, to be sure, of Bunge and Born.

- *Bunge and Born*[16]

Bunge and Born is, even in commodity trading, no run-of-the-mill case. A conglomerate of family interests, a major trader *cum* industrialist, the most stateless of the stateless groups, Bunge still remains shrouded in mystery.

The company was founded in Amsterdam in 1818 to trade with the Dutch colonies in spices, leather and skins. After moving to Antwerp in 1851, it began to trade in grains.

In 1880, while Edward Bunge remained in Antwerp, his brother Ernest left to settle in Argentina where he first of all participated in the founding of a bank before creating, in 1884, with his brother-in-law George Born, a grain export firm called Bunge and Born. In 1897, two other associates, Alfredo Hirsch and Jorge Oster joined the business. Before long, Bunge and Born was the largest exporter of Argentinian grain (with one-third of the country's total exports in the Twenties). The company relied heavily on its partner in Antwerp, and on P.N. Gray, a Chicago trading firm acquired in those early days. Meanwhile, Edward Bunge, who had remained in Antwerp, was becoming fully integrated into the business class of Belgium: rubber tree plantations in the Congo from 1890, in Malaysia in 1903, railways in China. . . At the same time, the group began to industrialize (mills in Argentina in 1902, oilseed crushing in 1925).

After the death of Edward Bunge in 1927, the group focused increasingly on South America and developed its industrial operations in that part of the continent. In 1974, after the kidnapping of the Born brothers by the Argentinian Montoneros (for which the company was obliged to pay a ransom of $60 million), the headquarters of Bunge and Born was transferred from Buenos Aires to Sao Paulo.

Today, according to Catherine Laurent and Raul Green, 'there is reason to believe that the Bunge and Born group, which has a foothold in 80 countries, enjoys a turnover of over $10 billion and employs over 60,000 people around the world'[17]. Moreover, the value of its assets is estimated at over $1 billion. But a deep mystery continues to surround the very structure of the group which is, in fact, a galaxy of independent companies linked to each other by 'family ties': the Borns, the Hirschs, the Brachts in Belgium, the La Tour d'Auvergne in France, provide the link between the scattered elements of this huge empire (which at the top includes holdings in the Dutch Antilles).

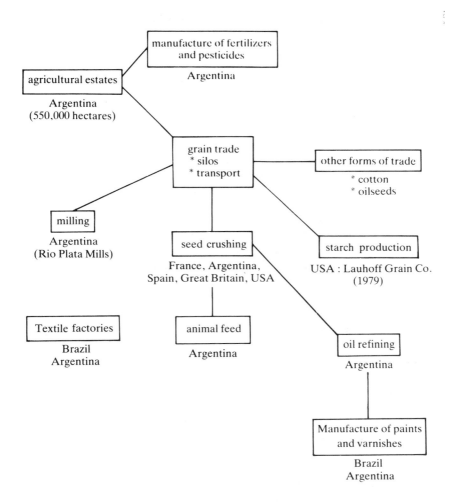

Figure 7.6 Diversification of Bunge and Born

The industrial diversification of the group has been far from spectacular: the first agro-food company of South America, Bunge has, in the last years, played its trump-card — oilseeds — to the hilt and is probably the leading crusher in the world today. In Brazil since 1967

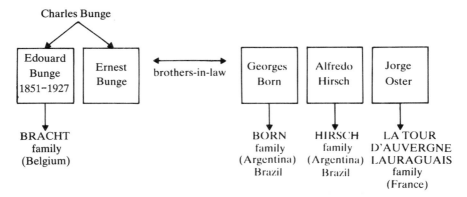

Figure 7.7 The founders of Bunge and Born and a few of the successor families

(*Sanbra* and *Samrig*), Bunge invested in the United States from 1977, in Spain and very recently in France with the taking over of the CNTA (along with its four factories, one of which is *Bordeaux-Oléagineux*), in Great Britain (buying of J. Bibbys for £14 million in October 1983).

Outside the oilseeds sector, Bunge has large interests in chemicals (with Bayer in Argentina), milling, and cotton trading.

Recently, the group, which is always co-managed by family representatives, appeared to be withdrawing from the purely trading sector of its activities. Many a rumour circulated about the selling out of trading activities. For the time being, they seem to be groundless.

- *André et Companie*

Of all the great grain traders, *André* is probably the most discreet[18]. In 1877, Georges André established a small trade in grain and cakes, and was already one of the principal grain importers in Switzerland by 1914. Soon after, a network was formed to cover Europe (1920), then Argentina (1927) and the United States (1937). After the war, *André* developed its shipping activities as well as the merchanting of industrial machinery. It is at present, with a turnover of 10 to 12 billion Swiss francs, the fourth largest firm in Switzerland.

In grain, *André* accounts for 8 to 10% of international trade. The structure of the group is rather difficult to come to grips with, the different firms being theoretically independent. An example of this is Garnac, founded in the United States in 1937 by Frederik Hediger, an employee of *André,* and which is, officially, merely an associate of *André* in the United States; the same goes for *Plata Cereal* in Argentina. In 1977, Garnac had a turnover of $1.5 billion and controlled a dozen silos in the United States (purchase of the Midwestern Grain Company). In the U.S.A., *André* also controls 50% of Adnac (along with Archer Daniel Midlands).

The group also owns ships (about fifteen, 40% of the Swiss fleet, about 500,000 dwt as well as industrial interests (milling, spinning, machine-tools) in South America (especially in Argentina). *André* is also one of the specialists of counter trading with the East Bloc countries (through its department FINCO).

Furthermore, *André* is very active in the coffee and cocoa trades.

- *The other traders*

A certain number of firms gravitate around the 'majors'. These are either small international firms or large bilateral ones.

Among the first we should mention three newcomers which have attempted to deprive some of the large firms of their markets. *Philipp Brothers* has been adopting, since 1978, the same policy put into practice in sugar: forcing its way through invitations to tender in order to make its presence felt, building up its own team from elements snatched from the competition. . . The result was, at the outset, a costly one, but Phibro profited remarkably from the embargo on exports to the USSR in 1980. The company refused to have its contracts bought by the C.C.C.[19] and was able to work for the Russians with total impunity during the spring of 1980. In 1981 and at the beginning of 1982, however, Phibro's tactics proved to be rather expensive and in the recent past the group has considerably reduced its grain presence. In 1979, Philipp Brothers had dealt in actuals amounting to 5 million tonnes of grain and soya; for 1981, the estimate was 20 million tonnes.

Marc Rich entered the grain trade rather late in the game, founding Richco Grain in 1980 and buying the international assets of the Dutch

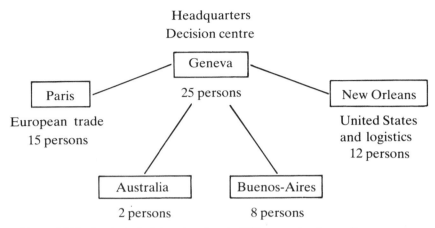

Figure 7.8 *Tradigrains'* administrative chart in 1980: example of a small structure

group, Granaria, in 1981. Richco benefited in its expansion from the
privileged relations which Marc Rich had in the Middle East: it is
almost the exclusive supplier of barley to the Kingdom of Saudi
Arabia. Despite the problems which the group started to experience in
1983, Richco managed to maintain its position and is now a world
trader in its own right, with a dimension very near *André*'s and Louis
Dreyfus's. With *Tradigrains*, we find once more one of the most
famous grain trading teams in the business, which, under the direction
of Gérard Emler, was sucessively Goldschmidt, and Cook Europe,
before constituting Tradigrains. The latter is linked to Tradimer, and
financed first by Arab and Pakistani shipping interests (the Gokal
family), and recently by the Saudi Pharaon. Tradimer is a small
organization which has rapidly come to occupy a place worthy of note
on the international scene (7 million tonnes handled in 1980).

   Among the great 'ethnocentric firms', the Japanese and the Italians
deserve special mention.

   It has not escaped our attention that the *sogo shosa* generally
engage in the provision of Japan's grain supplies. Some of them have
also become involved in off-shore activities. Thus in 1980, *Marubeni*
announced 70% off-shore activities with 4 million tonnes of wheat,

4 million tonnes of secondary grains, 2.3 million tonnes of soybeans. There is also *Mitsui,* which bought up a good part of Cook's logistic assets in the United States and has a subsidiary in Antwerp, and *Mitsubishi* and *Sumitumo* which own export elevators in the United States.

Table 7.6 The main *sogo shosa* involved in the grain trade

Company	Products	Main subsidiaries
Mitsubishi	grain, colza, palm-oil	Koppel Inc. (1979: elevator silos)
Mitsui	grain, meat	Gulf Coast Grain Inc. United Grain Co. (Vancouver) Pacific Grain International Corn Cy. (Antwerp)
C. Itoh	palm-oil	
Marubeni	grain, palm-oil	Columbia Grain Inc. (silo in Portland)

For a long time the Italian grain market was the most open in Europe, notably to firms of American origin. This very speculative market is dominated by a few firms which are also present in milling and in the semolina industry. . . The most important is the *Feruzzi* group.

At the outset, Serafino Feruzzi was a small grain merchant in Ravenna in post-war Italy. He took advantage of the special conditions created in the Italian ports by the European grain regulations to develop a steady flow of imports from the United States. Estimates have it that Feruzzi now handles 4.5 milion tonnes of grain per year, a little more than half of it in Italy, representing about half of the country's imports. This is supported by an impressive silo infrastructure in Italy, in the United States (Artfer Inc) and in Argentina, of freight cars and barges (in the U.S.A.) and of grain carriers (600,000 tonnes dwt). Moreover, Feruzzi is, through its subsidiary *Italiana Olii e Risi,* the most important Italian soybean crusher, and is now investing in Spain in this field.

In the midst of the very peculiar circumstances arising from the collapse of certain Italian financial groups (Bastogi, Monti), Feruzzi has been able to build up an enormous industrial base first in cement and concrete, then in sugar: Feruzzi controls the main Italian producer

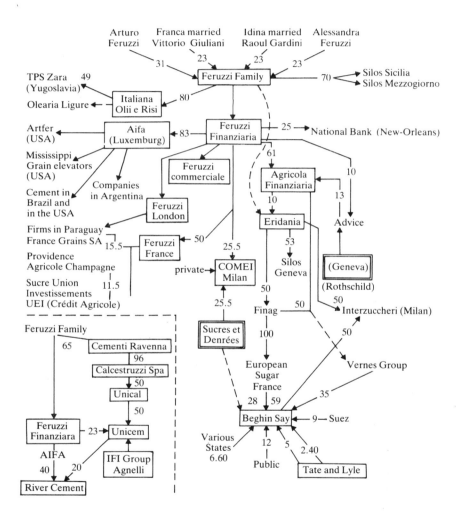

Figure 7.9 The Feruzzi group. This illustrates the complexity of European financial relationships

Eridania, the principal French producer *Beghin Say*, and in the autumn of 1986, was involved in the battle for the control of the only British producer, the British Sugar Corporation, owned since 1983 by S. and W. Berisford. Finally Serafino Feruzzi has invested massive sums in land and the group owns enormous estates in Italy, in the United States and in South America (over 800,000 hectares, and near to 150,000 heads of cattle!).

Until 1979, the group was a collection of independent companies owned by Serrafino Feruzzi (who remained deep down inside a grain merchant, never failing to make his Wednesday trip to the Grain Exchange in Milan). When he died in an accident, his four children began to reorganize the 'Feruzzi empire' around holdings, some of whose capital was sold out to the Geneva-based *Société Financière Rothschild* in 1982. In 1981, the Feruzzi turnover was some $4 billion for a cash flow of $210 million, and in 1985, it was estimated at around $8 billion.

Although the relative importance of Italian trade has decreased in the past few years, the same does not go for Germany. Concentrated around Hamburg, German trading, has developed, on the basis of new trades such as manioc.

Alfred Toppfer is the biggest German firm and the world's sixth trader. Founded in 1920 in Hamburg, Alfred Toppfer was carrying out, at the end of the seventies, about 8% of the world grain trade (17.4 million tonnes in 1975–76 for a turnover of 12.1 billion DM), and was particularly present in East Germany (50% of the grain imports of that country). Moreover, the firm controls a large fleet as well as animal feed plants and livestock breeding facilities in Germany. Around 1967–77, Toppfer made a few bad deals, lost 8 million DM in the bankruptcy of the Herstatt bank, and probably more with the collapse of the shipping market. It was then that, in December 1978, a certain number of European and American cooperative unions bought out 50% of the firm's capital (excluding industrial assets) (see above).

Peter Cremer, also from Hamburg, specializes in trade with South-East Asia and deals above all in oilseeds and their by-products, as well as rice and manioc. . . The firm controls crushing facilities in Thailand (manioc pellet factories), Indonesia (manioc), Phillipines (copra), in Zaire (vegetable oil-mills), and in 1977 the tonnage it shipped, from Hamburg alone, was 2.5 million tonnes.

Strongly marked by the cooperative storage monopoly set up by the *Office du Blé* (Wheat Board) in 1936, French business has become much more dispersed since the collapse of Goldschmidt in 1968. Until then, the Goldschmidt firm had been the major French exporter, owning a world infrastructure, oriented more than elsewhere towards the East Bloc countries, with exports amounting to 600,000 tonnes, and trading over 1 million tonnes on the international market. Only *Soufflet Frères* is now beginning to have an international status. We should also cite *G. et P. Lévy*, the *CAM* company, *Soules*. . .

It should be noted that the peculiarities of intra-European trade, the difficulties arising from the complexity of the European Community regulations and the absence of hedging opportunities (despite the existence of 'lines' on wheat f.o.b. Creil for example), have permitted a host of European firms to specialize in a field in which the 'giants' are apt to misdirect what little energy they expend (Bunge disengaged itself from Europe around 1975).

Among American firms, the name of *Canagra* has recently emerged as one of the few able of doing business on an international scale.

Among the traders of producing countries, we should also mention *Pioneer* in Canada, *Interbras* for Brazilian soya, and *Cobec* for grain. In Argentina, the *Sasetru* group went out of business in 1981, and the biggest national trader there is *Nidera*.

But the operators increasingly tend to come from fields either upstream or downstream of trade.

The upstream and dowstream approaches

Upstream of trade, the producers, regrouped in cooperatives and cooperative unions, have often attempted to to go beyond their traditional roles as mere exporters. As a result, there have been many attempts, but, to date, rather few successes.

There are, generally speaking, a few large national structures capable of tackling the international market: UNCAC and UGCAF in France, Farmland and Farmaco in the United States, Cebeco in the Netherlands, DRWZ in Germany. But more often than not they lack the means to do more than place the produce of their members in a f.o.b. position.

In the United States, some of the most important cooperatives grouped together in 1966 to form *Farmers Export*. Thanks to the power of its members[20], Farmers Export was, in 1980, the fourth exporter of grain in the United States (after Cargill, Conti and Louis Dreyfus) with a turnover of $3.8 billion. From 1978, in an effort to sustain its development (purchase of Cook's silo in Galveston. . .), Farmers Export tackled trade and the basis market after having employed a number of former traders[21]. A few badly controlled speculative moves led to losses of $35 million and caused the company to cut down on its operations at the beginning of 1981. In any event, every large cooperative in the United States tends to have its own export activities.

In Canada, as in Brazil, the role played by government propor-tionately limits the export activities of the cooperatives[22].

In Europe, the cooperatives are exporters (France), but especially importers of animal feeds. A number of these cooperatives have tried to establish direct links in order to short-circuit the trading sector (the *Eurograins* group in 1966). Others have sought to form an alliance with traders or infiltrate trading circles: we have already mentioned the purchase of 50% of Toppfer International's capital which allowed the participating cooperatives to profit from Toppfer's international logis-tics. But do the advantages justify such an investment? We do not believe so and make no secret of our scepticism which has grown since the collapse in 1976 of the *Union Française de Céréales* (UFC), created by UGCAF and Louis Dreyfus and of which the latter took consider-able advantage in making a comeback in the international grain trade. Similarly, international cooperative projects revived from time to time by the *Alliance Coopérative Internationale*, cannot be taken seri-ously[23].

Downstream, a certain number of grain users have attempted on more than one occasion to develop trading activities, and very often the division is rather blurred, so easy is it for the purchase of raw materials and the re-sale of semi-finished goods to become integrated into trade.

In the case of the U.S.A., most firms downstream have been led to set up their own collection networks. From there to using them for other purposes and to adding export silos was only a short step, whichit was taken by millers such a *Pillsbury* or *Peavey*, and crushers like *Central Soya* or *Archer Daniel Midlands*.

Pillsbury had already been mentioned in 1978 in connection with the

purchasing of the Cook assets, but the former already owned a
capacity of 60 million bushels in storage facilities in the United States.
Peavey effected, from its export installations, 5% of the American
exports (300 million bushels in 1981)[24]. Central Soya and ADM are
also very present on the soya market as is another crusher, *Anderson
Clayton*, through its subsidiary based in Switzerland.

In oilseeds, *Unilever* very often takes a double position, through its
subsidiary Tropical Sales Products (but the latter often acts independently).

Finally in Europe, milling firms such as *Rank Hovis Mac Dougal,
Spillers* (member of the Dalgety group and which controls the French
trader *Lecureur*) often engage in trading activities.

Note also that the grain business has, through its renown, attracted
interests often far removed from the agro-food world: this is the case of
the oil group *Elf-Aquitaine* which, however, never concretized its
intentions.

But our, for the moment very general, description embracing grains
as a whole, deserves to be qualified in a few specific cases.

Some special products

● *Rice*

The world rice trade is probably one of the most dangerous that
exists: it has no futures market[25], international trade being marginal in
relation to world production (about 5%), and the integrity of the
operators is more than dubious. The rice market has two centres of
gravity: the United States, the world's biggest exporter, and Bangkok,
the hub of Asian trade. One of the principal axes of trade is the
Asia–Africa axis. In this very speculative trade, carried out on a
case-by-case basis and dominated by foreign Chinese interests, the
great traders have not managed to make their weight felt (except for
Continental perhaps and Cargill), and have consequently stepped
aside in favour of the small firms, centered, as often as not, around
individuals. Prominent among these 'rice adventurers' we find the
American firm *Connel Rice and Sugar* and the French firms *Action*
(owned by Boris Chabbert) and *Riz et Denrées* which are apparently
the largest in the world. The latter dominate notably the African trade

(where they have been installed for some time now in competition with *Ipitrade*, owned by J.-B. Doumeng, which has a great deal of political clout in a number of countries). Recently, Richco has been quite active in the rice trade too.

- *Manioc and its by-products*

This is a relatively new trade flow due to the development of animal feed inside the EEC and to certain 'loopholes' in the European grain regulations: the EEC guarantees in fact to its grain producers a price which is generally higher than that of the world market. And as it is short on secondary grain (especially corn), the EEC is obliged to import such grain and levy a tax on it to bring the price into line with European prices. But the European Community regulations did not foresee the growth which was to take place in grain substitution products such as manioc, or corn gluten feed (waste from the processing of corn). From the middle of the seventies, there was a phenomenal increase in imports of Thai manioc and later of American corn gluten feed. At the root of these trades we find a number of German traders (*Toppfer, Peter Cremer, Krohn*. . .) and Japanese capital which has been responsible for creating the necessary infrastructure in Thailand: 200,000 tonne ships ply the waters between Thailand and Rotterdam or Hamburg. At present, it seems that the German firms' stranglehold on these trades is still strong, although their importance tends to be on the decline[26].

- *Oilseeds*

If our general analysis can be applied to the oilseeds complex, then its specific peculiarities and the geography of its trades, would explain the presence of certain firms on the world level for given oils or fats.

Apart from the 'majors', the most important oilseed trader was until not long ago, *Noga Import-Export* in Geneva. Noga was established by Nessim David Gaon, a Sudanese-born Jew, naturalized Swiss[27]. Gaon considerably expanded his oil activities in the seventies but his mistake was to invest too heavily in Nigeria. In January 1984, the military which had taken power in a coup, prohibited all activity by Noga's Nigerian subsidiaries (which are responsible, inter alia, for 80% of the country's imports) and froze all payments due for work which Noga was carrying out at that time (construction of a hotel, ports, railways). This default posed serious financial problems for Noga: the firm had $600 million in liabilities with a number of banks). In June 1984, the group's activities in the trade sector had diminished considerably but the personal fortune of Nessim Gaon ($250 million) is enough reason to believe that the Nigerian affair will be but another episode in his adventurous career. . .

The field of oilseeds has moreover, also been the stage of quite a number of no less spectacular collapses: without going as far back as the crash of the Allied Crude Vegetable Oil Refining Corp. of the American, Tino de Angelis, in 1963, we could cite in France the problems already mentioned of the CNTA and the Marseilles trader *Frahuiles* in 1983, or the collapse in 1984 of the Parisian trader *Agroshipping*.

Among the other firms present in oilseeds, there are *Nidera* (Argentina), *C. Itoh* for palm-oil, as well as the Malaysian firm of British origin, *Sime Darby* (which bought out the British company Faure Fairclough in 1975), *Anderson Clayton* for cotton oil, *Interco* for copra. . .In the field of oilseeds, there is evidence of an increasing tendency to integrate trade and production (in palm oil especially), and to do more and more trade and crushing, as Cargill's and Bunge's strategies show.

Finally, we should perhaps mention the international meat trade, which in certain respects remains very similar to the grain–oilseeds complex. It is an ill-known sector, but one in which we can find the majors (Louis Dreyfus especially). In France there is *Biret*, founded in 1885 around an abattoir in the Vendée and linked to the cooperative world (ULN and *Bocaviande*); it marketed 60,000 tonnes in 1980 (turnover of one billion francs) and has branches in Argentina, Uruguay and in the Middle East. Other French companies are: *Socopa*, linked to the cooperative world and to *Interagra*, and *Sogeviandes* of the *Sucres et Denrées* group.

The activities of the majors in the business, unfailingly oriented downstream, and especially towards stock-breeding, should incite the latter (Cargill and MBPLX for example) to penetrate increasingly into the meat trade which still remains extremely atomized.

For dairy products, the situation on the world market is rather similar. International trade, outside the large, more or less integrated groups such as Nestlé or Carnation[28] is carried out by very small trading structures which only rarely have regular trade flows. For France and the EEC (which dominate the market with New Zealand), there is *Francexpa* (subsidiary of Louis Dreyfus), *Sogelait* (subsidiary of *Sucres et Denrées* which, in 1982, bought out 28% of the capital of *Unilait*, the firm which organizes the export activities of the French cooperatives) and the British firm *A.H. Philpot and Sons*. Founded in 1963, *Francexpa* (turnover of 1.6 billion francs in 1983) markets over 200,000 tonnes of dairy products per year and began its industrialization process around 1980.

We have now come to the end of this analysis of international trade in grain and oilseeds. This is probably one of the leading sectors of international commodity trade, one of the most concentrated, and one which has given birth to some of the most powerful firms in the business whose activities go well beyond trade, from industry to international finance.

But what we consider the most important is that the great grain shippers have become the main elements of dynamism in the chain at an international level, even at a time when many 'new' interests are trying to penetrate their oligopoly.

Chapter 8

THE SUGAR TRADE

Sugar is unique among agricultural products: it can be produced almost everywhere in the world since it can take the form of cane sugar produced in the tropics and sugar produced from beet in the temperate zones. Linked to a very western diet, sugar consumption has a tendency to grow steadily (20 kg per capita per annum as against 5 kg at the dawn of the century) but with radical disparities due less to shortages than to eating habits: over 40 kg per capita in the Western countries and less than 5 kg in Africa and Asia.

However, the general increase in consumption (through sectors such as beverages and confectionery) is gradually inducing a worldwide tendency to on-the-spot consumption and a relative — or perhaps even absolute — reduction in the share of the product entering international trade. From a foodstuff which has classically been a symbol of the unequal trade existing within the colonial framework, sugar is increasingly becoming a product of direct consumption in whose economy foreign trade has become gradually marginalized. Out of a world production which has varied in the past few years between 90 and 100 million tonnes, trade accounts for a mere 25–30 million tonnes; but the free market share shrinks even more when one subtracts the quantities handled under the Cuba–COMECON agreement (3 million tonnes), the sugar protocol of the Lomé Convention (1.4 million), the American import quotas (2 million) and various

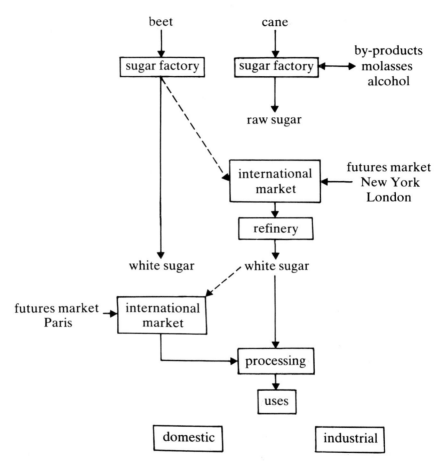

Figure 8.1 The sugar chain

long-term agreements. In fact, the free-market accounts for barely 18 million tonnes.

International trade in sugar can be carried out in two forms: white (or refined sugar), and brown (or raw sugar). This difference is the product of the entire colonial sugar heritage. In the 19th century, the cane sugar produced in the plantations of the West Indies was transported in its raw state for refining in the harbour refineries of Europe and North America. The same applied for German beet sugar which was initially refined in Great Britain. Gradually, however, technical innovations in beet sugar production enabled manufacturers to produce white sugar in the sugar factory itself. A parallel evolution was, however, not forthcoming in the case of cane, though not so much for technical reasons as for commercial and logistic ones: commercial first of all because the great sugar markets are raw sugar markets (New York and London), and because the producers of sugar cane have become accustomed to exporting raw sugar to the refining facilities existing in the countries (essentially in the United States, Canada, Great Britain and Japan). The logistic reason is that, for the time being, although raw sugar can be transported in bulk (since 1955), refined sugar has to be transported in bags, implying increased storage and handling costs.

At present, therefore, the sugar market is twofold: a market for raw sugar produced exclusively from sugar cane and a market for refined sugar produced from beet, or refined from cane and reexported.

The sugar trade

For a long time, the distinctive feature of the sugar trade has been its relative integration into the metropolitan refineries with the role of the middleman being limited to brokerage and representing the producer's interests (factors). Note, moreover, that this representative activity has survived in two important cases: Australia and South Africa, all of whose exports pass through the hands of two brokers: Czarnikow for Australia and Man for South Africa.

For the rest, international trade really appeared in the fifties. The position enjoyed by Cuba on the free market permitted the Cuban, Julio Lobo, to literally dominate the world sugar market (as a result of the effective control which Lobo exercised over Cuban exports). Castro's rise to power weakened Lobo's grip on the market. Having taken refuge in New York, his company could no longer maintain its hold on the market and collapsed in 1964–65. In Cuba he was replaced by a French trader of Moroccan origin, Maurice Varsano, whose firm,

Sucres et Denrées rapidly became one of the top world traders alongside the traditional Anglo-Saxon firms and the newcomers from refining (Tate and Lyle) or from international trade (Phibro and Marc Rich).

In the past few years, international sugar trade has opened up considerably with the appearance of many companies which have shaken the established hierarchies. In 1972, the British refining firm Tate and Lyle began to carry out large trading activities. From 1976, it was the turn of Philipp Brothers whose future seemed somewhat in jeopardy in 1981. Apart from these more or less perennial appearances, two firms dominate the sugar trade: Ed. and F. Man and *Sucres et Denrées*.

Table 8.1 The main international sugar traders

Ed. and F. Man (G.B.)	over 3 million tonnes
Sucres et Denrées (France)	over 3 million tonnes
(+ Westway, Comfin)	
Philip Brothers (U.S.A.)	
Tate and Lyle (G.B.)	
Woodhouse, Drake and Carey (G.B.)	
Golodetz (U.S.A.)	
Czarnikow Rionda (U.S.A.)	
C. Czarnikow (G.B.)	
Richco Sugar (Marc Rich)(Switzerland)	

• *Ed. and F. Man*

Founded in 1783, 'The House of Man', is one of the oldest trading houses in the business. At the outset a broker in sugar and a manufacturer of casks for transporting it[1], James Man's firm became more of a broker in tropical produce (a West Indian broker) in the 19th century before further specializing in a few products in the 20th century: sugar, cocoa, coffee, rum, tea and spices. During the fifties and sixties, the firm evolved gradually from broking to trade. It has, however, continued to carry out an important activity as a broker for certain products and has notably remained a broker for South African exports.

Although controlled by a company based in Bermuda, Man is still a partnership. Its main fields of activity are sugar (probably the major world trader handling more than three million tonnes, or 20% of world trade), coffee, cocoa and a few other products such as spices and orange juice. Moreover, Man recently tackled the oil trade (Premier Man) and the money market (Anderson Man, Tradman). The firm also owns interests in Brazilian coffee plantations (Agribahia). In 1983, the entire group generated profits of over £30 million with the aid of some 200 employees. In 1985 Man bought the Dutch molasses trader, Van Kinniken.

- *Sucres et Denrées*

The other major in the international sugar trade is of a totally different nature, and one which is strongly marked by the personality of its founder, Maurice Varsano (1916–1980).

Maurice Varsano began his professional activities in Morocco at the end of the thirties. After the Second World War, he became a wholesale merchant especially in tea and, on a secondary basis, in sugar. Around 1950, Morocco's sole supplier of sugar was Cuba and this brought Varsano into contact with the former and with its principal trader at the time, Julio Lobo, the 'Napoleon of sugar'.

In 1952 Maurice Varsano moved to Paris and developed what was until then no more than a small representative office: *Sucres et Denrées*. Until 1959, the company was struggling to survive. Varsano's big break came with the Cuban revolution: Cuba lost its guaranteed price quota to the United States and found itself isolated on the international trading scene. Varsano succeeded in gaining Fidel Castro's confidence and very soon *Sucres et Denrées* took charge of a portion of the island's foreign trade: exports of sugar and imports of foodstuffs (especially dairy products). With this base, *Sucres et Denrées* began a rapid development, creating privileged links with the Philippines and carving out a niche for itself on the import markets of Japan and the United States. In 1966 its subsidiary Amerop was the leading importer of sugar to the United States. Moreover, in 1968 *Sucres et Denrées* bought shares in a big sugar plantation firm in Puerto Rico, *Central Aguirre*, with a view to vertical integration: it was not a success. Later, *Sucres et Denrées* completed its network especially in Europe for trading refined sugar. Other products were gradually included in the range handled: molasses, meat, milk, coffee, cocoa and, finally, precious metals.

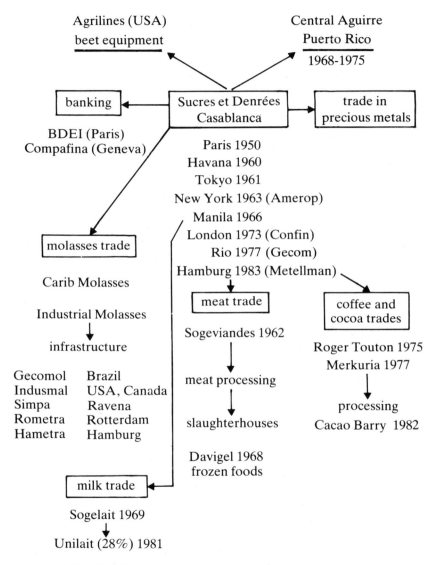

Figure 8.2 The diversification of *Sucre et Denrées* (dates are those on which activity began)

At the death of Maurice Varsano (in November 1980) the management of the firm (whose capital remains in the hands of the family and staff) was assumed by a board of directors composed of Max Benhamou, Elie Coriat and Jacques Bachelier, extended since to include Maurice's son, Serge Varsano.

At present, *Sucres et Denrées*, with a consolidated turnover of over 19.6 billion French francs represents:

– one of the major world traders in sugar (3 to 4 million tonnes per year) but without any major diversification within the chain (only one firm engaged in the distribution of beet production and irrigation equipment in the United States). *Sucres et Denrées* operates from Paris (especially for refined sugar), London (broking and activities across the Commonwealth area), New York (purchases and futures operations), from Rio de Janeiro. . .

– one of the main traders in molasses (see below).

– for a number of years now, a trader in cocoa and coffee. In 1975, *Sucres et Denrées* bought out the Bordeaux trader Touton, implicated in the bankruptcy of the Borie group. Then in 1977 it associated with a firm created in 1974, Merkuria, acquiring 50% of its capital. Finally in 1982, in association with the French cooperative group, *Sucre Union*, it took control of *Cacao Barry*, one of the world's main cocoa grinders[2] (which was experiencing serious financial difficulties at the time). and in 1985 it bought from Unilever its cocoa grinding subsidiary in Holland, Bensdorp, making the group the world's biggest cocoa grinder and strengthening its trading activities.

– finally the firm is an important operator on two very special markets: meat (since the take-over of the Goldschmidt team in 1967) and milk (since the days when it handled Cuba's imports). The arrival of *Sucres et Denrées* (under the name of *Sogeviandes*) on such a traditional and atomized sector as that of meat in France, not only rapidly ensured the group an important place in exports but, above all, encouraged it to develop an industrial strategy: abattoirs (Egletons and Fleurs), production of frozen minced-meat steaks and the distribution of frozen foods (purchase of 50% of the David company and creation of *Davigel*). In 1986, *Sucre et Denrées* sold off its interests in *Davigel* (which in fact was more and more orientated towards frozen foods and fish), but took over the second French meat packer, *Bocaviande*.

Table 8.2 The financial situation of *Sucres et Denrées* and its main subsidiaries in 1980 (in millions of French francs unless otherwise stated)

Consolidated turnover		12,072	
Net profits		28	
Consolidated equity		304	
Net group equity		183	

Main subsidiaries:		Turnover	Net Results
Sugar	*Compagnie Commerciale Sucres et Denrées*	5,932	6.20
	Westway Trading Corp.	652	0.40
	Comfin Co. Ltd.	112	0.10
Coffee–cocoa	Merkuria	950	1.80
	Roger Touton	546	1.30
	Cacao Barry (since 1982)	2,100	
Meats and frozen products	*Sogeviandes*	630	1.90
	David et Fils (50%) (sold 1986)	473	5.40
	Bocaviande (1986)		
Dairy products	*Sogelait*	265	3.70
Banks	BDEI		3.30
	Compafina (65%)		10.80

The entire development of *Sucres et Denrées* has been marked by the extraordinary personality of its founder, Maurice Varsano, one of the most remarkable post-war traders on the international scene. Trained on the job and highly pragmatic, Maurice Varsano (who, till the end of his days, had his office practically in the rooms of the trading department itself) had succeeded in creating, based upon his original colleagues from Morocco, a remarkable team managing a broad system of delegated powers; such was his personal charm that he was equally at ease with Fidel Castro in Havana as he was with Marcos in Manilla. Along with Ephraïrgulies (from Berisford), Ned Cook or Marc Rich, Maurice Varsano was probably one of the most striking personalities engaged in trade over the last twenty years[3]. At present one-third of the capital of *Sucres et Denrées* is retained by the Varsano family, one-third by the Roboh family and one-third by the staff.

- *Tate and Lyle*[4]

Of all the commodity trading firms existing today, Tate and Lyle is the only case which has not followed the development pattern which we have described: from an industrial firm it has evolved into a trading firm! Tate and Lyle was a British refining firm until, just after the war, it embarked on quasi vertical integration of the sugar chain: plantations in Jamaica, Trinidad, Belize, Zambia and Rhodesia, a sugar shipping firm, refineries in Great Britain, in Canada, in Rhodesia, manufacture of machinery for the production of sugar, trade and storage of molasses (see below). From 1965, decolonization and the evolution of industrial and shipping structures led Tate and Lyle to abandon (or to be abandoned by) a large number of its activities. The company succeeded, however, in creating new centres of profit in engineering, research and trade.

Tate and Lyle had a very special position on the sugar market, that of a large buyer with a monopoly in actuals on the London futures market and also present in Canada. From 1967 the various purchasing departments of the group's companies began to take positions on the market (through a subsidiary in Bermuda). The group's trading activities continued to grow especially from 1970–72 as a result of the sugar market boom. Tate and Lyle Trading sky-rocketed to the top of the international market (with three million tonnes) but had a reputation for being a rather speculative firm, which rarely carried out a complete trading operation, preferring to associate with other traders. At present it would appear that the sugar-trading activities of Tate and Lyle are rather limited as far as actuals are concerned but especially important in futures. From sugar, Tate and Lyle attempted to diversify, with varying degrees of success, into other products. Apart from molasses and alcohol (see above) the firm also dabbled in oils and fats (abandoned in 1973), seeds (abandoned in 1978), grain (purchase of Cook G.B. also with limited success) and finally in coffee where Tate and Lyle seems to have made a small breakthrough.

What deserves our attention is the place which trade has come to occupy in the group's profits: from 18% in 1973 it shot up to 61% in 1975 and 1976, and on to 77% in 1980, before declining again. Tate and Lyle thus demonstrates the paradox of a long-established industrial firm, with over 10,000 employees, three-quarters of whose profits are generated by the activities of a dozen traders!

- *Philipp Brothers*

We will come back later to what was, for a long time, the leading firm in international commodity trade. Sugar was the first agricultural product tackled by Philipp Bros in 1976. Thanks to its large financial assets, this company lost no time in becoming the world's leading trader with five million tonnes in 1980. In 1981, however, Phibro allegedly lost $50 to $80 million in sugar and its activities have, since then, been substantially reduced. In any event, a great deal of criticism has been levelled at Phibro by its competitors for its tactics, which consisted of throwing its weight around in order to compel recognition, and the company's spectacular growth seems to have been very artificial and costly.

Note that the other great metal trader, Marc Rich, also began to trade in sugar in 1980 but its activities seem to have tailed off in 1983.

- *The other Anglo-Saxon traders*

Among the other major trading firms, note the Golodetz group in the United States (also present on the metal, wood, and dairy products markets), Czarnikow-Rionda which no longer has any connections with the British firm C. Czarnikow[5], one of the last great sugar brokers (especially for Australia) whose trading activities are quite limited (less than one million tonnes). In London, there is also Woodhouse, Drake and Carey, and S. and W. Berisford. The Japanese firms (Mitsui and others), are not very active except in the provision of supplies for Japan. The Asian sphere is dominated in any event by the Chinese group, Kuok Brothers based in Malaysia and Hong Kong. In France, the *Jean Lion* group, founded in 1934, specializes in refined sugar (turnover in 1983, 1.3 billion francs).

All in all, the sugar trade appears rather concentrated around three or four large firms, which, although not very industrialized, have diversified considerably into other products.

The molasses trade

Molasses is the main by-product of sugar. It is a viscous liquid with a high sugar content used mainly in the production of animal feedstocks and in the distillation of alcohol. Of a world production estimated at 30 million tonnes, international trade handles 6 to 7 million tonnes. Given the cumbersome nature of the product as well as its low unit value ($100 per tonne at the end of 1983), traders have to own the required storage and transport infrastructure. The great logistic problem of molasses is the difficulty implied in valorizing a product which is often practically useless at the production stage. Trade in molasses is therefore very concentrated and specialized, with one firm responsible for 50% of the trade.

● *United Molasses*

A subsidiary of Tate and Lyle since 1965, United Molasses has dominated the world molasses market since the thirties, at present trading from 3 to 3.5 million tonnes per year. United Molasses has branches worldwide as well as storage capacity (almost 800,000 liquid tonnes) both in the producing countries (Africa, South America, Mauritius. . .) and on the main import market (Pacific Molasses and Knappen Molasses in the United States). On the other hand, United Molasses has gradually dismantled its molasses tanker fleet and has diversified instead into the creation of storage installations for liquids.

● *Socomel–Carib Molasses*

Sucre et Denrées' molasses activities were born of a joint venture with the Cuban State in 1970 — Carib Molasses[6]. Its control over Cuban exports subsequently put *Sucres et Denrées* on the path to an incredible growth, notably after it had bought out and American firm, Industrial Molasses, in 1968. Like United Molasses, *Sucres et Denrées* saw fit to create an entire logistic infrastructure and even invested in animal feed in the United States.

● *The other traders*

The third-ranking world trader is a Dutch firm, Van Ginniken, now part of the Man group. Other operators in this sector are the major grain traders like Cargill, Louis Dreyfus (associated in France with United Molasses). . .

Table 8.3 The main molasses trading firms

Tate and Lyle	United Molasses (50%)	3 to 3.5 million tonnes
	Pacific Molasses	
Sucres et	Socomel	2
Denrées	Carib Molasses	
	Industrial Molasses	
Ed.and F. Man	Van Ginniken	1
Cargill		
Namolco (Switzerland)		

Thus molasses is in all probability one of the few products which absolutely require the setting up of a storage infrastructure. The molasses trade is therefore characterized by low competitiveness and rather constant margins despite the absence of a futures market — a situation which certainly does not hold true for the alcohol trade.

The alcohol trade

There are two main means of producing alcohol: the distilling of agricultural products (notably molasses) [alcohol from fermentation] and the processing of hydrocarbons [synthetic alcohol]. World production is estimated at 88 million hectolitres, 8 to 10 million of which are traded. The alcohol trade is probably one of the most secretive in the world of international trade. Its main characteristic is the dominant position occupied by one of the Louis Dreyfus subsidiaries[7], SOFECIA (70% of the market). In 1968–1972 Tate and Lyle broke this quasi-monopoly by creating a subsidiary in Geneva (Unalco). This turned out to be a failure and the British firm lost £500,000 in Argentina in 1971 and another £500,000 in 1978 by liquidating its stock (which it sold out to Sofecia). Alcohol therefore presents the curious case of a monopoly–monopsony held by a trading firm!

Chapter 9

THE COFFEE AND COCOA TRADES

Coffee and cocoa are two products whose economic circuits are sufficiently linked for us to treat them together: they are produced in the same tropical zones (and the same countries, especially Brazil and the Ivory Coast), they share similar consumption patterns (beverages, although coffee has an 'indispensable' character which cocoa does not have), are often processed and distributed by the same firms (Nestlé, General Foods), and finally, they face the same obstacles in the stabilization of an international market on which international agreements are more or less efficient.

In trade, coffee and cocoa have been historically linked within the group known as 'tropical produce' handled by specialized traders and brokers in most of the large Western countries. Of course, the big operators subsequently tended towards specialization in one main product, but in general, coffee and cocoa were maintained, whenever possible, together: a trading team stationed in Africa can deal simultaneously both in coffee and in cocoa (at no added logistic cost). In both cases, traders have also had a tendency to invest in the different stages of production and in the first or second stages of processing. It should therefore come as no surprise to the reader to find a number of familiar names recurring throughout this analysis: Gill and Duffus, ACLI, Jacobs–Interfood and of course, *Nestlé*.

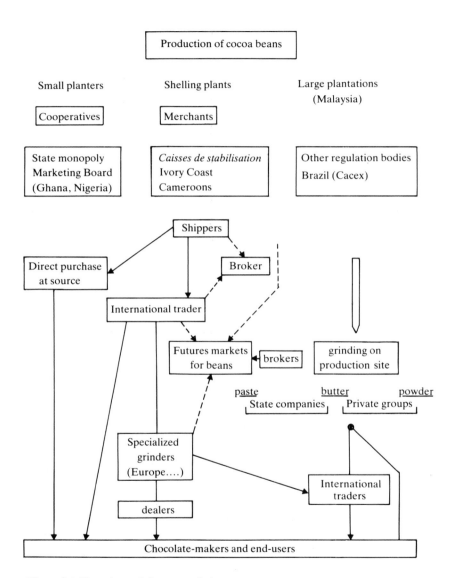

Figure 9.1 Flow-chart of the cocoa chain

The cocoa trade

Cocoa production begins with the splitting of the cocoa pod to release the beans which, once roasted, are ready to enter international trade. Nowadays, however, more and more producing countries have been striving to increase their share of the added value of their commodities and tend to export semi-finished products (butter, powder, paste) which at present occupy no small place in international trade. In the long-run this evolution could threaten the position of the large grinders, traditionally installed in the consumer markets in Northern Europe and in the United States.

Historically, the cocoa trade was very characteristic of the barter economy. The production of cocoa, very much centred around Africa was, and still is, mainly the occupation of small-scale farmers. The trading posts of a number of European companies would buy up the produce and transport it to the coast from where it would be shipped to Europe. A number of firms were active in this trade, among them: John Holt, the SCOA, the *Compagnie Française du Niger*, to mention only the most important. When, after the Second World War, the colonial governments, and later the independent governments which succeeded them, decided to set up Marketing Boards and stabilization funds, these companies most often discontinued all activity and were replaced — on the national level, and with an infinite variety of bodies from country to country — by shippers or transit agents accredited by the local governments. On the international scene, it was the era of the emergence of a small number of firms till then present in the trade of semi-finished products (Gill and Duffus), or in brokerage.

At present, cocoa is probably one of the sectors where concentration is at its most intense : three firms account for three-quarters of all trade. There is no denying that this extreme concentration is matched by a significant concentration of supply (through the stabilization funds and marketing boards) and of the processing industries whose links with trade cannot be overlooked.

Most firms trading in cocoa are also present in the product's industrial concatenation (since 1940 in the case of Gill and Duffus). Over the past few years, they have even extended their investments to the grinding industry which they now control to a considerable degree. They have not however, gone as far as chocolate production. It must be noted that at this level, we are entering the sector of high-consumption products for which a totally different structure is required.

On the other hand, a similar trend in semi-finished goods recently showed a marked acceleration (see Table 9.1).

As can be seen, save for the chocolate manufacturers who generally work in a vertically integrated context, most of the independent grinders have been taken over by trading firms: this trend is to be observed, not only in the traditional grinding activities on the production sites, but also in the new set-ups in the producing countries[1].

Table 9.1 The main groups engaged in the grinding of cocoa beans

Grinders		
Gill and Duffus	Joanes (Brazil)	23,000 t.
	British Cocoa Mills	15,000 t.
	49% West African Mills (Ghana)	35,000 t.
S. and W. Berisford	Wessanen (Holland, 1980)	40 to 45,000 t.
	Kascho (Berlin)	
General Cocoa	Gerkens (Holland, 1972)	10,000 t.
(Golodetz family)	Stuhrmann (Holland, 1972)	10,000 t.
	11.25% Chadler (Brazil)	
	with Hersheys (U.S.A.)	
W.R. Grace	De Zaan (Holland)	64,000 t.
	Ambrosia (U.S.A.)	30,000 t.
	Allied Cocoa Industries	36,000 t.
	(Singapore, 1984)	
Unilever	Bensdorp (Holland and FRG, 1985)	
Sucres et Denrées	*Cacao Barry* (France,	
	Cameroons, Ivory Coast,	
	Brazil, 1982)	
Barretto de Araujo		
(Brazil)	linked to Lewis and Peat	40,000 t.
Hamester (FRG)		25,000 t.
Monheim (Van Hou-		
ten–Trumpf) (FRG)		30,000 t.
General Foods (U.S.A.)	(Walter Baker – U.S.A.)	40,000 t. (1974)
Chocolate manufacturers	(total utilization of beans)	
Herschey's (U.S.A.)		80,000 t.
Cadbury Schweppes (G.B.)		80,000 t.
Rowntree MacIntosh (G.B.)		70,000 t.
Mars (U.S.A., G.B., Holland)		110,000 t.
Nestlé		150,000 t.

● *Gill and Duffus*

The most important international trader in cocoa is — a fact which is rare among commodity trading companies — a limited company quoted on the London Exchange.

Table 9.2 The main international cocoa traders

Country	Group	Name of specia- lized subsidiaries	Tonnage traded
G.B.	Dalgety	Gill and Duffus Ltd, Pacol	200 to 300,000 t.
G.B.	S. and W. Berisford	J.H. Rayner	200 to 300,000 t.
U.S.A.–G.B.	Philipp Brothers	Cocoa Merchants	200 to 300,000 t.
France	*Sucre et Denrées*	Merkuria, Westway Roger Touton	160,000 t.
U.S.A.	Golodetz	General Cocoa	
U.S.A.	ACLI–Cargill	ACLI Cocoa	
G.B.	Paterson Simons Ewart		
France	*Tardivat*		
G.B.	Ed. and F. Man	Holco	

A family undertaking founded in 1907, Gill and Duffus went public in 1950 and remained under the direction of one of the descendants of the founding families until 1985, when, having suffered heavy losses during the previous years (with a turnover reaching £1.89 billion in 1985), it agreed to a £125 million take-over bid by the agro-food group Dalgety.

The cocoa trade began, for Gill and Duffus, in 1929 and grew astronomically from 1962 after the purchase of another cocoa trader, Pacol Ltd. Around 1975, the Gill and Duffus group was by far the world's leading cocoa trader with tonnages amounting to almost one half of world trade. Since then its position as a trader has eroded somewhat and it is likely that its 'share' of the market has also diminished.

The company's strength lies in the size of its network and the contacts which it maintains with 'countries of origin' (the Ivory Coast through the shipper, CAPA). From 1947, in fact, the company set up operations in Ghana and in Brazil and, in the course of time, proceeded to develop grinding activities. Gill and Duffus has notably

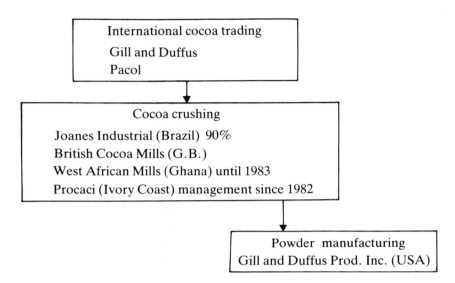

Figure 9.2 The Gill and Duffus group in cocoa

set up an entire information collection network which endows it with the most sophisticated statistical service in the entire cocoa world.

Moreover, the ‚Gill and Duffus Cocoa Market Report is one of the leading authorities on the cocoa market. It is a relatively independent service which provides forecasts on harvests and on the world production–consumption balance on a bi-monthly basis. Gill and Duffus, nicknamed ‘Gill and Bluffuss’ by some, has often been accused of manipulating its information to improve its positions on the market. Most people, however, do not think this possible; the very credibility of the report hinges on its objectivity and judging from the statements of even the company’s sharpest competitors, the statistics published by Gill and Duffus are the most reliable available on the market today. Nevertheless, it is obvious that having access to certain forecasts before the rest of the market presents an undeniable advantage.

From the trading point of view, Gill and Duffus, and Pacol are totally independent and are run like two completely distinct firms. In fact, in the cocoa trade itself, Pacol is more important than Gill and Duffus. The two companies operate in competition with each other, with a limited amount of task-sharing: Gill and Duffus Inc. in the United States, Pacol in Paris and in the franc-pegged area for example.

As far as trade is concerned, the group is managed in the classical manner with almost automatic hedging on the futures and money markets, as well as a fixed ceiling on open positions for each company or company group. There seems to be no centralization between Gill and Pacol even though their managing executives are always informed of the positions held by the entire group. At any given moment the maximum position which the group may have open is 10,000 tonnes (5,000 at most from London) — a rather small quantity which demonstrates the amount of control exercised. This control had been further tightened since it was discovered that the Hong Kong subsidiary had lost £7 million because it had failed to ensure an adequate follow-up of its operations.

The firm's processing activities go back a long way (Ghana, Brazil, Great Britain) but they have grown considerably since 1980 (development in the United States, rumours pointing to the acquisition of the Dutch butter producer, De Zaan, in 1981, although the financial end of the negotiations with the owner, W.R. Grace, came to nothing; assuming the management of PROCACI (Abidjan), which until then had had very close ties to the Interfood group). The degree of integration displayed by the firms varies: although British Cocoa Mills and Procaci are managed (especially on the purchase–sales level) from London, Joanes, on the other hand, is totally independent. In 1986, Gill and Duffus lost its management contract in Ivory Coast.

Gill and Duffus' efforts to diversify into different products have met with little success; since the group was born in the spice trade this department has, of course, lost none of its importance. Pacol and Gill and Duffus are also big traders in rubber and coffee respectively, but the firm's diversification into chemicals and non-ferrous metals misfired. In 1982, Gill and Duffus resumed activities in grain and sugar (Geneva and New York) and continued along the trading path by becoming a broker on the new futures markets in London for oil and financial assets and by setting up operations in Chicago (Agra-Trading Co.).

But Gill and Duffus' strength resides, without a doubt, in cocoa although its position is now weaker than it was a few years ago. This decline was undoubtedly due to the arrival of new competitors on the market (especially Berisford) but also to errors of management and more generally to the many problems encountered by a firm which still had its family structures, trying to adapt to the imperatives of risk management on increasingly uncertain markets. The merger with Dalgety might give it a new impetus.

Table 9.3 The Gill and Duffus accounts at 31.12.1982 (in 1984 the turnover was £1.89 billion for a taxable profit of £17.1 million)

Turnover	(£1 billion)
shared between:	
(clients' nationality, in %)	
– Great Britain	16.70
– Europe	28.30
– North America	50.10
– Rest of the world	4.90
– pre-tax profits	£12.9 million
Cash flow	£16.8 million
Cash flow after extraordinary operations	£19.6 million
– Working capital	£87 million
– Total financial costs of loans under 5 years	£13.9 million

● *S. and W. Berisford*

Like Gill and Duffus, Berisford is a publicly-quoted firm whose capital is also divided among more than 17,000 shareholders[2]. At the outset, Berisford was a 'domestic' sugar trader based in Manchester, and had somewhat diversified its activities, becoming involved in the British agri-foostuffs industry.

Berisford's international development coincided with the arrival of Ephraïm Margulies at its helm. He is another legendary personality in the trading world (a practising Jew, wild horses could not get him to trade on a Saturday!) with a solid reputation as a daring operator who has no qualms about sitting tight on a very large open position.

Under the baton of Margulies, himself trained in the cocoa trade, Berisford (under the name 'Rayner') incisively tackled this market, and landed the 'contract of the century' in 1980, (100,000 tonnes which were stored by the Ivory Coast). The Rayner–Berisford connection is seen with mixed feelings on the cocoa market: there is general agreement that it has a high percentage of speculative activities both in actuals and in paper; there has been mention of numerous cases of more or less successful squeezes, especially on the May due dates. Rayner also had an unsavoury reputation as far as delivery of actuals was concerned, often demanding changes in the date or the quality.

Table 9.4 The S. and W. Berisford group in cocoa

| *Cocoa trading* |
| J.K.Rayner (G.B.) |
| Lonray (USA) |
| Continaf (G.B.) |
| *Cocoa transformation* |
| Wessanen (Holland) |
| Kaschokakao (Berlin) |

But in a few years Berisford's position on the cocoa market improved to such an extent that certain observers believe that, with its direct (Continaf) and indirect subsidiaries, Berisford has managed, in the interval, to wrench the top position in the cocoa trade from Gill and Duffus. This claim is very difficult to substantiate and is in any event of little import. Nevertheless, for a firm which started from nothing in 1970, the growth of the group has truly been inpressive.

Berisford's strategy in cocoa has been an industrial one: the acquisition of Wessanen in the Netherlands (after the agro-foodstuffs group went bankrupt) and the development of *Kascho-Kakao* in Berlin.

But the firm's most spectacular growth has not taken place in cocoa but in other commodities, particularly in sugar. Since 1980, the Berisford group has been very active in the sugar market and in July 1982, after a stock-exchange battle which lasted for more than a year, it spent over £250 million to acquire the only British sugar producer, The British Sugar Corporation (output of 1.1 million tonnes of sugar), driving up the item 'fixed assets' from £43 to £387 million! Berisford is also present in coffee (plantation in Papua New Guinea), dried fruits, tea, oilseeds and rubber (since 1982) and finally in non-ferrous metals (but mainly as a broker on the London Metal Exchange).

Table 9.5 The Berisford accounts (30.9.1982) (note that in 1982 the chairman received a salary of £101,000 plus commissions (£2 to £5 million)

– Turnover	£2.727 billion	
– Pre-tax profits	£54.7 million	
shared between:	Turnover (£ million)	gross profit
international trade	1,788	40
British Sugar Corporation (from its acquisition, i.e. three months before)	90	13.50
food industry and metal reprocessing	842	10
financial and real-estate activities	7	1
geographical distribution (%)		
Great Britain	35.80	
Europe	35.80	
North America	22.60	
Rest of the world	5.80	
– Working capital	£105 million	
– Cash flow	£62 million	
– Financial charges (for less than 5 years)	£29.8 million	

Apart from the B.S.C., Berisford also controls a few industrial (metal reprocessing) and foodstuff activities (canning plants, meat products, spices, wool and leather. . .).

The picture did seem quite rosy until 1985. However, the battle over the B.S.C. had exhausted the commodity trader which could no longer bear the financial burden. Early in 1986, Margulies announced his intention to sell Berisford. The idea was that the new owner would keep the B.S.C. and sell back the trading rooms to Margulies and his team, who could then go private. After minor skirmishes, two offers (at the time of writing) have been submitted to Britain's Monopolies Commission: one from Feruzzi and the other from Tate and Lyle. Whoever won, the Berisford trading comnpany would regain its freedom, but would probably find itself operating on a much smaller scale than before 1982.

- *Cocoa Merchants*

Cocoa Merchants was a relatively prosperous British firm when, in 1982, its owners sold out to Philipp Brothers.

At the time, Anthony Weldon, one of the leading figures in the cocoa world, with a reputation for having excellent contacts with the countries of origin (Brazil, Africa), was at the helm of Cocoa Merchants. Phibro's acquisition of the company was partly due to the former's desire to acquire Weldon's services.

Cocoa Merchants is rather special in that its directors insist on making a trade margin of 1%. Moreover it refuses to do intra-trade business. The firm gives a great deal of importance to its contacts in the countries of origin and with the consumers. Cocoa Merchants is a shipper in Brazil and in Malaysia and has contacts with a shipper in the Cameroons. It is the major exporter of Malaysian cocoa (with purchases going up to five years in advance). It is also the main supplier of the USSR and Poland.

Cocoa Merchants is the exception among the large firms in that it has no industrial investments. This is manifestly the philosophy of the firm, and one which is shared, moreover, by Philipp Brothers.

But at the beginning of 1984, Cocoa Merchants, heavily engaged in South-East Asia, was dealt a hard blow by the bankruptcy of Allied Cocoa Industries in Singapore. Cocoa Merchants was forced to make a deposit of £5 million for exceptional losses and Anthony Weldon resigned. This episode demonstrates once again the problems encountered by Philipp Bros in its diversification endeavours (sugar, grain. . .).

- *Sucres et Denrées*

Sucres et Denrées' arrival in the cocoa trade is rather recent, going back to the seventies when it bought Merkuria, a small coffee and cocoa trading firm of Dutch origin. In 1977 it bought Touton, a Bordeaux trader with close links to Africa and in 1980, *Cacao Barry,* second cocoa grinder in the world (turnover in 1983, 2 billion francs)[3].

Since 1977, *Sucres et Denrées* has sought to establish a position on the cocoa market by paying particular attention to the development of its investments in the United States (Westway–Merkuria) and in

Figure 9.3 The *Sucres et Denrées* group in cocoa

London (Comfin). The group still appears to be somewhat heterogeneous and continues to have a strong presence in French-speaking
Africa (shipper in the Ivory Coast). With the purchase of *Cacao Barry*
— which has lost none of its independence in the process — the group
has grown to a significant size. But curiously enough, *Sucres et Denrées*
has never been counted among the major traders by the London trading
circles (most likely because, in cocoa, the firm's activities are dispersed
among many names the link between which is not always obvious).

● *General Cocoa*

General Cocoa is a subsidiary of the Golodetz group. Little is known
about the Golodetz except that they were a Russian trading family

which at some point in time had settled in New York. The family must have scattered considerably over the years since General Cocoa New York is not owned by the same interests as General Cocoa Amsterdam, the latter being by far the more important. It was General Cocoa Amsterdam which bought out the cocoa butter producers, Gerkens and Stuhrman, around 1972 and General Cocoa Paris is also a subsidiary of the Amsterdam company.

Outside the Netherlands, the General Cocoa group (or groups) has reportedly experienced a decline in activities over the past few years.

- *Holco*

Until 1981, Holco was the British subsidiary of Internatio-Muller, a large Dutch international trading company formerly based in Java.

In 1981, Internatio disengaged itself from the trading sector and sold Holco to Ed. and F. Man, the world's leading sugar trader. Man — which is still a partnership — thereby gained a foothold in the cocoa trade. Holco is a medium-size firm with a reputation for having a rather large — and speculative — presence on the market.

Other important traders are Volkart, *André*, through its Marseilles subsidiary, and the French–Ivory Coast group *Tardivat.* . .

- *The downstream firms*

It is rather difficult for the users to make a distinction between their genuine supply requirements and their trading activities. A firm like *Interfood* (Switzerland, the Tobler and Suchard brands) which recently merged with the Swiss roaster, Jacobs, has an indisputably large trading activity. The same goes for *Nestlé* and for Herschey (United States) or Mars (United States). At the end of the seventies, the British firm Rowntree MacIntosh almost disappeared as a result of badly controlled speculation on the cocoa market.

The influence of the downstream — and even upstream — structures on trade, though substantial for cocoa, is even greater for coffee where trading structures seem to be much weaker.

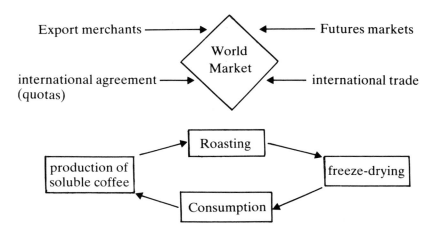

Figure 9.4 Flow-chart of the coffee chain

The coffee trade

Produced often in the same geographic zones as cocoa (South America, Africa), coffee also goes through a first processing stage on the spot (processing of berries) before being exported. For technical reasons, roasting can really only be carried out in the consumer zones. The prospects of making soluble coffee, entertained by a number of producing countries, have so far not been able to to get off the ground (a maximum of 10% of Brazil's exports) owing to the tightness of the consumer markets which are dominated by a few large roaster–distributors (General Foods, *Nestlé*). On the other hand, the consumption patterns for coffee are very different from those of cocoa since the former has come to occupy an essential place in the Western diet and since the consumer brooks no substitution.

The historical evolution of the coffee trade is identical to that of cocoa and more often than not both products are handled by the very same operators. The main difference can be seen in terms of a downstream concentration of the coffee industry within an oligopoly of specialized firms and a few other firms which — thanks to their marketing approach — are present on most of the consumer markets. Because of the power wielded by these firms, the coffee trade has remained much more dispersed than that of coffee. Futhermore, world trade in coffee has long been 'regionalized', especially around the United States–Brazil and Colombia axis which, even today, promotes direct relations.

The links existing between trade and roasting vary a lot. In fact, it would not be exaggerated to assume that all roasters, which do not engage in direct distribution to the public at large, engage in trade (Rothfos is a case in point). On the other hand, firms which are traders in the strict sense of the term, have pratically never gone on to the roasting sector although they have often integrated gathering activities (especially in Brazil).

Table 9.6 The main coffee traders

Company	Group	Estimates of the share of world trade		Share of US imports in 1978	
		%	million bags	%	million bags
Rothfos		10	5		
ACLI	Cargill	10		7.10	1.40
Volkart		5	3	2	0.40
Jack Aron	Goldman-Sachs			7.60	1.50

(For the American import figures: *Uker's International Tea and Coffee Buyer's Guide* 1982–83).

Table 9.7 The main coffee roasters and distributors

U.S.A.	market share in 1983	beans and ground coffee	soluble coffee
	General Foods (Maxwell)	34.30	44.30
	Procter and Gamble	24.90	17.60
	Nestlé–Hills	7.40	25.80
Europe	Douwe Egberts (65% Consolidated Foods) Van Nelle (Standard Brands) Jacobs–Interfood (controls *Jacques Vabre. . .*) *Nestlé* General Foods (Legal, Maxwell. . .) Eduscho		

● *ACLI*

For a long time ACLI has dominated the international scene in coffee, and even if recent events have forced it to reduce its activities in this sector, we think it logical to mention it in first place. The founders of ACLI were the Israel family, French and German Jews, who started a coffee trading business in New Orleans (Leon Israel Bros.) in 1898, and another firm in New York in 1913, A.C. Israel Commodity Company. In the meantime they had expanded to Brazil (1908). It was not until 1971 that the two companies fused to form ACLI International. The chairman was A.C. Israel (ACE) who had been chairman of the famous Wall Street commission house, Bache, until 1966 and also controls the family fortune (estimated at some $40 million). He also holds, among other posts, the chairmanship of Peoples Drugstores, a large chain of stores and pharmacies in the United States. Before long, ACLI had extended its activities to South America, especially Brazil (where the Israel family owns 4,000 hectares of land) and Colombia (where the *Compania Cafeteria de Manizales* controls six roasting factories and is one of the three largest private exporters of Colombian coffee). ACLI is also present in the cocoa, rubber, soya, sugar and fertilizer sectors (it was one of the world's leading traders in fertilizers) and shipping brokerage (ACLI Marine). All in all the firm used to employ some 2,000 persons.

But in 1980, it seeems that the firm suffered a number of serious failures. Although it is difficult to affirm anything with certainty, it seems that ACLI's problems began with the crash of the silver market due to the manipulations of the Hunt Brothers. ACLI, associated with Naji Nahas, a Lebanese financier operating in Brazil who had also been affected, had apparently tried to get back on its feet and had instead increased its losses on the coffee, cocoa and sugar markets. There has been talk of overall losses in the region of $85 million. It therefore came as no surprise to learn of the firm's take-over in the summer of 1981, by a Wall Street firm, Donaldson, Lufkin and Jenrette (DLJ, the sixth largest publicly-quoted financial firm), until then supported in part by Saudi capital. In return, the Israel family received $22 million worth of DLJ shares, making it the largest shareholder with 18% of the capital, and A.C. Israel became vice-president of DLJ. There is every reason to believe that the firm had, in fact, collapsed: the sugar and soya departments and later ACLI Marine, were closed and in coffee, ACLI lost so much ground that in the summer of 1982 it was no longer considered an important factor on the market; finally, A.C. Israel was forced to abandon his executive functions in the spring of the following year.

The (totally relative) 'fall' of ACLI is another illustration of the extreme volatility of trading activities (which always, whether one wants it or not, have a speculative dimension). It is no less an illustration of the precariousness of the classifications and percentages which we are striving to present in these pages: The 'ACLI empire' was worth no more than $22 million when it collapsed!

But the ACLI story did not finish there. The union with DLJ was less than harmonious, at least as far as the trade sector was concerned. In May 1984, it was learned that DLJ was planning to cede three of the ACLI group companies to Cargill: ACLI Coffee, ACLI Cocoa and ACLI Ores, retaining, however, the commission house department. Cargill paid an estimated $85 million for its ticket to the coffee and cocoa trades, the cementing of its networks in South America and Africa. We can do no more than wait and see if Cargill–ACLI will manage to recover its position as a major coffee trader.

- *Rothfos*

Bernard Rothfos, from Hamburg, started out as a roaster and gradually developed activities in the trading sector. Although, by the autumn of 1982, it had become the world's leading trader, the roasting activity remains an essential part of operations. In 1980 Rothfos had a turnover of 1.5 million DM and handled 5 million bags of coffee.

- *Gebrüder Volkart*

In 1851, two brothers from Winterthur in Switzerland, Salomon and Johann Georg Volkart, set up a firm to trade with British India and opened an office in Bombay. For a century they pursued their activities, trading with India and Sri Lanka. Independence and the Indian government's declared will to promote the development of local capitalism, caused them to progressively limit their activities on the sub-continent[4]. Since then Volkart has become an international trader for three products in particular: coffee, cocoa, and cotton, on whose markets it ranks among the best in the business. Volkart handled about 3 million bags in 1980, that is, 5% of world trade. Depending on the year, the group's turnover ranges from 2 to 3 billion Swiss francs.

- *Jack Aron*

This American company which was founded in 1898, deals in two distinct products: on the one hand precious metals and on the other, coffee, for which it is one of the principal American operators. In 1981, it was also bought out by a Wall Street firm, Goldman Sachs, essentially for its activities on the markets for gold, other precious metals and foreign exchange.

Other trading companies active in coffee are: Gill and Duffus–Pacol, Berisford–Rayner, Woodhouse Drake and Carey, Man, Tardivat (France) which owns a coffee engineering subsidiary (Gerico), and numerous firms from the North of Germany. Among the relatively rare newcomers we could mention, apart from *Sucres et Denrées* with Merkuria, Tate and Lyle, which, after having bought out and then resold 30% of the shares of a New Orleans trader (International Coffee Corporation), still owns a plantation in Brazil and controls a Spanish trading firm, *Intra-café*. Finally, next to the international traders, we must mention the existence of numerous export firms (in South America), such as the *Tristao* group in Brazil[5], and import companies (especially in the United States).

- *Upstream and downstream activities*

Among the producers, it is probably in South America that the awareness of the vagaries of the international market is the greatest. As early as the inter-war period, producers from the state of Sao Paulo had organized themselves and taken the unilateral decision to limit supply on the international market. In Brazil especially, powerful 'cooperatives'[6] have arisen. One of them, *Coper Sucar,* controlled by the Attala family (until 1980) did not hesitate to buy out a New Orleans importer, Hills Brothers, in 1978 (resold to *Nestlé* in 1984). Liem Sioe Liong, the Chinese group from Indonesia, paid $38 million in 1983 for the Dutch company Hagemeyer, one of whose principal activities was trade in coffee and particularly the import of Indonesian coffee into the United States[7]. On another level, we must mention the efforts made internationally to create a marketing body — and in particular one able to operate on the futures markets — common to all South American producers; first came *Café Mundial,* then *Pancafé,* the arm of the famous Bogota group from 1979 to 1980.

Most of the large roaster-distributors engage in trade either directly or indirectly , but their activities in the sector are difficult to identify as such: this is the case with Nestlé, Procter and Gamble (through American Coffee and Folger), Douwe Egberts, Jacobs (which amalgamated in 1982 with the Swiss chocolate producer Interfood) and Brooke Bond Liebig.

International trade in coffee is clearly much more 'open' than that of many other commodities. When all is said and done it would not be unjustified to state that trade in coffee is marginal, given the dynamism of the exporters (especially South American) and the power of the roasters and the packer-distributors — a set-up which only serves to make it more speculative as recent movements amply illustrate.

Coffee is, in the final analysis, a counter-argument to our thesis that international trade has really developed only where there were no forces capable of assuming its function.

Chapter 10

THE NON-FERROUS METAL TRADE

Compiling an analytic table of the ore and metal trades is more problematic than devising one for grains, for example. There are many reasons for this: first of all the large number of products and substances involved (Philipp Brothers trades in over 150 different items), each corresponding to a specific market, reflecting a greater or lesser degree of trade and, within the latter, the particular positions of the different firms ranging from a giant like Philipp Brothers to private firms which are well placed on the market of a specific minor metal. Furthermore, in this instance, the frontiers of trade appear particularly blurred: upstream, the great mining companies which are still important in the Western countries, but which now only have an engineering and advisory role in the developing countries, have, for the most part, integrated their trading activities which are by no means easy to distinguish from their principal activity. Downstream, a number of metallurgists have been drawn to trade because of their processing activity.

Trade in metals is therefore very heterogenous and the role of trade within these economies, extremely variable. In most cases, it has remained more of an instrument than an agent. There is no denying its indispensable role; yet, given the economic and financial powers acting upstream and downstream (and although they are beyond comparison with those in the agro-foodstuffs chains), it has not been called upon to

J

act as a dynamism-inducing factor within the product-system (except perhaps in specific sectors such as reprocessing and transport logistics. . .). On the contrary, trade has very often been integrated by firms up and downstream. For this reason the classification which we are about to propose for the ore and metal trade, is rather special:

– a small number of large firms covering the entire world and a large range of products: Philipp Brothers, Marc Rich, Associated Metals and Minerals . . .;
– the specialized subsidiaries of the large mining (Billiton, Noranda, Péchiney) or metallurgic firms (*Metallgesellschaft*, Amalgamated Metals. . .);
– a very large number of small firms active in a specific product or on a specific market.

But this 'classification' needs to be put into perspective to take into account the differences existing between the markets for metals and those for ores:

– on the one hand, there are the metal 'majors' quoted on the futures market, on the LME or COMEX (copper, tin, lead, zinc, silver, and to a lesser extent, aluminium and nickel);
– the so-called minor metals on the mostly tight free market often dominated by producer oligopolies;
– a few extremely bulky products which are often subject to direct negotiations (coal, iron ore, manganese, phosphates);
– finally precious metals.

The heterogeneity of both the operators, and the product handled makes it difficult to go beyond a description of the broad structural outlines. We shall therefore restrict ourselves deliberately to this type of approach without going into a detailed description of any given market.

The major traders

One firm symbolizes more than any other both the metal trade and far beyond it, the power and the limits of international commodity trading — Philipp Brothers, the largest trader in the world, in terms of turnover.

- Philipp Brothers

Philipp Brothers, founded in Hamburg by two brothers, Oscar and Julius Philipp, started out as a metal trading firm around the middle of the 19th century. At the beginning of this century they moved to England where they bought a small steel firm, Derby and Co. In 1914, a cousin, Siegfried Bendheim, founded a subsidiary in New York which, before long, was to become the group's parent company as a result of the First World War. Philipp Bros developed both in America and in Europe remaining under the direction of the founding families (generally Jews of German origin): Siegfried Bendheim was succeeded by Siegfried Ullman and, after the war and until very recently, by Ludwig Jesselsson.

However, the history of the firm — and of the different names which it has had — has been much more eventful than the mere growth of a metal trading firm would normally be. In 1960, when a number of the company's partners were seeking to recover liquidities, the Lazard bank proposed an amalgamation with a public company: Mineral and Chemical Corp. of America (specialized in non-metallurgic ores such as kaolin). The main shareholder of the new company (which kept the name of Minerals and Chemical and within which Philipp Brothers became an independent division) was Charles Engelhard who also controlled Engelhard Industries, one of the main refiners of precious metals in the world. In 1967 Engelhard decided to amalgamate Engelhard and Mineral and Chemical. The new company, Engelhard Mineral and Metal Corporation, headed by himself, therefore comprised three divisions which were rather dissimilar and heterogenous from all points of view. Philipp Brothers, under the direction of Ludwig Jesselsson, remained very independent leaving almost no room for symbiosis between the three entities. On the other hand, in 1960, 'Phibro' was unable to prevent Charles Engelhard to sell, one year before his death, almost one third of the company's capital to one of his personal friends, the South-African Harry Oppenheimer, in 1960.

But from 1972–73, Philipp Brothers's growth took on extraordinary proportions. Suitably positioned to take advantage of changes on the oil market and the general buoyancy of the commodity markets, the firm's turnover rose from $1.2 billion in 1971 to $5 billion in 1975 and $23.6 billion in 1980 and its after-tax profits climbed from $26 million in 1971 to $97 million in 1975 and to $466 million in 1980.

Table 10.1 Some financial data on Philipp Brothers (as a division of Engelhard before 1980, with Salomon Brothers from 1981) (in $ million)

Year	Turn-over	Net profit	Fixed assets	Equity yield
1971	1,216	26	1.9	0.2
1972	1,551	24	3.1	0.16
1973	2,436	35	3.8	0.2
1974	4,574	89	21	0.37
1975	5,066	97	40	0.3
1976	5,782	95	61.4	0.23
1977	6,572	88	67.9	0.19
1978	9,125	100	70.1	0.18
1979	16,401	301	93.8	0.35
1980	23,691	466	433.1	0.37
1981	25,655	298		
1982	26,703	434	493	0.24
1983	29,757	617	427	0.27

Source: Annual Reports

Two very special points in its trajectory deserve special attention: the 1973–75 period and the commodity crisis: Philipp Brothers was able to take up position on the oil market[1], rapidly becoming the leading 'free' trader in the world (with the exception of government trading and of the majors) with an 'oil turnover' of $6 billion in 1979.

Not only was Philipp Brothers therefore superbly placed to profit from the second oil shock (1979–80), but it had not lost the opportunity to extend the scope of its activities in the meantime; needless to say, non-ferrous metals remained the company's stock-in-trade but Philipp Brothers also dealt in coal, fertilizers, cement, fuels and petrochemicals, pig iron and a range of agricultural products, diversifying into sugar in 1976. By means of contracts with producers[2], a financially burdensome policy of undercutting the competition, and a team of traders on its payroll, Philipp Brothers rapidly became the world's leading sugar trader (5 million tonnes in 1980). But, at the beginning of 1981, Phibro — long on the market — was caught unaware by the steady fall in prices and reportedly sustained losses of $50 to $80 million in the affair. The result was a notable reduction in the company's sugar activities. In 1978 came grain (10 million tonnes in 1981) for which Philipp Brothers does not seem to have attained a real profitablity threshold (apart from the period following the American embargo in January 1980), and finally cocoa in 1981 with the acquisition of a long-established British trading firm, Cocoa Merchants, which, as we know, went through a rough period in 1984. From a trading staff of 900 in 1970, the Philipp Brothers count rose to 2,400 in 1980 (4,500 employees in all). Globally, the share of petroleum remained preponderant, accounting not only for half of the turnover (which does not mean a great deal) but also for 20–25% of the profits in 1980.

Table 10.2 Share in % of oil and copper transactions in the turnover of the entire Engelhard group

Year	Oil (crude oil, petroleum products, oil transport)	Copper (concentrated ores, metal)	Phibro's share in Engelhard's turnover
1971	less than 10	25	77.00
1972	less than 10	28	79.00
1973	less than 10	33	78.70
1974	19	23	84.20
1975	31	11	88.90
1976	32	14	88.70
1977	36	9	89.30
1978	50		89.60
1979	45		90

Source: Annual Reports, form 1.OK

The growth of Phibro could hardly be matched by the other Engelhard divisions and in some years it accounted for 80–90% of the group's turnover and 70–80% of its profits. Within the Engelhard company, where the problem of the succession to the post of CEO then occupied by Milton Rosenthal, was at its height, the relationship became so tense that in April 1981, the de-merging of Engelhard Corp. and Phibro Corp. was announced. Phibro thus assumed its total independence under the direction of Ludwig Jesselsson and notably of David Tendler (who had joined the company in 1961 and had been, until 1975, the manager of the Tokyo office).

Four months later Phibro announced a new diversification this time into the 'supreme commodity' par excellence: money, and bought Salomon Brothers, the fourth largest Wall Street firm, for a little more than $500 million. Founded in 1910, the latter had retained its partnership structure all along and was one of the most famous firms in New York high finance, deftly marrying the functions of broker, stockbroker, banker. . . In 1980, Salomon had handled $1 trillion worth of securities and had provided finance to the tune of $50 billion. The director of its economic services, Henry Kaufman, is considered one of the gurus of Wall Street[3]. For Phibro this meant completing the range of activities and products handled. As David Tendler said at the time: 'Salomon gives us the ultimate limitless world to trade — money — while we were in the finite world of commodities where the supply is limited'[4]. Until then Phibro had owned one bank in Zug, Switzerland and another in Hongkong. In the spring of 1981, there were rumours about the purchase of an insurance company in Milwaukee, but Phibro's offer was turned down.

The Phibro–Salomon arrangement turned out to be one of the largest, most efficient and best performing in international finance at the time. With a total capital of $1.5 billion, it was bigger than Merryl Lynch ($1.1 billion). It was almost unequalled in the field of international trade worldwide. But it remained to be seen whether the grafting of two such highly individual companies would hold and if there would really be enough complementarity to form the world's first 'merchant bank' (in the literal sense of the term).

But the graft did not take, or at least did so badly. From the very start, one thing was, or at least seemed, clear: Phibro was buying Salomon Brothers and David Tendler, alone, was to be Chief Executive Officer and Chairman.

However the commodity price tumble was soon to make it clear that Salomon and not Phibro was the group's main centre of profit with the result that the former's boss, John Guttfreund, was made co-chairman in 1982.

Table 10.3 Distribution of profits for the Phibro–Salomon group between 1981 and 1983 (in $ million)

Pre-tax profits	1981	1982	1983
Phibro	364	222	307
– losses on industrial assets sold by Phibro at the end of 1983	(78)	(100)	(58)
– financial charges on long-term debts (Phibro)	(52)	(49)	(47)
Salomon	80	421	463

At the beginning of 1984, tensions mounted between Guttfreund, Tendler and O'Tally, the director of Phibro-Energy. On the 22nd May, the company announced that it was studying, in collaboration with Lazard, the feasibility of a separation: Salomon and oil on one side (together or apart), the remaining commodities with Phibro, on the other. This new Phibro, without oil, would be bought out by its directors with David Tendler at the helm and would become a private company. It was to be a clear-cut divorce: Phibro also stood to gain the advantage of recovering the status of a private company and the concommitant discretion which is so dear to the trader. But less than a week later, it was disclosed that the project, deemed too expensive, had been abandoned.

However, the conflict remained: Salomon considered the costs generated by Phibro for the maintenance of its world network, too high. The dispute seems to have been finally settled in favour of Salomon and at the end of July 1984, John Guttfreund was named the group's sole chief executive officer over the head of Tendler, who announced his decision to leave the group in autumn of that year as Guttfreund set about pruning out the Phibro executives. Later he began to reorganize the whole company keeping only the desks and offices which were showing a profit. In 1985, to comply with anti-apartheid feelings that hurt some of Salomon's financial operations, he ordered the closure of all its South African offices. When one knows the importance of South Africa in the metal trade, one begins to realize the constraints imposed thereby upon Phibro. At the same time, most secondary offices (such as Paris) were closed, and aproximately half of the traders left the company.

Finally, in 1986 John Guttfreund announced that the company would be named 'Salomon Inc.', without any reference to Phibro: sad end of a century-long story!

At present, Phibro is still a trader of some importance in oil, some metals, cocoa and rubber. But nothing is left that could be compared with the glorious days of 1982! The future looks rather bleak.

Phibro had otherwise very little infrastructure and has, all in all, diversified little. Until 1977, it controlled a phosphate fertilizer plant in Florida, and a zinc refinery in Oklahoma. . . From 1979, the company began to take an interest in logistic problems: shipping first of all (it ran a fleet of 38 ships in 1980), domestic transport and storage facilities for Pittsburg coal in the United States[5], an import terminal for cement in California. . . After the fall of the Hunts in

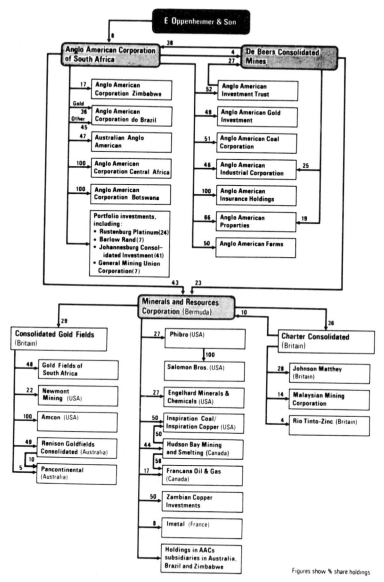

Figure 10.1 The financial ties between the Oppenheimer group, Phibro, Johnson Matthey. . . (*The Economist*, 1 May, 1982). (From the French edition of this book)

1980, Phibro decided to buy up their oil interests in the Beaufort Sea (Canada)[6].

In 1983, all of the company's investments were liquidated in conformity with the group's fundamental philosophy — to keep fixed assets at the bare minimum.

No description would be complete without an outline of Phibro's capital structure. Since 1969 the Anglo-American–De Beers group controls 28% of Engelhard's and subsequently of Phibro's capital[7]. The transaction was carried out through a subsidiary in Bermuda, Mineral and Resources Corporation (Minorco) which holds the group's interests in Consolidated Gold Fields and Charter Consolidated. Minorco recently became the group's investment arm for the United States (coal and copper mines, fertilizer plants. . .). Although the foregoing activities are highly complementary to those in which Phibro engages, there was practically no synergy between the trader and the South-African group. The remaining capital is distributed among the public, with the thirty main directors controlling about 5%. the merger with Salomon has not altered much this structure, although Anglo-American has reduced its participation in the company.

Philipp Brothers demonstrated an astounding growth rate over the past ten years. But the future of such a firm — in a state of total flux — is difficult to predict: it has remained above all a firm of traders. Its strength resides in men, but so does its weakness: this was abundantly clear in 1974 with the departure of the Marc Rich team; it happened again in 1982 with the departure of a number of vice-presidents (Benjamin Bollag, Phibro's executive vice-president until September 1982, took away a number of colleagues to form a new company, Bomar Resources, with the aid of Rothschild capital). At the end of 1984, it was David Tendler who left. And in 1985–86, many veteran traders stepped away too. In two years time, Guttfreund had destroyed what Jesselsson had built in thirty. The mythical alliance between the banker and the trader has turned short. Only the future will tell whether Phibro will at all survive!

- *Marc Rich*

Marc Rich and Co is probably, the adventure of Ned Cook aside, the firm which best symbolizes the legendary saga of the trader–adventurers in the wake of the great commodities crisis at the beginning of the seventies. In both cases, we find the same elements, worthy of a B-category suspense film: exceptional men with trading in their blood, possessed of an irrisistible charisma, on the brink of megalomania, fascinating everyone around them, men who in a few short years have built empires which collapse with the first recession. The last element is missing in the case of Marc Rich who, in 1986, seemed to be on the way to recovery.

Born to a Jewish family in Belgium in 1934, Marc Rich accompanied his parents when they fled Europe to New York in 1940. His father had interests in a Bolivian bank and owned a jute bag factory. After less than brilliant studies, Marc Rich joined Philipp Brothers in 1952 and spent 21 years with the company, moving up from the correspondence division where he was first employed as a clerk to the post of director of the petroleum department in 1973. He got his first break on the mercury market around 1955, was later transferred to Bolivia, the Netherlands and then to Spain. It was from Spain that he began, around 1955, to deal in the oil business in association with another Phibro executive in Zug, Pinkus Green. Rich and Green were able to take advantage of the radical change in the oil market in the early seventies, earning considerable sums for Philipp Brothers. What happened then remains moot: were Marc Rich's hopes for promotion to the post of managing-director of Philipp Brothers after Ludwig Jesselsson, dashed, or was it true that he had made exorbitant demands for a profit-linked salary bonus (Rich and Green allegedly requested $500,000 each at the time)?

Whatever that may be, Marc Rich and Pinkus Green left Philipp Brothers in November 1973 and with the aid of a few other refugees, created Marc Rich A.G. in Zug (Switzerland) with an initial capital of $350,000. The new firm grew at a fantastic rate: relying on precious friendships in Arab oil circles, Marc Rich was able to take advantage of the opening up of the oil market. Later, recruiting a number of erstwhile Phibro employees, Rich expanded to the ore and metal markets and lost no time in becoming the world's leading trader in bauxite and aluminium. Rich rapidly acquired a reputation for being a very speculative firm. In 1981–82, it was behind Malaysia's manoeuvres on the tin market: acting on behalf of a group most likely inspired by Malysian mining interests (Malaysian Mining Corporation) who were growing irritated by the difficulties encountered at the time by the international agreement, and relying on Gulf capital, Marc Rich, who counted among his employees one of the most famous traders on the tin market, David Zaidner, kept the market bullish over the entire winter of 1981–82, and even managed to drive the major houses of the London Metal Exchange to the brink of disaster at the end of February 1982. After modification of the market rules and probably bowing to pressure brought to bear by the Malaysians, who had not wanted the affair to go that far, Marc Rich was gradually forced to liquidate his position, though not before he had pocketed some hefty profits for himself. The example inspired no small number of imitators: when, at the end of 1982, the Chilean copper corporation Codelco wished to bolster prices (by buying on the New York futures market COMEX, this time) it went through Marc Rich. But the operation was unsuccessful.

At the end of that year, 1982, fortune seemed to be smiling on Marc Rich and his associates: the group had become the second world trader in oil, ores and metals, on an equal footing with and even surpassing the leader, Philipp Brothers, in many respects. Rich and Green appeared, besides, to nurture a stubborn hatred for their former employer, and seemed to calculate many of their moves according to those made by Phibro: entry into the sugar and later the grain trade. In grain, Marc Rich was able to put his Arab contacts to good use: Richco Grain was able, in a short space of time to become the barley 'king' of Saudi Arabia (barley imports into that country are subsidized and often reach dizzy heights). In 1981, Richco bought out the international division of the Dutch trader, Granaria, to secure a base in Europe. The profits of Marc Rich A.G., in Zug alone, amounted to $367 million in 1979 and 1980 (pre-tax), $110 million in 1982 (net profits) despite the noticeable lag in activity on the commodity markets. Its turnover was estimated then, at more than $10 billion.

In 1981, Marc Rich, in a private capacity, with the Texan magnate Marvin Davis, bought the cinema company 20th Century Fox for $722 million. Not a bad record for a man whose company was barely six years old!

As far as its commercial methods are concerned, Marc Rich does not, however, enjoy a very good reputation: the growth of the firm, based initially on the oil market boom, was fuelled, from 1980, by more dubious practices: there was talk of dealings with Iran during the worst days of the American Embassy hostage affair in Teheran. Similarly, Rich was present in Angola at the height of the civil war and in the United States itself, he took advantage of the complexity of the American oil legislation to funnel barrels of oil through more or less ficticious companies (the so-called 'daisy chains' to whitewash its exact origin).These transactions, which enabled him to export his profits through a Panama-based company, caught the attention of the American tax authorities. In April 1982, a grand jury enquiry was opened to investigate Marc Rich. The American tax authorities estimated that in 1980 Rich had sold in the region of $345 million worth of oil to its American subsidiary, which had reported a loss of $110 million on the re-sale of the same. Since these declared losses were used to cover the profits of the rest of the company, the latter's actions were considered tantamount to tax evasion.

At the beginning, the company took an insolent stance: Marc Rich A.G. was a Swiss company and Swiss law forbade it to answer an enquiry from the American law enforcement authorities. The latter were slow at first, but things began to speed up in June 1983. On June 29 in fact, a judge sentenced Marc Rich to a fine of $50,000 per day, as long as he refused to present the documents. On the first of August, the same judge ordered that $55 million worth of the company's assets be frozen.

However, Marc Rich had received an injunction from the Swiss courts forbidding him to hand over, to the Americans, any of the documents pertaining to Marc Rich A.G. The Swiss obviously did not appreciate being treated by the Americans like an 'ordinary Central American State'. 'We are not a banana republic', was the headline of one Zurich weekly, *Finanz und Wirtschaft*!

Moreover, on the 30th of June, Marc Rich's American subsidiary was sold out to a few senior executives and changed its name to Clarendon Ltd. Clarendon was suposed to take over Marc Rich's trading activites in non-ferrous metals for its own account. But the American courts countered by including Clarendon in the freeze of the group's assets.

At the beginning of August, as he began to perceive the risks posed by a closing of the American market, Marc Rich decided to hand over the requested documents. All went well until the 10th of August, when the American customs authorities at Kennedy Airport seized two suitcases of documents which Marc Rich was about to send to Zurich. Two days later, the Swiss police retorted with a raid in Zug and symbolically seized the documents demanded by the American courts.

Switzerland was now turning the affair into a test of honour and Marc Rich found himself somewhat caught in his own trap.

Not wishing to get involved in such a dangerous and politicized affair, the American banks gradually reduced their credit lines to Clarendon whose activities practically ground to a halt in the autumn of 1983. Meanwhile, the American judges had widened the scope of their enquiry and were now accusing Marc Rich of contravening the embargo declared by the American government against Iran during the hostage affair. This was no longer a crime against the tax authorities, it was a crime against the nation. . . Warrants for the arrest of Marc Rich and Pinkus Green were issued, but they refused to appear before the New York jurisdiction. They were accused inter alia, of having evaded taxes to the tune of $48 million, the biggest fraud in the history of the United States.

In fact, at the end of September, Marc Rich acquired Spanish nationality (the reader will recall that he had once directed the Phibro office in Madrid). Spain's extradition agreement with the United States is in fact rather lax. . . Sometime later, Green acquired Bolivian nationality.

The entire affair had serious repercussions for the group: practically forbidden to operate in the United States, ostracized by the American banks, a number of subsidiaries were forced to close: Richco Bullion which was active on the foreign exchange and precious metals markets in London, Richco Sugar in sugar and Clarendon Ltd. in New York. Rich's Paris office also closed its doors. But the group was much more resilient than would have been thought at a first glance. Without the United States, and despite the departure of a number of its somewhat demoralized traders, Marc Rich remained the second world trader in oil (thanks to the Gulf countries), in ores and metals, and was still an important actor on the grain market. In 1983, its turnover was allegedly in the region of $6 billion and bankers put the value of the firm at between $600 and $800 million. In this success, the quality of the contacts which Marc Rich entertains with some of the great princely families of the Gulf, undoubtedly played no mean role.

At the beginning of October 1984, Marc Rich took the only alternative open to him, if he wanted to safeguard the future of the group: come to a settlement with the American government. The bill they presented him was a loaded one: $150 million in fines on the tax evasion charge, plus $21 million in daily fines calculated from 1983 and

Figure 10.2 Caricature published in *The Economist* (20 August 1983) at the time of the Marc Rich affair. (From the French edition of this book)

a few other minor charges producing a grand total of $172 million. On the other hand, Rich and Green still stand accused and have to restrict their movements to a few 'friendly' countries.

Since then, Marc Rich's subsidiaries have returned to the U.S.A., and the company profited much from Phibro's troubles. In December 1985 it even bought an oil refinery in Florida. Richco seems to have well maintained its grain activities, venturing also into new areas, such as rice.

Few people know anything about this 'Spaniard from Zug', this 'trader–adventurer', who in a short space of ten years succeeded in building an empire which the American authorities have barely managed to shake. Alongside a Varsano, a Margulies, a Gaon, and others of their ilk, Marc Rich is in all probability one of the most fascinating figures in the international commodity trade.

- *Asoma*

The New York-based Asoma — or more precisely the Associated Metals and Minerals Corporation — is better known under the name of the Lissauer group, the name of the founder and of the family which still controls it today. The Lissauer company was founded in Cologne at the dawn of the century[8]. In the twenties it was transferred to New York where it was directed until his death on the 15th May 1984, by

Franz Lissauer, grandson of the founder (who has been succeeded by his nephew Stefan Eliel). The name crops up relatively seldom since the different national subsidiaries appear to function independently: Leopold Lazarus in London, *Transafer* in Paris, *Rheinischer Erz* in Köln. . . Here we are also dealing with a company which has diversified little: one reprocessing plant (basically tin) in Texas, 50% of the capital of a ferro-silicum producer in Norway (Orkla), trading activities in coal and chemicals. . . Asoma's turnover (in ores and metals) is estimated at $2 to $3 billion. From 1983, the company was having serious problems and sustained heavy losses. As a result, Asoma was forced to give up a number of its activities in 1984 (fertilizer with the sale of Bomar Resources) and reduce its own capital to $60 million.

- *Hochschild*

This company was the brainchild of a German Jew who, sent to South America at the dawn of the century, founded mining companies there (*Mantos Bancos* in Chile). Hochschild, controlled by a holding company in Panama, Consolidated Mining and Industries, then began to grow rapidly. In mining, its subsidiary, *Empresas Sud-Americanas Consolidas,* controls copper mines in Chile, nickel and phosphates in Brazil, and silver in Peru. The trading division is known under the names Samincorp in New York, Exsud in London, Sudamin in Brussels and also encompasses industrial activities (antimony in France, tantalum and carbon in the United States). In 1984, the trading division separated from the mining company, which was sold to the Anglo-American group (again!) and was bought out by its president, Ladislav von Hoffmann, backed by close financial interests.

We are witnessing here, as in the case of Asoma and even of Phibro, a reduction of structures, a separation of trade from the rest of the group's activities.

- *The other traders*

Commercial Metals is a Texan firm based in Dallas. Founded in 1914 around a reprocessing site, Commercial Metals developed considerably in the trade sector in the past few years and at present probably constitutes the fourth largest international network for oil and metals (turnover in 1981, $1.3 billion). CMC was responsible, for example, for the sale of 25,000 tonnes of bauxite from the People's Republic of China to the American strategic stockpile (it is also one of the main aluminium traders in the world). CMC first diversified into petroleum, and then into petroleum products and most recently into agricultural products.

Among the other great trade-based networks, there is Heine Brothers (founded in Melbourne in 1865), Gerald Metals (founded in 1962 by former trader Gerald Lennard with two industrial subsidiaries in the United States — refining of precious metals and reprocessing), Bomar Resources, founded in 1982 by former Phibro directors allegedly backed by Rothschild capital and who dream of becoming another Marc Rich.

Apart from these international firms, there are a number of subsidiaries belonging to traders specialized in other products: C. Tennant, founded in 1825 and now owned by Cargill, J.H. Rayner of the Berisford group, Gill and Duffus, Continental. . . In 1985, the Golodetz group closed its metal trading subsidiary, Lonconex.

Here too, the Japanese trading firms are a special case. Most of the *sogo shosa* have in fact, substantial activities in the field of ores and metals and are even financially involved in numerous mining projects in Australia and Brazil.

Table 10.4 The Japanese presence on the London Metal Exchange

Firms with a seat on the LME	Shareholders
Ametalco Trading	Amax and Sumitumo
Anglo Chemical Metals	Phibro (75%) + Mitsui (25%)
Tennant	Consolidated Gold Fields (75%) + Marubeni (25%)
Triland	Mitsubishi (60%)

But beyond this, as demonstrated by Table 10.4, the Japanese traders are also present on the LME. It would seem, however, that there too, they have remained rather Nippon-centric.

The upstream and downstream presence

Here we are entering a field where it is extremely difficult to draw a clear dividing line between industrial or mining activities and trading ones.

An analysis of the distribution of seats on the London Metal Exchange (which is not necessarily a good criterion) would give the following picture:

– mining firms: Amax, Péchiney, Imetal, Noranda, Consolidated Gold Fields, International Minerals and Chemicals;
– metallurgical firms: Billiton, *Metallgesellschaft*, Preussag, Britannia Lead, Lead Industries.

Most of the mining firms (which have often become companies servicing the mining activity) have trading subsidiaries. This is true of the two main French mining groups, *Péchiney* and *Imétal*. In July 1982 Péchiney created Péchiney International Trading regrouping its different subsidiaries (Intsel, PTC Partners) and a British firm, Brandeis Goldschmidt, acquired for £30 million in 1981 from the S.G. Warburg group. Imetal, through its subsidiaries Minemet and Entores, also engaged in substantial trading activities. It is also true of a number of American (Phelps Dodge, Arsaco, the Marmon group (mines in South America) with its subsidiary Cerro Sales. . .) and Canadian firms (Noranda Mines which owned until 1985 one of the oldest metal trading firms, Rudolf Wolff). . . Government enterprises of the producing countries have begun to engage in trading activities: MMC Metals for Malysia and Memaco Trading for Zambia have opened offices in London; MMC Metals had a seat on the London Metal Exchange, but left it after the tin crash of October 1985. Note also the existence on the London Metal Exchange of Medtist, controlled by an Indian trader, Raj Kumar Bagri.

The two metallurgical firms with the largest trading activities are German companies, the *Metallgesellschaft* and Preussag.

Originally from Frankfurt, the *Metallgesellschaft* was one of the first European transnational corporations in metals in 1914. Founded in 1881 by Wilhelm Merton (a British citizen) as an arm of the British Metal Corporation, it was initially a metal trading company.

But before long it industrialized to the point where the trading activity was relegated to second place (an itinerary which many large traders follow nowadays).

After the Second World War, reparations took away many of its subsidiaries especially those in Belgium (now the famous Hoboken metal refining firm). At present, its activities are focused on non-ferrous metallurgy (in Germany and Austria), mining (Canada and New Guinea), engineering (with the international construction firm,

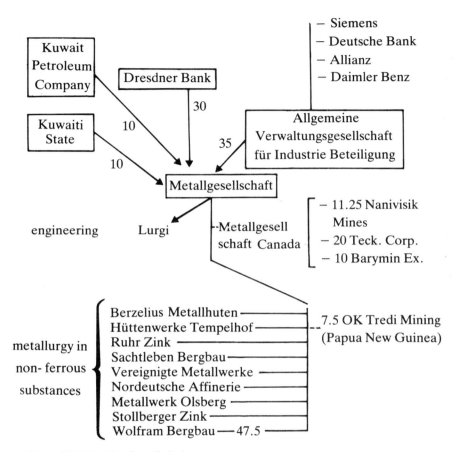

Figure 10.3 The *Metallgesellschaft* group

Lurgi) and of course trading (the *Metallgesellschaft* has the Number
One seat on the London Metal Exchange). Its trading activities
accounted for some 40% of a total turnover of 11 billion DM in
1982–83. The firm's capital is divided among Kuwaiti interests (20%),
the Dresdner Bank and a holding company regrouping some of the
biggest names in German finance and industry (Figure 10.3).

Moreover, there have recently been rumours about a sizable interest taken by the foremost German industrial firm, Veba, itself controlled by the Federal government.

Preussag (turnover in 1980, 3.5 billion DM) is much more diversified than the *Metallgesellschaft*. Originally a refiner of metals, the group has substantial interests in the energy sector (oil and coal) which it cemented in 1981 with the purchase of C. Deilman, in transport and in construction. Its trading activities acquired a worldwide dimension with the purchase of 85% of the capital of Amalgamated Metal Corporation in September 1978. AMC is, in all likelihood, the fifth world trader in metals and was formerly the trading arm of the Patino mining group, famous for its Bolivian tin mines. These origins have ensured AMC an important place on the tin market and in its metallurgy (tin refining in Malaysia and Australia) and curiously enough, a minority Malaysian participation in its capital[9].

Other metallurgists are the *Société Générale des Minerais*, an arm of the vast grouping created under a bank, the *Société Générale de Belgique,* controlling interests from Hoboken to the Zaire province of Katanga, the Swedish firm Boliden (which controls the American trader Leonard J. Buck), the Billiton group (tin refining, controlled at present by Royal Dutch Shell) and in France, *Alliages d'Etain et Dérivés*, the leading French tin trader. . .

All in all, both miners and metallurgists remain very active and present in the trade of ores and metals: either for considerations of internal strategy due in general to the very strong synergy existing between their primary activities (in particular refining) and trade, or for reasons of the external strategy to which their financial power entitles them (Péchiney, Preussag, Noranda to mention only the most outstanding).

However, despite the presence of industrial groups and of few trading majors, there is still ample room for a host of small companies present on very specific markets.

The special markets

We shall take two examples to better illustrate our point: the case of minor metals and that of precious metals.

Minor metals are understood to be all metallic substances which are generally not quoted on the futures market. The London-based Minor Metals Society, the trade association concerned by these metals, includes in its list: antimony, cadmium, bismuth, mercury, nickel, selenium and recently, cobalt, molybdenum, germanium and indium. Until 1969 these were confidential markets controlled by a few big producers; the operators comprised a few English houses which essentially sold the by-products of their major metal contracts. 1969 was a year of psychological rupture with the strike which paralysed Inco (International Nickel of Canada). The markets suddenly opened up and the number of interested operators rose from less than ten to over fifty, techniques evolved from back-to-back operations to paper transactions between traders (such as the one related in the famouse 'sardine trading' joke of old). Moreover, these tight markets rapidly fell prey to manipulations (the case of bismuth in 1974). It would appear that the effervescent period which had enabled a host of small firms to develop came to an end in 1977 and many a bankruptcy has been reported since then.

The market for precious metals is totally different because of the financial magnitude and monetary significance of the transactions carried out there: speculation is also, generally speaking, more rampant on such markets (see the Hunt affair!). A number of firms (which often come quite near to being merchant banks) are specialized in trade in the strict sense of the term, i.e. in bullion dealing. In London there is Mocatta Goldsmid, N.M. Rothschild, Samuel Montagu, Sharps Pixley, Ayrton Metals (subsidiary of Impala, the platinum mining company), in New York Mocatta, Phibro, Jack Aron (already mentioned in the context of the coffee trade), in France the *Compagnie des Métaux Précieux* (recently bought out by Phibro's former partner, Engelhard), the *Comptoir Lyon Allemand Louyot* (founded in 1815). . .

Here too, the trading and processing activities are closely linked to each other: Johnson Matthey (turnover in 1981, £765 million), one of the five members fixing the price of gold in London, owner of a seat on the London Metal Exchange and having important banking activities, is also one of the principal refiners of precious metals in the chemical industry and in jewellery. Like Philipp Brothers, Johnson Matthey indirectly forms part of the Oppenheimer group (28% of its shares belong to Charter Consolidated). At the beginning of 1982 it bought out Wallace Brothers Commodities, a trader which specialized in agricultural products, from the Brooke Bond group, thereby enlarging the scope of its activities. However, in the autumn of 1984, Johnson Matthey Bankers, the group's merchant bank subsidiary went out of business and was bailed out and taken over for a token £1 by the Bank of England. This did not prevent the group from suffering from J.M.B.'s losses.

The ore and metal trade therefore generally demonstrates a much more heterogenous pattern than the agricultural sector (where specialization is greater). Firms do not have the same degree of power *vis-à-vis* the market given the importance of upstream and downstream (at least for the main metals). And in the final analysis, the few world-size firms owed their phenomenal growth of the seventies, in particular to the energy sector. It remains to be seen whether this growth will be lasting and will stabilize and to what extent the balance of power within the metal product-systems will remain in place.

Chapter 11

TRADE IN SOME OTHER MAJOR COMMODITIES

The aim of this book is not to give an *exhaustive* view of commodity trading nor a systematic analysis of *all* products. However, in order to enhance the analyses made in the preceding chapters, we would like to give a few explanations about a number of products which are particularly exemplary or about which we have privileged information. We shall discuss in turn, agricultural commodities such as cotton, hard fibres and rubber, some tropical products (tea and bananas), tobacco and shall end with oil. There are few links between these various analyses save for a number of names which we are sure the reader will recognize.

Cotton

World production of cotton has a rather peculiar geopolitical configuration which is practically unique in the field of commodities: the main producers are the USSR, China and the United States (almost 60% of the world production is shared between these three parties), followed by India, Brazil, Turkey, Pakistan and so forth. The main exporters are the United States (31%), the USSR (20%) and Turkey (5%). . .

Involved in imports are the developed countries (especially Japan with 16%), a number of developing countries such as South Korea, Hong Kong and China. The strategic points of the cotton trade are therefore the United States (P.L. 480 also plays a role in cotton), the USSR, Japan. . .

Cotton is usually traded in the form of bales of raw cotton. The first stage of transformation is spinning followed by the weaving and knitting of textiles (more or less mixed at this stage). The geography of cotton processing has undergone a radical transformation since the beginning of the century.

Spinning is done increasingly in the developing producing countries but also in non-producing countries (South East Asia). The markets for raw cotton have shifted to the detriment especially of what was once the major world market in the 19th century, Liverpool, where a futures market was set up in 1860. From 1871, it had to face stiff competition from the New York futures market (but only for American cottons). At present the only futures market in existence, that of New York, deals exclusively with the domestic market and paradoxically, international trade now takes place without any direct possibilities for hedging.

The structure of international trade is still determined by the history and geography of cotton: the old firms of Liverpool have gradually given way to the American traders concentrated around Memphis, whilst a substantial portion of trade remains in the hands of the Japanese. The Japanese case aside, trade plays a very negligible industrial role within the cotton chain: a number of firms have ginning activities (especially in South America) but there is next to no synergy with the textile industry (in either direction). The most characteristic feature is, in the final analysis, the increasing role assumed by the grain merchants for mainly geographical reasons.

- *Cargill*

Since 1981, Cargill has been by far the major world trader in cotton. Back in the sixties, Cargill had acquired a large firm in Memphis, Hohenberg Brothers. In March 1981 it bought Ralli Bros. from the Bowater group (wood and paper pulp) for £12 million.

Of Greek origin, the Ralli family made its debut in the 19th century in the cotton, silk, bacon and indigo trades between Great Britain and India (in 1818 John and Eustratio Ralli were in London, Auguste in Marseilles, Thomas in Constantinople, and Pandia in Odessa).

Table 11.1 The main world traders in raw cotton

Cargill: subsidiaries Ralli Brothers (G.B.)	over 10%
Hohenberg (U.S.A.)	
Volkart (Switzerland)	5%
McFadden–Valmac (U.S.A.)	5%
W.B. Dunavant (U.S.A.)	
Bunge and Born (Brazil–U.S.A.–Argentina)	
Anderson-Clayton (U.S.A.)	
Allenberg Cotton (U.S.A.)–Louis Dreyfus	
Weil Brothers (U.S.A.)	
H. Molsen and Co. (U.S.A.–FRG)	
Cotton Import-Export Co. (U.S.A.)	
The Japanese firms:	
Toyo Menka	5%
Sumitumo	5%
C. Itoh	
Marubeni	
Nichimen	

Sources: UNCTAD, *Fibres et Textiles: Dimensions du pouvoir des sociétés transnationales*, TD/B/C.1/219 (and private data).

In 1851 offices were opened in India, starting with Calcutta. From its powerful base in India, the firm gradually specialized in cotton, buying out a Liverpool trader, Reynolds and Gibson, in 1962 and amalgamating a short time later with another trader, Smith Coney and Barett. In 1980, Ralli Brothers was the leading world trader in cotton (with an estimated turnover of £500 million): in 1972, Ralli organized a sale of no less than 500,000 bales of American cotton to the People's Republic of China! Ralli recently embarked on an industrialization process: acquisition in 1977 of the California Compress Company (storage, ginning, and bale pressing) and of the British Cotton Growing Association Ltd. in 1973 (factories and production of cotton oil in Nigeria, Sudan, Malawi and Pakistan). Moreover, Ralli is involved in wood trading (Hunter Fowles), jute, hard fibres, rubber and linen (Malcom Maclaine).

In 1959 Ralli had been bought out by a finance company, General Guarantee Corporation owned by Sir Isaac Wolfson. In 1969, the latter sold Ralli to Slater Walker Securities, then run by the famous Jim Slater.

After the bankruptcy of the Slater Walker group in 1972 Ralli was bought out again, this time by the Bowater company whose principal centre of activity is wood and paper pulp. The graft between the industrial group and the trading firm did not take and in 1981, Bowater, in the grip of financial woes, sold Ralli to Cargill.

With Hohenberg, Cargill was already the sixth world trader (according to a 1981 UNCTAD study). With Ralli, it became by far the largest world trader with a volume of actuals amounting to over two million bales. Logically the group's position should be consolidated if the synergy between the commercial networks is effective (which is not all that certain).

- *Volkart*

This Winterthur firm, already mentioned in coffee, is also the world's second trader in cotton (one million bales), with operations in Dallas, Mexico (where it has ginning activities) and in Japan. In India and in Pakistan, Volkart has minority shares in spinning and in the textile industry (but due to past events, no longer maintains a policy of vertical integration).

Among the other trading firms, note especially the position occupied by those from the grain sector: Bunge and Born particularly active in South America, Anderson Clayton in Brazil, Louis Dreyfus through Allenberg Brothers[1].

The peculiar position of the Japanese firms is due both to the importance of their import activities and to their history: a number of them began trading in cotton in the 19th century.

As in other sectors, most of them have have remained relatively 'Nippon-centered', with the exception of Toyo Menka, active especially on the American market and Sumitumo, active on the Russian market.

As we have already pointed out, the influence of the textile industry is negligible in the cotton trade (a few direct purchases are made from the USSR by firms such as Courtauld's). On the other hand, the role of the American cooperatives is indisputable and they account for an important share of American exports. The two most important are the Plains Cotton Cooperative Association and, especially, CALCOT-AMCOT of California with sales offices in South East Asia and Japan.

Till now relatively regionalized, there are indications that international trade in cotton is becoming increasingly concentrated around a few multiproduct firms and the Japanese *sogo shosa*.

Hard fibres

The major hard fibres are sisal, henequen, abaca and coconut. Sisal and henequen have very similar characteristics and constitute the basic raw material used in the twine industry. These products are of little importance in international trade but they play a major role in the exports of countries like Tanzania and Kenya. Moreover, sisal provides an interesting example of post-colonial evolution. In East Africa in particular, sisal had been relatively integrated by the European and especially British companies, but this integration has been challenged in recent times especially by the policy pursued by Tanzania.

Two-thirds of the fibre and 80% of the twine production is sold on the free market (outside long-term or barter agreements). The sisal market apparently fluctuates wildly; the main quotations being published by the leading world trader, the British firm, Wigglesworth Ltd.

Table 11.2 The main world traders in sisal and sisal manufactures

	share of the sisal trade	share of the trade in sisal products
Wigglesworth and Co. (G.B.)	19.00	8.10
Landauer (Fibres) Int. Co.	17.20	
Malcolm Maclaine (Ralli–Cargill group)	6.60	4.80
Hindley Co. (G.B.)	7.80	8.90
Dalgety Int. Trading	4.00	

(Source: UNCTAD, *The marketing of hard fibres: areas for international cooperation*, TD/B/C.1/PSC/21, Geneva, 1981).

The world sisal trade is dominated by five firms of British origin which carry out 70% of the free trade in fibres and 30% of that of twine (Table 11.2). Of these firms, three (Wiggleworth, Dalgety and Landauer) have interests in plantations in Tanzania and Kenya. Most of them have exclusive agreements with plantations and twine factories: Wigglesworth, Landauer, Dalgety and Ralli in East Africa and Hindley in Brazil.

Of these five firms, three have remained independent (Hindley, Wigglesworth and Landauer which have, moreover, combined their twine activities) whereas two of them are the subsidiaries of large-scale trading groups: Dalgety and Cargill (through Ralli under the names of Malcolm Maclaine and Smith Conney and Barett).

In a sector which is marked by competition from synthetic fibres, trade has remained a central element of the marketing system despite the 'socialization' policy pursued by Tanzania.

Natural rubber

Natural rubber, produced from the rubber tree, comes essentially from South East Asia (Malaysia, Indonesia and Thailand especially) and marginally from Africa (Liberia) and South America. Despite competition from synthetic products the main user remains the tyre industry. International trade is divided into three parts: intra-government trade, direct sales (vertical integration of certain tyre manufacturers such as Firestone in Liberia or sales through the management agencies of the Malaysian plantations) and free trade.

In fact, given the problems of collection and the first processing of latex, then of the leaves and balls of rubber, international trade has centred around an Asiatic pole on the one hand (Singapore, Kuala Lumpur) and the consumption centres (London, New York) on the other.

In the production zones, the trader, who is often also a planter, buys produce from the village trader, then processes and packages it before selling it to the international trader. Based in Singapore, and controlled by foreign Chinese interests, the Lee Rubber group is the main Asian trader in rubber responsible for at least 10% of the world tonnages. In Malaysia, Lee Rubber, a producer (40,000 hectares), collector and industrial power, carries out 32% of the rubber collection operations. Lee is also present in Indonesia and Thailand. Globally, the group handles 500,000 tonnes of rubber and reportedly has a turnover of over $1 billion per year in this field. Lee, however, is reputedly more industry than trade oriented, more conservative than venturesome like the other big Chinese groups (Kuok, Liem)[2].

Table 11.3 The main international traders in natural rubber

— Asia trade
Lee Rubber (Singapore)
— Western trade
Safic Alcan (1983 t.o. : 2.6m FF)
Gill and Duffus/Pacol
ACLI
Maclaine Watson/Ralli (Cargill)

Among the western traders, we find numerous firms which have already been mentioned for other products such as Gill and Duffus–Pacol, ACLI, the subsidiaries of the Cargill–Ralli group. . . The top position in the trade is, however, occupied by a specialized firm: the French company, *Safic Alcan*.

The successor of a trading firm for tropical produce (Hecht), *Safic Alcan* is, in tonnage terms, the second world trader after Lee. Present in Singapore and Kuala Lumpur as well as in New York and London, *Safic Alcan* handles practically only rubber and latex (with the exception of palm-oil from Malaysia, a product which is complementary to rubber) and owns small industrial infrastructures in France. From 1968 to 1981, *Safic Alcan* was under the control of the group, *Chargeurs Réunis* (though it was still being run by the members of the Alcan family). When the *Pricel* group, owned by Jérome Seydoux, bought *Chargeurs Réunis*, it sold the 50.27% participation owned by *Chargeurs Réunis* for 43 million francs to Unifin BV, subsidiary of the Luxemburg firm, IFI International, itself an industrial holding company of the Agnelli family (30% of Fiat). It is still too early to say whether the Italian group has strategic intentions in the trading field. *Safic Alcan* remains in any event one of the all too rare successes of the French in international trade.

Wood and forestry products

On the one hand, it is impossible to speak of an international trade in timber and forestry products: there are, in fact, only a number of relatively compartmentalized markets (tropical timber, resinous woods, timber for trituration. . .). On the other hand, the forestry economy is still characterized by extensive vertical integration ranging from plantations to first processing into pannels or the production of pulp and then of paper.

From the point of view of trade, two elements are of particular importance: on the one hand the role of the international trading companies, which have concessions in Africa and in South East Asia : the SCAC, SCOA for France in Africa, the East Asiatic, Jardine Matheson and the Japanese firms in South East Asia[3]. On the other hand, in the case of the resinous woods where they have a great deal of clout, the Russians have set-up joint companies with traders in most of the European countries: an example in France is *Rubois*, founded in 1968 between Export Khleb and two French firms, *Nielsen et Bernier*, and *Konow et Smith*. For the rest, trade in timber is very much scattered among a host of operators with brokers playing a rather important role.

Tea

Tea is probably one of the only major agricultural products which cannot be handled on a futures market for practical reasons: in fact quality tends to vary considerably (even between neighbouring tea gardens, somewhat like fine wines!) and it is difficult to store for more than six months. Finally, since each distributor carries out its own blending operations, he will settle for nothing less than a tea of a precise origin. The situation here is no different from that of coffee where the distributor's trump-card is the brand which plays an enormous role in consumer reaction.

The peculiarity of the tea market is that it is the last (along with that of wool) to function under the auction system. Historically, the most important auctions were those of London (the main consumer centre). But gradually, since independence, those organized by the producing countries (Calcutta, Colombo, Monbasa and more recently Singapore) have become more important in terms of quantity.

During the auctions themselves, it is the brokers who intervene: either, as in London, to organize the sales themselves (there are five selling brokers playing a role rather similar to that of the auctioneer) or to act as buying brokers for the major trading-packaging firms. This is because there is practically no independent trade but rather an oligopoly of firms who control the product up to the stage of consumption and whose names are well-known to housewives (British especially in so far as the British market is still the largest in the world):

Table 11.4 The main tea trader-packagers of British origin

Group	Company	Founding date	Share of the market in 1973	Plantations in
Unilever	Lipton's & Co. Colonial, Elephant	1871	13%	Malawi, India
	Brooke Bond	1861		Kenya, Tanzania
Allied Lyons	Lyons	1886	13%	
Associated British Foods	Twining's			
Cadbury Schweppes	Typhoo			

There is no doubt that these firms exert a much greater influence on the market than did the classical traders (about which the Tea Boards of the various producing countries used to complain). But here we are practically in an industrial setting and the trader-packager's added-value is undeniable. The acquisition of Brooke Bond Liebig by Unilever in 1984 has rendered the sector even more concentrated and placed Unilever in a dominant position on the world scene. A similar (but very different as far as origins are concerned) situation obtains in bananas.

Bananas

Just as there has been a sugar-cane 'civilization', we could say that there was — and still is — a banana 'civilization' as illustrated by the

caricature of the banana republics of Central America dominated by
the all-powerful North American firms described by Miguel Angel
Asturias in *El Señor Presidente*.

This image has evolved considerably. The all-powerful United Fruit
Company which controlled 75% of world trade in 1945 has encountered competition on its own territory from new operators; most of the
companies have been led to surrender ownership of their plantations.
They continue, however, to retain substantial leverage in packaging,
transport and ripening operations.

United fruit, Standard Fruit, and Del Monte, all three subsidiaries
of powerful American agro-foodstuffs firms, account for 70% of the
international trade in bananas (the major exception being the French
franc area where the trade is managed by the *Comité Interprofessionnel Bananier*). The strength of these companies is now anchored less in
the control of production (which they no longer have) but rather in
their technical know-how of the logistics of the product (a delicate
field) and in the control of marketing channels in the consumer
countries.

It is this hold on distribution which precipitated the downfall of a
joint enterprise set up by the UBEC (Union of Banana Exporting
Countries) countries, *Communbanana*. Moreover, the three majors
can afford to boycott a country when relations deteriorate (see the case
of Panama recently boycotted by United Fruit).

In 1984, the companies succeeded in imposing considerable tax
reductions on the producing countries, going as far as their total
suppression in Guatemala.

Table 11.5 The main banana trading companies

Group	Company	Share of the world market in 1973	Plantations controlled (hectares)
United Brands	United Fruit	35%	26,000 (Costa Rica, Pa-nama, Honduras)
Castle and Cook	Standard Fruit	25%	13,125 (Costa Rica, Ecuador, Honduras)
	Del Monte	10%	6,367 (Costa Rica, Guatemala, Philippines)

As is the case for tea, a highly industrialized trading sector has a great deal of clout on the product's market: a situation which is not very different from that of tobacco.

Tobacco

Here too, we are dealing with a product for which the added value accruing to the packager, creator of the brand, is of capital importance. Nevertheless, between the production stage and the oligopoly of cigarette manufacturers[4], there is a very active and more or less independent trading sector.

These operators buy leaf tobacco which they package and process for resale to the cigar and cigarette manufacturers (although some of them also carry out direct purchases). Here too, trade plays an undeniably industrial role: drying of tobacco leaves, sorting according to quality. . .

Six firms, essentially of American origin, carry out 90% of world trade in tobacco:

Table 11.6 The main traders dealing in tobacco leaves

Company	Group
Universal Leaf Transcontinental Leaf Tobacco Debrill Brothers Export Leaf Tobacco Kulen Kampf A.C. Monk & Co.	British American Tobacco

Universal Leaf is the leading world trader and a highly diversified industrial firm with over 12,500 employees (turnover in the tobacco sector alone in 1976: $700 million). Among the other major traders note the presence of a subsidiary of B.A.T., Export Leaf and those of Imperial Tobacco. In 1976 the distribution of tobacoo purchases at auctions held in the United States was:

Universal Leaf	25%
Export Leaf	18 to 20%
R.J. Reynolds (manufacturer)	18 to 20%
Debrill Brothers	15%
A.C. Monk	10%

This table should provide some idea of the distribution on the world market.

In this precise case, trade owes its importance to its technical nature and probably to the low value of the real cost of tobacco in the total cost of cigarettes (even before tax) an incentive which has led the major manufacturers to show an interest in this sector.

Phosphates and fertilizers

Here we go back to the mineral and industrial field. Raw fertilizer can generally take any of three main forms: potassium, nitrates, and phosphates (without counting the double and even triple combinations). The basic raw materials employed are phosphates, potassium and sulphur.

The main market, that of phosphates, functions integrally on the basis of annual negotiations between producers (especially Phosrock in the United States and the *Office Chérifien des Phosphates* in Morocco) and fertilizer manufacturers. There is no international phosphate trade as such. There are, however, for each consumer country, trading companies which handle the majority of the fertilizer products destined essentially for small manufacturers. Their share of the market is on the increase in so far as producers are seeking to add value to their raw materials to the utmost by processing them on the spot (phosphates into phosphoric acid and even into superphosphates). Many large trading companies have recently opened fertilizer departments. The most significant importers include Noranda in Canada, Boliden in Sweden and in Switzerland, the Japanese *sogo shosa*. . . Among the trading firms we find once more Philipp Brothers (in Great Britain), Marc Rich (in Italy), Tennant Trading (subsidiary of Consolidated Gold Fields in Great Britain), Amalgamated (in Japan), the Hochschild group, ACLI. . .

There is no doubt a great deal of room left in this sector for the activities of the trading companies which should gradually expand here as they did in the oil market.

Oil

Because of its importance in world trade, oil cannot be analysed as a classical commodity. And yet, the recent behaviour of the crude-oil market would tempt one, all else being equal, to consider it 'a market like any other' which has evolved in three phases: a cartel of companies (the same type as the aluminium or banana oligopolies) replaced to some degree (on the level of crude-oil) by a cartel of nations — the most efficient to date — whose progressive deregulation has facilitated the expansion of the hitherto marginal free market. This free market has acquired a new dynamism with the opening of the futures markets in London and New York, although the latter still have to show proof of their efficiency. But even before, at the beginning of the seventies, the expansion of the free market had attracted new operators which were in a much better position than the classical traders to assume the intrinsic risks.

The first was indisputably Philipp Brothers which then began its prodigious growth of the seventies. From 1974 Marc Rich, who, the reader will recall, was formerly the head of the oil division at Philipp Brothers, based the development of his firm on oil. At present, these two firms are of equal importance on the oil market, which accounts for half of their respective turnovers, and dominate the free market in oil. Alongside them there are small specialized firms such as Transworld, controlled by Dutch capital but registered in Bermuda, Vitol of Rotterdam, Gatoil of Dallas or Oasis Petroleum. Most of the classical oil companies also engage in trade, but more often than not, do so within the group itself (Exxon International, Shell International Trading. . .). Curiously enough, the trading majors of other commodities have, with the exception of Phibro, taken little advantage of the oil manna: Cargill took a minor risk in the sector with Tradax Petroleum (a loan of almost $50 million to an oil company), Hochschild controls the Schlubach company and Ed. and F. Man has associated with a small British company to form Premier Man, but all in all their impact continues to be modest. The problem with oil is that, apart from the classical risk of price fluctuations, the freight risk is much higher than for any other commodity (Marc Rich, like Phibro, saw fit to invest in a shipping fleet).

In any event, the oil market is still in the initial stages of its evolution: it seems hardly likely that OPEC will succeed in resuming control of the market and maintaining monopoly domination. On the other hand, it is difficult to imagine that a radical evolution towards a totally free market whose every convulsion will threaten the international economic balance, will ever materialize. The expanse between the two situations is vast enough for the future of trade to remain relatively uncertain. Because of the size of the market and the volume of transactions handled, it has (and will most likely continue to serve as) a formidable launch-pad for the trading structures which have developed in this sector.

CONCLUSION

The aim of this book was to describe international trade in commodities with special reference to the operators therein — the international traders — about which little is known. It was the author's desire to present as impassionate and objective a description as possible, attempting to bring forward reliable material on these often mysterious, but yet essential links in the international trading chain.

The purpose of this conclusion is less to pass judgement (the author has no delusions about how influential his judgement is likely to be) than to put a number of theses in the balance and to attempt to answer the ultimate question: how useful, how efficient is trade?

Let us first take a look at the most common criticisms levelled against international trading:

(1) The trader is a parasite whose function is of no social use. He could easily be replaced by State trading bodies.

(2) The concentration of trade leads to the creation of oligopolies which are dangerous to the freedom of trade in the long-term and can lead to the manipulation of prices on the world level.

(3) The trading function is costly for the product chain and correspondingly reduces the price paid to the producer.

(4) International trade is a vector of imperialism in the developing countries encouraging policies of export-oriented growth, which are

often dangerous and lead to a greater dependence on the part of the developing countries.

These opinions are relatively widespread and are shared by people more or less everywhere without a marked distinction as to ideology or policy[1]. They are, moreover, strengthened by the veil of silence, even of mystery which the international traders love to drape aroung themselves: 'if they were not guilty, they would have nothing to hide', is the general opinion! Let us study each of these criticisms separately and try to do them justice.

(1) On the usefulness of the trading function:

We feel that the trader has a physical role to play: that of managing the flow of commodities both in time and in space in a universe characterized by instability. It is this very instability which in the final analysis, provides the *raison d'être* of trade. In a stable economic setting, the activity of the trader would lose a great deal of its usefulness: at best, he would become involved in storage or transport. But the commodity markets have been characterized — especially since 1973 — by a chronic instability and the failure of even minimal efforts to check this instability on the world level. Since then, the trader has come into his own: it is he who is capable of assuming the direct and related risks of the market. But would it not be possible for the producers, consumers or even governments to replace him? We do not see this as being possible in the present circumstances. The international market of a given commodity must be seen as a whole and the maximum chances of success can only be ensured through a global approach. The only feasible solution would be the creation of a supranational trade authority and not the take-over of trade functions by national public or private firms: the few example we have of direct inter-governmental trade (whether in the South, the North or the East), are hardly convincing if seen from the point of view of the strict economic profitablity and not in their political context[2].

We therefore have no doubts as to the utility of the trading function. But there is no denying that the function itself can have its disadvantages: the presence of the trader could cut off the producer or the consumer from the international market; some people believe that the purchasing activity of the trader slows down the reactions of supply in relation to demand and causes a delay in production in relation to the potential of the market (notably in a downturn period)[3]. This may be true but we see the effect as being limited to a few products and to relatively short periods of time. This being as it is, the danger involved in the filtering role played by the trader, is unquestionable especially for markets which are not equipped with a futures market which is acknowledged to be efficient.

(2) This leads us to the problem of the effective power wielded by trading. There is clearly no direct link between the trader's cut and the effective price of a product on the international market. What motivates him is the difference which he will make between the two prices, whatever their level.

In any event, when a product is quoted on the futures market, the size of its market is such that no one trading firm, no matter how powerful, will risk trying to force the prices in one direction or the other in the medium-term[4]. A trading firm can, at best, use its positions to influence the market in the short term (by means of spreads or straddles) though not without exposing itself to enormous risks (the Cook and ACLI examples. . .). For products with tighter markets and *a fortiori* devoid of a futures market, the room for manoeuvre left to the trader — or to any operator for that matter — is clearly much greater. It should not be forgotten, however, that the trader has nothing to gain — unlike the producer or consumer — from manipulating the prices.

Although the extreme concentration of certain physical markets in the hands of a few firms could instill fears of the establishment of an oligopoly or oligopsony (or both) we have no example at hand of such collusive practices. On the contrary, trade, especially in the major products, is an extremely competitive activity functioning generally on the verge of profitablity (with the exclusion of all speculative activity). It is, nonetheless, always possible for a firm to have a privileged non-competitive position in a given country, but then this has much more to do with the internal structures of the country in question.

It would, however, be false to say that the trader has no influence on prices: a trading company usually has access to a great deal of intelligence (which it can manipulate at the risk of ruining its reputation for reliability) and, by the size of its own operations, can pull the market for a time in one direction or the other. In tight markets, it can, if it has the means, attempt a corner even though this type of

manoeuvre is carried out most often by armchair traders or speculators.

Let us recapitulate on this major issue: the trader has no influence on
the formation of medium and long term price trends for products
which are traded on a futures market. In the short term, its influence is
certain but of lesser importance for the producers and consumers. For
other products, the situation can vary considerably, the hold which the
traders have on such markets can often ensure them real yields simply
because they are established there. There is no denying that in the
present state of things, a vast, efficient and well-supervised futures
market is still the best guarantee of transparency of operations in a
given product[5].

(3) As to the exact cost of the trader's intervention, it must be quite
clear that the profit made by the trader is much less of a commercial
nature than of a speculative one. In many cases, it would not be
incorrect to say that the cost of the trader's intervention is supported
by the private speculator who acts as his counterpart on the futures
market. When all is said and done, it is the futures market which
financially supports the activity of the trader. The picture should not,
however, be excessively idealized since the 'speculative' role of the
trader is probably an additional factor in the instablity of prices. In any
case it is certain that the function of the trader is in most cases not very
costly for the chain of a given product.

(4) There is no room for doubt as to the 'influence' which the trader
has in many developing countries; international trade is most at ease
when administrative structures are permeable and transparent. The
more a country like the United States is able to control its trade (and
even it has not been able to prevent the frauds committed in the Gulf of
Mexico), the more difficult it is to do so for most of the Third World
countries who are time and again solicited by 'dream merchants'. It is
certain that the interest of the trader who — as we have seen — is very
often industrialized upstream or downstream, lies in opening the
economy and the markets of a country as far as possible to international trade, although it may not necessarily be in the best interest of
the country concerned. This influence is particularly apparent in the
agro-foodstuffs business, in the choice of rural development policies
and of the direction in which food consumption should evolve. The aim
of the trader is to have as large and unregulated a market as possible.

In the pursuit of this aim he comes up against varying degrees of regulation which he either fights or penetrates[6].

In the final analysis, the problem is less that of the influence of trade than that of the inability of the administrative apparatus to utilize it.

Moreover, it is certain that commodity trade is far from being a uniform whole, that next to the nearly fifty major companies which this book has described at length, there are many dangerous operators whose sole concern is immediate profit and not the long term policy of a firm: men who carry out one more or less shady operation, only to disappear and reappear with a new address. The trading world is replete with such examples, the names of which are well known even if they are not mentioned in these pages. There is probably still a need for education and for the inculcation of moral values: education about the real state of affairs on the international commodity markets, and bringing in, both within and without[7], a healthy dose of ethics.

International trade in commodities therefore has an important 'mechanical' role to play in the unstable universe of world markets. But this is not all. The general trend of the past twenty years has been an extreme concentration around a few multi-product firms: new-comers have been rare, profiting in general from the opening of new markets. At present, however, the dynamism of these firms largely surpasses the narrow framework of commodities in two spheres:

– an exhaustive industrialization of the product chain or chains leading, little by little, to a radical transformation of the firm and making it one of the most dynamic agents of the trading world;

– an expansion of the international finance sector ranging from the creation of giant services conglomerates to international trade: commercial, logistic, financial. . .(although the events of 1984 have demonstrated the real limits of such associations).

The first case takes us to the classical field of the industrial trans-national companies but on a scale and with a logic rarely attained before (the Cargill example).

The second case puts the finger on what will probably be the reality of tomorrow: transnationals in the service sector grouping the efficiency of trade, the financial clout of banks, the contribution of research (Phibro): the felicitous crossing on the world scale of a trading room, a Wall Street firm, a laboratory and a marketing service!

Whatever the future may hold in store, the twenty odd mysterious, little known and discrete firms which 'make' the international trade in commodities, will have a role to play in it. They are already showing themselves to be one of the most dynamic forces of the capitalist system.

BIBLIOGRAPHY AND SOURCES

This book is practically the first to be written on this subject. Journalists, often rather prolific, have chosen to be relatively close-mouthed on the subject. The reader will therefore not be surprised to learn that the major part of our sources has been oral: the bibliography gives a few clues, a few indications, but remains, as is to be expected, very short!

Chapter 1

Evolution of practices, methods and structures of international trade since the 11th century

This chapter has no claim to originality, since the author has merely taken a fresh look at a certain number of elements. We have made considerable use of the remarkable works by Fernand BRAUDEL, *The Mediterranean and the Mediterranean World in the Age of Philip II*, London, New York, 1972, and *Civilization and Capitalism, 15th–18th Century*, London, New York, 1982–1984, as well as the *Fontana Economic History of Europe*, 6 volumes, London, New York, 1971–1976, edited by Carlo CIPOLLA.

On the first forms of trade, J.N. BALL, *Merchants and Merchandise*, London, 1977; on the British East India Companies, the works by

K.N. CHAUDHURY, *The Trading World of Asia and the English East India Company*, Cambridge, 1978.

For the other periods, the main source was G.L. REES, *Britain's Commodity Markets*, London 1975, and a number of works on the geography and commerce of the times (mentioned in footnotes), as well as numerous company monographs.

Chapter 2

The different functions in international trade

Apart from many studies and general articles (especially the report of the French *Conseil Economique et Social* entitled: *Les sociétés de commerce international*, Paris, 1982, we have made considerable use of the annual reports published by various firms as well as a few existing monographs.

Chapter 3

An approach to world commodity markets

This chapter is but a brief reminder. For more detailed information consult the five volumes published by Editions Economica: MOUTON, CHALMIN (eds.), *Matières premières et échanges internationaux*, Volumes I to V, 1980, 1982, 1983, 1984, as well as P. CHALMIN, *Les marchés mondiaux des matières premières*, Paris, P.U.F., 1984.

Chapters 4 to 6

The trader's function
The trader's many jobs
Classification and evolution of trading

Essentially oral sources and a few press clippings.

Chapter 7

The grain trade

Two books provide a well-documented analysis of this topic: MOR-GAN (Dan), *Merchants of Grain*, New York, 1980; GILMORE (Ian), *Poor Harvest*, Longman, 1982. Also worthy of note is Raul GREEN, *Histoire d'un secret bien gardé, Bunge et Born*, Paris, 1984.

Apart from bits of information gleaned from the firms themselves, (private publications by Cargill, Louis Dreyfus, André, Peter Cremer) we have used the works of the North American Congress on Latin America (NACLA) and especially: 'US Grain Arsenal', *NACLA's Latin America and Empire report*, vol. IX, 7th October, 1975; Roger BRUBACH and P. FLYNN, *Agribusiness in the Americas*, New York, 1979.

Additional sources include an article in *Business Week* on Cargill (16th April, 1979), a study by Ricardo SIDICARO, 'Note sur le conglomérat Bunge et Born', GEREI–INRA, June 1975, an article in *Fortune* on 'Farmers Export' (20 April, 1981).

Chapter 8

The sugar trade

Here we should like to refer the reader essentially to our Ph.D. thesis: *L'Emergence d'une firme multinationale au sein de l'économie sucrière mondiale, Tate and Lyle 1860–1980*, University Paris IV, 1981, english version to be published in 1988 by Harwood Academic Publishers. We have also consulted LAMALLE (Jacques), *Le Roi du sucre*, Paris, 1980 (on Maurice Varsano), *Sucres et Denrées'* annual reports as well as the histories of firms like Ed. and F. Man (*The House of Man*, by Tim DUMAS, unpublished), Woodhouse, Drake and Carey (C.H. WOODHOUSE, *The Woodhouse Drakes and Careys*, London, 1977) and Czarnikow (JANES and SAYERS, *The Story of Czarnikow*, London, 1963). On *Sucres et Denrées*, see also the article written by Patrick du GENESTOUX, 'La Stratégie de Sucres et Denrées au sein de la filière sucre', in MOUTON (Claude), CHALMIN (Philippe), *Les marchés internationaux des matières premières*, Paris, 1982. On United Molasses, W.A. MENEIGHT, *A History of the United Molasses Company*, London, 1977.

Chapter 9

The coffee and cocoa trades

Our main sources are the annual reports of the companies themselves: Gill and Duffus, S. and W. Berisford, *Sucres et Denrées*, and a few small volumes published by ACLI, Volkart as well as parts of a specialized bi-monthly journal: *Cocoa and Coffee International* (London).

Chapter 10

The non-ferrous metals trade

The main sources are still the companies' annual reports: Philipp Brothers (formerly Engelhard), Commercial Metals, Amalgamated Metals, Preussag, *Metallgesellschaft*, Johnson Matthey. On Phibro we should mention two in-depth articles in *Business Week* (3rd September 1979) and *Institutional Investor* (December 1981). An article on Marc Rich in *Fortune* at the beginning of 1984, and a journalistic treatment by A. Craig COPETAS, *Metal Men*, New York, 1985.

We have also used the announcements and articles published in *Metal Bulletin* as well as a study published by that body: *Metal Traders of the World* (1980).

Chapter 11

Trade in some other major commodities

• On cotton, the main source was the UNCTAD report TD/B/C.1/2/ 9/, *Fibres et Textiles: dimensions du pouvoir des sociétés trans-nationales*, which the authors have since published elsewhere: Frédéric CLAIRMONTE and John CAVANAGH, *The World in their Web*, London, Zed Press, 1982. The ideas propounded by these works are less than objective and must at least be balanced by the reply of the American government to the UNCTAD report (TD/B/IPC/ COTTON/20, 19 March, 1981) and by a publication of the USDA: *How U.S. Cotton is sold for Export* (F.A.S. M-198, December 1980).

The author has also used the brochures published by Ralli and Volkart. Read also, Lucien MARCHAL, *L'Epopée du coton*, Brussels, 1959.

• On hard fibres: the UNCTAD report, *The marketing of hard fibres (sisal and henequen), areas for international cooperation*, TD/B/C.1/PSC/21 (Geneva,1981), written by Henri YOUNNES.

For rubber: the thesis written by the CNAM economist, Emile BORTOLATO, *Prix du caoutchouc naturel: Arbitrage entre pays producteurs et pays européens*, CNAM–Clermont-Ferrand, 1981, as well as annual reports from *Safic Alcan* and the study by Colin BARLOW, *The Natural Rubber Industry in Malaysia*, Kuala Lumpur, 1978.

• For tea: the brochure published by the WORLD DEVELOPMENT MOVEMENT, *The Tea Trade*, London, 1980.

• On bananas, different articles written by Frédéric CLAIRMONTE and especially his study for UNCTAD, TB/B/C.1/205, *The Marketing and Distribution System for Bananas*, Geneva, 1978.

• For tobacco, another study by UNCTAD, TD/B/C.1/205, *The Marketing and distribution of tobacco*, Geneva, 1978.

• For fertilizers and phosphates, UNCTAD TD/B/C.1/PSC/22, *The processing and marketing of phosphates, areas for international cooperation*, Geneva 1981.

NOTES

Introduction

1. The yearly reports on international trade published by GATT (General Agreement on Tariffs and Trade, based in Geneva) since 1954 clearly demonstrate this development.
2. At least for strictly commercial purposes. Speculation in commodities has always attracted considerable capital originating from outside trade and commerce.

Chapter 1

Evolution of practices, methods and structures of international trade since the 11th century

1. BRAUDEL (F.), *Civilization and Capitalism, 15th–18th Century,* Vol. II, *The Wheels of Commerce,* London, Collins, 1982, p. 434. It would seem in fact that large-scale trading was initially itinerary. Two of the names passed down to us are those of the 7th century Venetian Romano Mairano and the 8th century Genoese Benedetto Zaccaria. See also BERNARD (J.), 'Trade and Finance in the Middle Ages 900–1500,' in Carlo CIPOLLA (ed), *Fontana Economic History of Europe,* London, 1971, p. 307, and Michel BALARD, 'Gênes et la Mer Noire,' *Revue Historique,* Juillet–Septembre 1983, No 547, pp. 31–54.
2. BRAUDEL, *op. cit.,* pp. 448–450, and BALL (J.N.), *Merchants and Merchandise,* London 1977, pp. 34 *sq.* The name 'Merchants of the Staple' came from the stop-over (*étape*) made at Calais.
3. They were referred to as the Lombards because they came from towns such as Asti, Piacenza, Lucca and Siena. The term Lombard later became generic and synonymous with financial activities (e.g. Lombard Street in London).
4. Especially after the election of Charles V to the Imperial throne in 1519 (Ball, *op. cit.,* pp. 106 *sq.*).

5. GLAMAN (Kristof), 'European Trade 1500–1750,' in Carlo CIPOLLA (ed.), *Fontana Economic History of Europe*, London, 1974, Vol.II, p.518.

6. Cited by Fernand BRAUDEL, *The Mediterranean and the Mediterranean World in the Age of Philip II*, London, Collins, 1972, p. 561.

7. Braudel, *Civilization and Capitalism*, p. 443.

8. On the East India Company, see: CHAUDHURY (K.N.), *The Trading World of Asia and the English India Company*, Cambridge, 1978, and *The Economic Development of India under the East India Company*, Cambridge, 1975.

9. FAURE (Edgar), *La Banqueroute de Law*, Paris, 1977.

10. Here again we are dealing with commercial imperialism. The company possessed a quasi-monopoly of the sale of manufactures and a monopsony of the purchase of indigenous raw materials.

PEARSON (Scott R.), *The Economic Imperialism of the Royal Niger Company*, Stanford, Food Research Institute, 1971. The monopoly of the Royal Niger Company lasted from 1886 to 1899. The Company then became the United Africa Company and is now part of the Unilever group.

11. The *Compagnie Olivier* set up operations in Ning Po in the vicinity of Shanghai in 1888 and became involved in the import–export trade with China.

On the beginnings of Butterfield and Swire, see MARINER and HYDE, *The Senior John Samuel Swire*, Liverpool, 1973.

12. The British seem to have been less 'protectionist' in India. Thus in 1851 the Volkart Brothers of Winterthur in Switzerland opened a branch office in Bombay from which they carried on a thriving business exporting commodities from India and Ceylon and importing consumer goods.

13. BERLAN (Bertrand), *Unilever, une multinationale discrète*, Paris, 1978, p. 87.

14. VAN DER VEE (R.), *Growth of the Antwerp Mart*, The Hague, 1963.

15. BARBOUR (Violet), *Capitalism in Amsterdam in the 18th century*, Baltimore, 1950.

16. BERGERON (Louis), *Banquiers, négociants et manufacturiers parisiens du Directoire à l'Empire*, Paris, 1978, pp. 287–288.

17. BRAUDEL, F., *Civilization and capitalism, op. cit.*, vol. III, *The Perspective of the World*, p. 231.

18. BEACHEY (R.W.), *The British West Indies Sugar Industry in the late 19th Century*, Oxford, 1957. Very often the planter was linked to a metropolitan merchant under the consignment system: in exchange for an advance on the harvest paid by the merchant, the planter would undertake to sell all his produce through him and to purchase all his supplies from him. This explains why many West Indian plantations gradually passed into the hands of British or French harbour merchants, especially from 1850 and in the aftermath of the crisis caused by the emancipation of the slaves.

19. ROTHSTEIN (Morton), 'Multinationals in the grain trade 1850–1914', in Jeremy ATTACK (ed.), *Business and Economic History*, 2nd series, XII, 1983, pp. 85–92.

20. STOUT (H.), 'The Toko from Rotterdam and what came after', in H. BAUDET (Ed.), *Trade World and World Trade: One Hundred Years of Internatio*, Rotterdam, 1963, pp. 28–29.

21. REES (G.L.), ßop. citß., p. 130.

22. *History and Activities of the Ralli Trading Group*, privately published, London, 1979.

23. Private publication of the Louis Dreyfus company (undated). In the interwar period, one of Léopold's sons, Louis Louis-Dreyfus, was to play a prominent role in French politics.

24. BOUVIER (Jean), *Naissance d'une Banque: Le Crédit Lyonnais*, Paris, 1968, p. 277.

25. MAURETTE, *op. cit.*, p.40.

26. ROTHSTEIN, *ibid.*, p. 88.

27. Raul H. GREEN, Catherine LAURENT, *Bunge et Born, histoire d'un secret bien gardé*, Paris, 1984.

28. See RAZOUS (Paul), *Cartels, trusts et diverses ententes de producteurs*, Paris, 1935; PLUMMER (Alfred), *Raw Materials and War Materials*, London, 1973; HARVEY (Charles E.), *The Rio Tinto Company (1873–1954)*, London, 1981.

29. The fact that most of the merchandise was transported in casks explains the importance of this profession whose members were often actively involved in trade. Tim DUMAS, *The House of Man*, unpublished document, ca. 1966.

30. WOODHOUSE (C.H.), *The Woodhouses, Drakes and Careys of Mincing Lane*, London, 1977.

31. Hurford JANES and H.J. SAYERS, *The Story of Czarnikow*, London, 1963.

32. *Les fils et les petits-fils de Maurice Duclos: 1874–1974*, privately published.

33. Archives of the Goldschmidt firm. The Goldschmidt code books, published in 1908, provide particularly interesting reading material: on the export end we find at least twenty American shippers, but on the import end in Italy, where Goldschmidt was particularly active, we find a considerable number of importers and, especially, a great many millers and pasta manufacturers (no less than 20 for the town of Florence alone).

34. GAFTA: Grain and Feed Trade Association, located in London at the Baltic Exchange.

35. See Jacques FIERAIN, *Les Raffineries de sucre des ports de France (XIXe début du XXe)*, Lille, 1976, p. 175 *sq*. Note that in those days brokerage firms were most often private firms and were therefore responsible to the extent of their own assets. In some of the articles published in the *Journal des Fabricants de Sucre* (JFS) in connection with the crash of 1905 we can find scenes worthy of Balzac's *César Birotteau*.

36. JANES and SAYERS, *op. cit.*, p. 79. Pepper was, however, perhaps a special case given the extremely speculative nature of the market. In 1935 one of London's brokerage firms, James and Shakespeare, tried to corner the pepper market after having successfully cornered the shellac market in 1934. Its failure led to the bankruptcy of many brokerage firms, among them, one of the oldest, Rolls and Sons (*ibid.*, p. 92 and A. DAUPHIN-MEUNIER, *La City de Londres*, Paris, 1940, p. 81).

37. Quoted in *Histoire du Commerce*, ed. by J. LACOUR-GAYET, Paris, 1952, Vol. V, p.127.

38. Charles RUFENACHT, *Le Café et les principaux marchés de matières premières*, Le Havre, 1945, p. 240.

39. Louis PIERREIN, *Industries traditionnelles du port de Marseille: Le cycle des sucres et des oléagineux*, Marseilles, 1975, p. 204.

40. *Joseph Travers and Sons: A Few Records of an Old Firm*, London, 1924, and *Chronicles of Cannon Street*, London, 1953. On the eve of the Second World War Travers employed 717 persons.

41. It is interesting to note that the first attempts in this direction were the result of private initiative. The first sugar negotiations were held among producer associations grouped in a cartel (Tarafa in 1925, Chadbourne in 1931, Thomas Chadbourne being the representative of the American banks controlling Cuban sugar production) before taking place on a state level (1936 and 1938).

42. Jean GOTTMAN, *Les Marchés des matières premières*, Paris, 1957, p. 86.

43. The first *caisses de stabilisation* were created after the Korean war by Pierre Moussa, then Director of Economic Affairs at the French Ministry for Overseas Territories and who became the last president of the Paribas bank before its nationalization in 1981.

44. Psalm XXIII, 'The Lord is my Shepherd, I shall not want' (published in the *West African Times* of Accra on August 5th, 1944 and kindly passed on to me by Mr. Bernard Reysset).

45. The Combined Food Board became the International Emergency Food Council at the constituent conference of the Food and Agricultural Organization (FAO) in Washington in May 1946. At that time, numerous projects for a World Food Board to manage and regulate world produce markets were circulating but none of them were pursued. In 1987, considering all the UNCTAD failures in recent years, such a project would certainly be something to look forward to.
46. It would be fitting to include here the Australian and South African exports which are handled by monopolies (CSR and Hullets), with the tacit agreement of the governments concerned.
47. Note the special case of Argentina which had centralized its trade under Perón and liberalised it after the fall from power of his second wife.
48. In his *Bourses de Commerce et marchés à terme de marchandises*, Paris, Dalloz, 1986.

Chapter 2

The different functions in international trade

1. But the London auctions are losing ground to the sales organised by the Tea Marketing Boards of the producing countries.
2. A branch, true enough, of de Beers (South Africa) the world's largest producer!
3. Let us contribute by quoting Pope Paul VI (as he received the Italian Brokers' Federation): 'Whoever counts the broker among the beneficial elements of society, is by no means mistaken.'
4. Successors of the sworn produce brokers (*courtiers de marchandises assermentés*) whose monopoly was revoked in 1866.
5. A seat on the Chicago Board of Trade is worth, at present, more than one on the New York Stock Exchange.
6. It is said in Chicago that 'when the analyst of Merryl Lynch coughs, the market catches a cold'.
7. Frédéric CLAIRMONTE, 'Les Economies libérales dans le piège du capitalisme financier', *Le Monde Diplomatique*, March 1982, and Philippe CHALMIN, 'La Montée en puissance du négoce international des matières premières dans les structures du capitalisme international', *Le Monde Diplomatique*, May 1982.
8. In 1974 the Crown Agents, having pursued a financial policy of a rather adventurous nature, (to say the least) were obliged to announce losses of £195 million which the British Government was forced to make good. In 1983, the Crown Agents were constrained to sell their headquarters' building to obtain liquidity. They had just lost the custom of the Sultanate of Brunei.
9. Such is also the case for the British company Tate and Lyle, which acts in this manner for the sugar projects it manages in various parts of the world.
10. See: Frédéric CLAIRMONTE, 'Les sogo shosas, fer de lance de l'offensive des intérêts japonais à l'étranger', *Le Monde Diplomatique*, February 1981. UNCTAD, *Fibres et Textiles: Dimension du pouvoir des sociétés transnationales*, Doc. TD/B/C1/129, 1981, pp. 71–83.
11. As regards Japan's oil supplies the *sogo shosa* have succeeded in the past few years in carving out a place for themselves among the 'majors' in the sector. In 1979, Mitsubishi imported 900,000 barrels per day, Mitsui 400,000, Marubeni 300,000. . . See Jeffrey SEGAL, 'The Rise of the *Sogo shosa*', *Petroleum Economist*, May 1981, pp. 201–204.
12. For example, C. Itoh is heavily involved in the development of Thailand's maize production. Another japanese company is presently developing 50,000 acres of wheat

and soya in the State of Mato Grosso and 124,000 acres in the State of Minas Gerais, both in Brazil. Mitsui is participating in a sugar project in Swaziland. In forestry, Sumitumo is present in Malaysia and Nissho Iwai in Papua New Guinea.

13. And in the opinion of most Japanese analysts this is what constitutes the essential strength of the *shosa*. Yasuo OKI, 'Sogo shosa's Role as a Sub-system of the International Economy', *JFTC*, Tokyo, 1980.

14. Some of the present-day Hamburg firms started their careers abroad: Melchers and Co. (Bremen) founded in China in 1806, Arnold Otto Meyer in Singapore in 1840 and C. Illies and Co. in Nagasaky in 1859.

15. This was often due to the fact that British firms lost their trade monopoly on the markets of the developed Commonwealth where local firms, sometimes of British origin, severed all links with the home country. Moreover, the decolonization process has, in many cases, been a brutal one. Booker McConnel, for example, at one time very active in the West Indies (especially in Guyana) has practically disappeared from the region and has considerably reduced its activities as an international trading company (in Africa and in the West Indies).

16. On the U.A.C. see the critical report written by Bertrand BERLAN in *Unilever, une multinationale discrète*, Paris, 1978, pp. 83–110.

17. Size-wise Lonrho could be considered an international trading company. In 1983, for example, its turnover was £2.4 billion.

18. See Stephanie JONES, *Two Centuries of Overseas Trading: The origins and Growth of the Inchcape Group*, London, Macmillan, 1986.

19. Hindered in his business activities by the American Civil War, John Samuel Swire, a cotton trader from Liverpool, opened an office in Shanghai in 1866. Swire Pacific is still controlled from London by John Swire and Sons.

20. *The East Asiatic Company Ltd.*, Copenhagen,1957.

21. East Asiatic is probably the largest international firm dealing in printing supplies.

22. The socialist countries have apparently set up no general international trading companies to date, but we cannot affirm with any degree of certainty that this is also the case as far as commodities are concerned.

23. *Optorg* was created in 1905 at the time of the French–Russian alliance to export to Russia. After the Russian Revolution in 1917 it shifted its attention to Asia. It later abandoned its activities in that part of the world and turned its attention fully to Africa.

Chapter 3

An approach to world commodity markets

1. See the fundamental study by Ray GOLDBERG, *Agribusiness Coordination*, Harvard, 1967 (on the agro-foodstuffs complex) and the special issue of *Annales des Mines*, 'Les Filières industrielles', January 1980.

2. One could also consider the definition of Christian Stoffaes: 'an industrial chain comprises all the stages in the production process which brings raw materials to satisfy an end need of the consumer whether this need takes the form of goods or services.'

3. A more detailed study of the subject matter discussed in this chapter can be found in: MOUTON, CHALMIN, (eds.), *Matières Premières et Echanges Internationaux*, Paris, Economica, 5 volumes published so far: I (1980), II (1980), III (1982), IV (1983), V (1984).

4. This statement needs to be qualified: though it is true that a processor (refiner) can be in a strong position, it is also often true that he is strapped by his dependence on others for his supplies. One must distinguish clearly between high technology processing and

the common processing procedures. We should also not lose sight of the fact that the processing capacity of various products constitutes a market in its own right, and that, in addition, the development of the reprocessing industry is beginning to give rise to a new set of problems.

5. The breakdown was as follows: Australia: Broken Hill group; Brazil: Bethlehem Steel (49%) and US Steel; Gabon: Comilog (US Steel 44%); Ghana: Union Carbide (nationalized in 1974); India: British Steel (nationalized); South Africa: the government and Anglo-Continental; Mexico: Bethlehem Steel (government participation in its capital since then); Zaire: Gecamines (state-owned).

6. A statement which should be qualified. Many industrial firms in the developed countries try to ensure supply from 'reliable' producing countries by means of financial and technical participation. The Japanese pursue a policy of this type for coal supplies in Australia and for iron ore in Brazil. This is also the policy of a number of German firms.

7. It is then commonly called a 'free' market as opposed to a producer market.

8. Whereas for most products, direct negotiations concern only delivery dates and quantities, the price being the free market price of the day.

Chapter 4

The trader's function

1. He later takes out a performance bond.

2. This case was initially devised for our seminar at the *Conservatoire National des Arts et Métiers* by two traders from the Louis Dreyfus company, Mr. Samuel and Mr. Belloin. We have taken the liberty of rewriting it using the same basic data. The case having been devised in 1982, some of the figures have changed as far as the Egyptian grain market is concerned. This does not impair its validity for our present purpose. In 1985, the Egyptian wheat market was the stake in a trade war fought between the major exporters, who were conquering markets from each other by heavy doses of subsidies and bonuses. Consequently, the price paid for her wheat by Egypt is now unrelated to prices made in Chicago.

3. The real freight rates at that time were in fact: 26, 26.50, 27, 27.50. We have, of our own accord, adopted rather exaggerated freight rates to make the outcome of the case more interesting.

4. The 'trader basis' is equivalent to the difference between the futures market price and the tender.

Chapter 5

The trader's many jobs

1. By way of example here are the salaries recorded for some American traders in 1976–77:

Philip Mac Caull (Director of Louis Dreyfus USA) $1,000,000

William Sparks (Executive Director, V.P. Cook Industries) $500,000

C.R. Parott (Vice-President, Cook Industries) $450 000.

These are of course exceptional cases of trading team directors. The best paid trader in 1983 was perhaps David Tendler, chairman of Philip Bros who was the third best paid US company director with a total of $6.9 million (*Business Week*, 7 May 1984).

2. Our information is drawn from reports and accounts of Cook Industries as well as from articles published in *Business Week*, the *Wall Street Journal* and *Fortune*. Some facts are also to be found in the study by Dan MORGAN, *Merchants of Grain*, New York, 1980.

3. An operation which they were to attempt again less successfully in 1979–80 on the silver market.

4. In theory a single individual was not allowed to take out a position of more than 3 million bushels. With 22 million, the Hunts were considerably in excess of that figure. But Cook would have had to be able to prove the commercial links between the different members of the family and that proved to be an exceedingly difficult task. Moreover, the Hunts went as far as the physical delivery of the contracts, and selling stocks ex-warehouse.

5. It seems that in 1975 Gill and Duffus used its position as statistician to cement its position as trader. The firm's forecasts were relatively incoherent in that year: by announcing, contrary to expectations, a grinding–production deficit for the first quarter of the year 1974–75, it caused a rise in prices (which, it is said, allowed Gill and Duffus to extricate itself from a difficult situation). In subsequent forecasts it reversed this movement by announcing increasing surpluses which was in fact what actually took place. In some circles, it was thereafter known as 'Gill and Bluffus'. Similarly, the French trader, *Sucres et Denrées* published in April 1980 an information circular containing a graph which compared the prices of 1974 and 1980. Was that a manoeuvre aimed at triggering off a price rise?

6. Dan MORGAN, *op. cit.*, p. 169.

7. Cargill has had close political ties notably with the Republicans (Nixon) but also with the Democrats: the two Minnesota senators in 1975, Hubert Humphrey, Vice-president under Johnson and Walter Mondale, Vice-president under Carter.

8. Richard E. CAVES, 'Organization, Scale and Performance of the Grain Trade', *Food Research Institute Studies* (Stanford), XVI, 3, 1977–78, pp.107–123.

9. Which is not the case for other commodities.

10. CAVES, *op. cit.*, p. 115.

11. The major elevators owned by Cargill in the United States are: Terre Haute (near to Reserve in Louisiana, 300 million bushels per year, 158,000 tonnes of grain, 36,000 tonnes of cakes, 45,000 tonnes of molasses), Norfolk (on the East coast, 200 million bushels per year), Toledo (on the Great Lakes, 40 million bushels) Duluth (also on the Great Lakes), 100 million bushels per year.

12. UNCTAD Document ȚD/B/C4/203.

13. In 1974 molasses was being quoted at $70 per tonne (as against $600 for sugar). In 1978 it was being quoted at $30 as compared with $150 for sugar.

14. *Société Européenne de Mélasses* in France, Pacific Molasses and Knappen Molasses in the United States, *Melasse Handels Gesellschaft* in the Federal Republic of Germany, Pure Cane Molasses Company in South Africa. . .

15. We shall return later to the processing firms which have widened the scope of their activities to trading.

16. These courts of arbitration nominate one or more experts to settle the case, the decision being referred to as an 'award'. This procedure is more rapid and efficient than going through the normal legal procedure.

17. This brought about a three months prison sentence, without bail, for Mac Caull, when he was president of Louis Dreyfus U.S.A. (Dan MORGAN, *op. cit.*, pp. 257–263).

18. Let us not dwell here on the insurance question. One can note, however, that many merchants are also acting as insurance brokers.

19. There is also a third type of freight contract: the trip charter, which is a voyage

charter where freight is deducted on the basis of time. Finally there are tonnage contracts where the ship-owner undertakes to transport a certain quantity of merchandise in a stipulated time and in specific lots.

20. The Nord Grain contract for grain shipments from North America, Amwelsh for coal shipments from the East Coast of the United States, African Phos, to name but a few.
21. Daniel BOURNAZAC, *Les grands courants des trafics maritimes mondiaux*, Paris, Ministère des Transports, 1979, pp. 10–12.
22. They are often expressed in terms of 'worldscale', worldscale being a reference base corresponding to a specific ship.
23. Since 1985 there exists a freight futures market in London (Biffex), quoting an index of dry cargo routes. But its use as a hedging device remains rather imprecise. In 1986, another market opened for tanker freights.
24. Annual report of the Engelhardt Mineral and Chemicals Corporation, 1979.
25. UNCTAD, *Le Contrôle du trafic de vrac sec par les sociétés transnationales*, document TD/ B/C 4.203, 20 May, 1980.
26. Alcoa: 138,000 dwt, Reynolds: 189,000 dwt, Alcan: 8,000 dwt.
27. The banker's confidence may be misplaced, as in the Cook case, but even there the latter's assets were sufficient to make good the losses. At the end of 1980 the executive in charge of the commodities section of a large French bank was dismissed overnight for having financed the speculative activities of a coffee trader, which could have resulted in some 15–20 million FF in losses for the bank.
28. H. de LA METTRIE, 'Réflexions d'un banquier sur quelques aspects du financement des flux internationaux de matières premières', in Claude MOUTON, Philippe CHALMIN, *op. cit.*, p. 80.
29. There are moreover a certain number of other sureties which the bank could be called upon to provide (within the framework of the EEC, specific sureties have to be supplied to the market regulatory bodies. . .).
30. A similar arrangement was of considerable assistance in 1980 to *Pancafé*, member of the Bogota group.
31. The futures market for foreign exchange should not be confused with that for merchandise.
32. Two of Conti commodity funds disappeared when the Chicago market collapsed in mid-December 1980. In 1984 again, Conti had to close two of its investment programmes after extremely heavy losses (several tens of millions of dollars).
33. Conference held at the *Centre de Recherches et d'Etudes sur les Marchés de Matières Premières*, Paris, 11th December,1980.

Chapter 6

Classification and evolution of trading

1. In 1978, for example, France boasted over 600 fruit and vegetable shippers, 1,800 grain and oilseeds traders, 6,000 livestock dealers. The directory published by the *Fédération des Syndicats du Commerce Exterieur* lists the names of 1,000 firms which carry out exclusively international activities.
2. The Cook accounts presented above, were based not on the turnover but on the 'margin', a margin of $100 million in 1974).
3. MICHALET, *Le capitalisme mondial*, Paris, 1978.
4. The small size of their national markets had encouraged the European traders to expand to the international arena at a much earlier stage than their American colleagues. The latter, however, subsequently developed at a much faster rate owing to the size of their domestic markets.

5. For historic reasons, the French grain cooperatives are grouped in two competing national unions: the UNCAC (*Union Nationale des Coopératives Agricoles Céréalières* or Maillot-Mac Mahon group) and the UGCAF (*Union Générale des Coopératives Agricoles Françaises* or La Fayette group).

6. J.-B. Doumeng's claim to represent the French agricultural cooperative movement was itself highly dubious. Note that the trading companies of the Doumeng group — *Interagra* and *Ipitrade* — have no links whatever with the cooperative world.

7. In the logical philosophy of a cooperative group whose priority must be to serve the interests of its members (we shall discuss at a later stage the losses incurred by Farmers Export).

8. This was the policy pursued by the Peruvian fish-meal monopoly, EPCHAP, which refused to deal with international traders and channeled its business exclusively through national brokers; the Philippines had a similar policy for coconut oil.

9. On this subject see UNCTAD, *Entreprises multinationales latino-américaines*, TD/B/C. 7/5O, 27 April 1982.

10. We should like to remind the reader of some of the members of the London Metal Exchange: Lead Industries, Entores (IMETAL group), Intsel (Péchiney group), Tennants (Consolidated Gold Fields), Ametalco (Amax), AMETS (RTZ), Anmercosa (Charter Consolidated), British American Metals Co. (Anaconda).

11. The Malaysian Mining Corporation left its seat after the tin market collapse of October 1985.

12. Goldschmidt and Charteris was originally the British subsidiary of the French grain trader, J.A. Goldschmidt, mentioned above.

13. In 1976 Phibro made its entry into the sugar trade with huge sums of capital (almost $15 million worth of investments in sugar refineries in the Philippines for example). In 1980 the company was one of the most important sugar traders in the world with an estimated 5 million tonnes. But in the course of 1980, owing to differences of opinion between Philipp Brothers and its sugar department (made up of newcomers), the former allegedly suffered huge losses ($80 million according to some observers). Most of its sugar department staff were obliged to resign and the company had to substantially reduce its activities in this sector. Similarly, in 1984, the new Phibro cocoa subsidiary, Cocoa Merchants, suffered heavy losses as a result of the bankruptcy of a Singapore cocoa grinder, and its directors were obliged to leave the group.

14. The evolution which we describe in these pages is a theoretical one which does not claim to trace the exact itinerary of a trading firm. Depending on the men and women who make up a firm and the environment in which it operates, the latter might stop at any one stage in the evolution which is presented here. Finally, our theoretical description takes into account primarily those firms which are a product of trading circles; firms which operate either upstream or downstream of trade have generally been quicker to step into the shoes of the international merchant.

15. This category could be extended to include a certain number of agencies responsible for trade between different blocs: *Interagra*, member of the J.-B. Doumeng group, for East–West trade. The great majority of these firms, save in exceptional circumstances, have very little influence on international trade.

16. Needless to say, the trading firms are experts in tax paradises such as Panama (Cargill-Tradax), Zug in Switzerland (Marc Rich), Bermuda. . .

17. Thanks to its oil activities, Marc Rich seems to have been in fact the last arrival.

Chapter 7

The grain trade

1. The case of rice is a special one and shall be treated apart.

2. See the remarkable study on this subject written by the journalist

Dan MORGAN, *Merchants of Grain*, New York, Viking Press, 1980. Note that Cook, who would have been on this list, disappeared in 1977 (see above). See also Richard GILMORE, *A Poor Harvest: The Clash of Policies and Interests in the Grain Trade*, Longman, 1982.

3. 'US Grain Arsenal', *NACLA's Latin America and Empire Report*, Vol. IX, No. 7, October 1975, pp. 21–29, and Roger Burbach, P. FLYNN, *Agribusiness in the Americas*, New York, NACLA, 1980 (chapter 13: 'Harvest of Profits, The World Empire of Cargill Inc.'). These authors contend that the major grain companies constitute an oligopoly in the collection and transport of grain by virtue of their stranglehold over the transport system.

4. In 1981, Tradax advanced an American refinery (Commonwealth Oil Refining) \$50 million on supplies .

5. According to internal sources , the trade margin had reached its maximum in 1973–74 with 2% and its minimum in 1968–69 with −0.26%. In 1982–83, the pre-tax cash flow was 1.6%.

6. UNCTAD Document TD/B/C-6/40 'Technological policies in the food industry'.

7. The two men at the head of Cargill at present illustrate this tendency: Whitney MacMillan is a pure trader, but the real strategist is a technician, M.D. McVay, a livestock specialist, who is surrounded mainly by managers.

8. Who, if anyone is interested in the minor details of history, has double French and American nationality.

9. In 1981, it was said that Continental Grain, in collaboration with Chia Tai International Investment of Hong Kong, was about to invest \$30 million in China to set up a feedstock production plant and to start livestock breeding operations in that country. An agreement had been reached with the province of Guang-Dong and the town of Shumchun on this subject. The plant was to have an installed capacity for feedstocks of 80,000 tonnes per year which could later be expanded to 360,000 tonnes. It is quite possible that Continental Grain will develop the entire project upstream of production (building abattoirs for pigs and poultry, and factories for meat processing), if asked to do so. Moreover, Conti's Argentinian subsidiary was building an oilseed crushing plant (\$30 million worth of investment) and that in Liverpool was doubling its capacity.

10. Louis Louis-Dreyfus played an important role in French political and economic affairs during the inter-war period.

11. Gérard Louis-Dreyfus also has both French and American citizenship.

12. Apparently after some difficulties in a sunflower business.

13. Even the first in terms of tonnage of food effectively produced (over 1 million tonnes).

14. We have not included the shares owned by the Dreyfus bank: 10% of Novotel, 14% of Borie. . .

15. Turnover in 1976–77, \$1.1 billion for the American subsidiary alone (Louis Dreyfus USA Inc). The average profits of the group from 1970 to 1975 amounted to 200 million French francs.

16. See Ricardo SIDIRACO, *Note sur le conglomérat Bunge et Born*, GEREI-INRA, June 1975; Raul GREEN and Catherine LAURENT, *Bunge et Born, histoire d'un secret bien gardé*, Paris, 1985.

17. The British subsidiary, Bunge and Co., had in 1985 a turnover of £1.15 billion, and showed profits of £3.86 million. It handles in Britain only 3 million tonnes of grain, sells 600,000 tonnes of fertilizers (through the Kenneth Wilson group) and just opened a new oilseed crushing mill, Bibby, with a capacity of 300,000 tonnes.

18. 'Blé, le tiers du commerce mondial passe par la Suisse', *Vers un développement solidaire*, November 1982.

19. When Jimmy Carter decreed his embargo on the 4th of January 1980, some 15

million tonnes of grain had already been sold but not yet delivered. The traders had hedged their forward contracts on Chicago in the course of their operations as they are wont to do. Since the embargo effectively cancelled these forward contracts, the traders found themselves in open upward tending position in Chicago, whereas it was clear that the market would inevitably turn downwards. The American government therefore decided to buy up the traders' contracts, in return for an undertaking not to try to replace these contracts with the Russians. Two firms refused to comply: Phibro and Central Soya.

20. Farmland Industries ranked 87th in order of turnover in *Fortune*'s list of the top 500 American firms. Others are Agri-Industries, Farm Bureau of Indiana. . .

21. 'A Farm Cooperative in the Hands of High Rollers', *Fortune*, 20 April, 1981.

22. The Brazilian cooperative Bantrade holds 10% of the capital of the oilseed crushing plant, *Bordeaux Oléagineux*.

23. All the more so as the motives of someone like J.-B. Doumeng in seeking to promote these projects, were not totally convincing. True enough, he had had a few genuine cooperative mandates (president of the Noé wine cooperative in Haute-Garonne), but the company he created and ran until his death, *Interagra* is strictly private and has no links whatever with the cooperative world.

24. In May 1982, Peavey, in difficulties, was bought out for $177 million by Conagra, a firm which was already present in grains, poultry and animal feed. . .

25. A rice futures market which opened in New Orleans in 1981 ceased to function in 1983 for want of business.

26. Voluntary restriction agreement between Thailand and the EEC.

27. Nessim Gaon is one of the main benefactors of the State of Israel (and especially of M. Shamir's party, the Likud). He was allegedly a 'civilian' member of the Israeli delegation to the Camp David negotiations. Gaon was also the founder of the small religious party 'Tami' which, in spring 1984, precipitated the political crisis in Israel by withdrawing its support from the Likud which was in power at the time. Certain observers see a clear link between the stance taken by Tami and the Iraeli government's refusal a few days earlier to guarantee a loan to the Noga group ("Nigerian Cold Shoulder may topple commodity 'empire'", *African Business*, June 1984).

28. In September 1984, *Nestlé* bought Carnation and since then dominates, unchallenged, the world market in dairy products.

Chapter 8

The sugar trade

1. Two very complementary professions in the 18th and at the beginning of the 19th century: the cask manufacturer organized the shipping of his products to the West Indies (with a cargo of general merchandise such as dried fish etc.,) making sure that the return cargo would be sugar.

2. In 1981, *Cacao Barry* had processed 120,000 tonnes in France and in Africa for a turnover of 2.1 billion francs. It had 2,400 employees on its payroll.

3. Another minor historic detail: Maurice Varsano's character is Grezillo in the novel written by Georges CONCHON, *Le Sucre*, Paris, 1976, and is played by a bald Michel Piccoli in the film based on the book.

4. For more details see our *Tate and Lyle: A history*, to be published in 1988 by Harwood Academic Publishers.

5. In 1984 Czarnikow, controlled by the families of the former presidents Rook and Liddiard, totally separated its trading and industrial activities (Lion Mark holdings) in

the food business. This activity alone brought in profits of £100,000 in 1982–83 and £2.5 million in 1983–84.

6. Fidel Castro reportedly told Maurice Varsano that this was to be a 'transideological' company.

7. Note moreover, that in a related but different sector, Louis Dreyfus owns the Cognac firm Castillon-Renaud.

Chapter 9

The coffee and cocoa trades

1. Grinding activities in the producing countries are, with a few exceptions — such as Ecuador — controlled by foreign interests: Barry in the Cameroons, in the Ivory Coast and in Brazil, Gill and Duffus in Brazil and in Ghana (minority), Cadbury in Ghana, Hershey in Brazil (minority), Nestlé in Brazil, André in the Ivory Coast. . .

2. The main shareholders of Berisford were in 1985 the insurance company, Prudential Corporation (6.46% of ordinary shares) and the members of the Berisford family (preferential shares).

3. Following the death of the son of the founder, Henri Lacarré, the future of *Cacao Barry* seemed uncertain. Confronted with a take-over bid from S.W. Berisford, the French government decided to seek a French solution uniting under the *Omnium Financier du Cacao, Sucres et Denrées* (74.4%), Alain Delaunoy's *Sucre Union* group (19.2%) and the Cameroonian government.

4. Volkart has, nevertheless, maintained distribution activities in India (Voltas founded in 1954 with the Tata group, is the leading Indian distribution firm with 9,000 employees). It is also present in the textile industry and, of course, in coffee (India's leading producer) and cotton. In Sri Lanka, Volkart exports and processes coconut-oil.

5. Note that in 1982, the American firm Anderson Clayton, specializing in fats, decided to abandon its activities as an exporter from Brazil (where it was one of the principal operators).

6. The term 'cooperative' is rather incorrect in this case!

7. The Liem Sioe Liong group is probably the most powerful and the least known of the Chinese groups of the 'diaspora'. Sixty-six years old and closely linked to the family of the Indonesian president Suharto (he is known as the 'president's Chinaman'), Liem made his debut in the forties as a trader in cloves. At present, his group (whose turnover is estimated at $10 billion), composed of companies which hardly ever bear his name or those of his associates, is mainly industrial, with activities ranging from flour-milling and iron and steel to cement, cars, and oilseeds. . . As an individual Liem is considered to be the richest man in Asia.

Chapter 10

The non-ferrous metals trade

1. Until 1974 the director of the petroleum department of Philipp Brothers was 'a gentleman called Marc Rich'.

2. For example the loans made by Phibrobank to the Philippines Sugar Mills.

3. He had predicted, inter alia, the rise in American interest rates in 1981.

4. Quoted in *The Economist*, August 8, 1982.

5. In 1978 coal exports from the north-east of the United States began to pose an extremely serious problem. In 1980, the waiting period at the coal port of Hampton Roads, was over six months. Phibro deemed it advisable at the time to invest in the management of transport rather than in the mines themselves (a stance taken by *Elf Aquitaine* around the same period).

6. Philipp Brothers had found itself in an unfavourable hedging position on the silver market in the aftermath of the Hunt manipulations: on 14 January, 1980, they had to respond to margin calls made by COMEX to the tune of $100 million. At that point they sold their silver actuals — under the market — to the Hunts (by reciprocally annulling futures contracts): 19 million ounces on the 14th of January, 11 million ounces on the 16th of January. The first contract (worth $665 million) was nearing due date on the 31st of March. By then the market had already collapsed, with the price of silver dropping from $50 to $6 per ounce. After a series of dramatic negotiations with the participation notably of Paul Volcker of the Federal Reserve Board and William Miller, Secretary of the Treasury, Philipp Brothers accepted by way of compensation, the Hunts' oil interests in the Beaufort Sea (but without much enthusiasm if we are to believe Milton Rosenthal). See Stephen FAY, *The Great Silver Bubble*, London, 1982.

7. Participation reduced from the summer of 1984 to 22%.

8. The reader will have noticed that the great majority of the metal traders (Philipp, Lissauer. . .) started off in Germany (we should also add to the list the *Metallgesellschaft*). Not wishing to theorize about a hypothetical 'descendancy' from the the Fuggers and the Welsers, we assume this to be the result of the importance of German metallurgy, the first in the world in the 19th century.

9. In 1981, Preussag sought to buy out the remaining 15% of AMC's shares which were not yet in its control, but its move was met by a violent counter take-over bid from *Permadolan Nasional* (fully owned by the Malaysian State) which managed to secure 9.63% of the AMC capital.

Chapter 11

Trade in some other major commodities

1. Before its collapse in 1977, Cook Industries had been one of the major international traders in cotton. Ned Cook had in fact started out as a cotton trader in the family firm in Memphis.

2. Colin BARLOW, *The National Rubber Industry of Malaysia*, Kuala Lumpur, 1978, p. 207. The Lee family controls inter alia the Overseas Chinese Banking Corporation; the group, founded in 1927 and controlled by the founder's three sons, has activities in palm-oil, pineapples, banking and real estate.

3. Here too, the *sogo shosa* play the most important role: Mitsubishi is active in Canada, C. Itoh in Brazil (where it produced pulp), Sumitumo in Malaysia, Nisho Iwai in Papua.

4. British American Tobacco, Imperial Tobacco, Philip Morris, R.J. Reynolds, Gulf and Western, Ruppert-Rembrandt-Rothmans, American Brands.

Conclusion

1. From the French farmers to the leaders of Third World countries as the late Indira Ghandi claiming in 1981 before the assembled FAO: 'When harvests are good, international prices fall. When they are bad, the market is manipulated to such an extent that profits are reaped by the traders and middlemen and not by the producers'. (Quoted in the *Financial Times*, 10 November, 1981).

2. It is a matter of significance here that the state trading agencies of the socialist countries (such as *Exportkhleb* in the USSR) practically always employ the services of international traders.

3. An opinion imparted to us by Dr. James Fry of Landell Mills Commodities in London.

4. We can, of course, think of the Hunt case, but their fortune combined with that of the Arab princes was colossal and despite it all their manoeuvre failed.

5. The ideal would, of course, be definitive stabilization, but in 1987 this is still utopian!

6. The case of the deregulation of the agricultural markets in Argentina after the fall of Isabelita Perón, is particularly enlightening as to the interest of certain major grain traders which wield enormous power in that country!

7. A problem addressed by the Swiss Commodity and Futures Association which groups traders based in Switzerland. We had put forward a draft agreement for control under the aegis of UNCTAD (*Journal of World Trade Law*), but the time seems to be far from ripe.

INDEX